LIGHT, SPACE & TIME
ESSAYS ON CAMERA CRAFT AND CREATIVITY

DAVID DUCHEMIN

rockynook

Light, Space & Time: Essays on Camera Craft and Creativity

David duChemin
www.davidduchemin.com

Editor: Ted Waitt
Project manager: Lisa Brazieal
Marketing coordinator: Katie Walker
Copyeditor: Cynthia Haynes
Interior and cover design: Aren Straiger
Interior layout: Kim Scott, Bumpy Design
Cover production: Aren Straiger
Cover photograph: David duChemin

Softcover ISBN: 979-8-88814-200-4
Hardcover ISBN: 979-8-88814-208-0

1st Edition (1st printing, October 2024)
© 2024 David duChemin
All photographs © David duChemin

Rocky Nook Inc.
1010 B Street, Suite 350
San Rafael, CA 94901
USA

www.rockynook.com

Distributed in the UK and Europe by Publishers Group UK
Distributed in the U.S. and all other territories by Publishers Group West

Library of Congress Control Number: 2023952038

Printed in Korea

To Jon,
With inexpressible gratitude for the adventure of our friendship.
Nakupenda, ndugu.

Contents

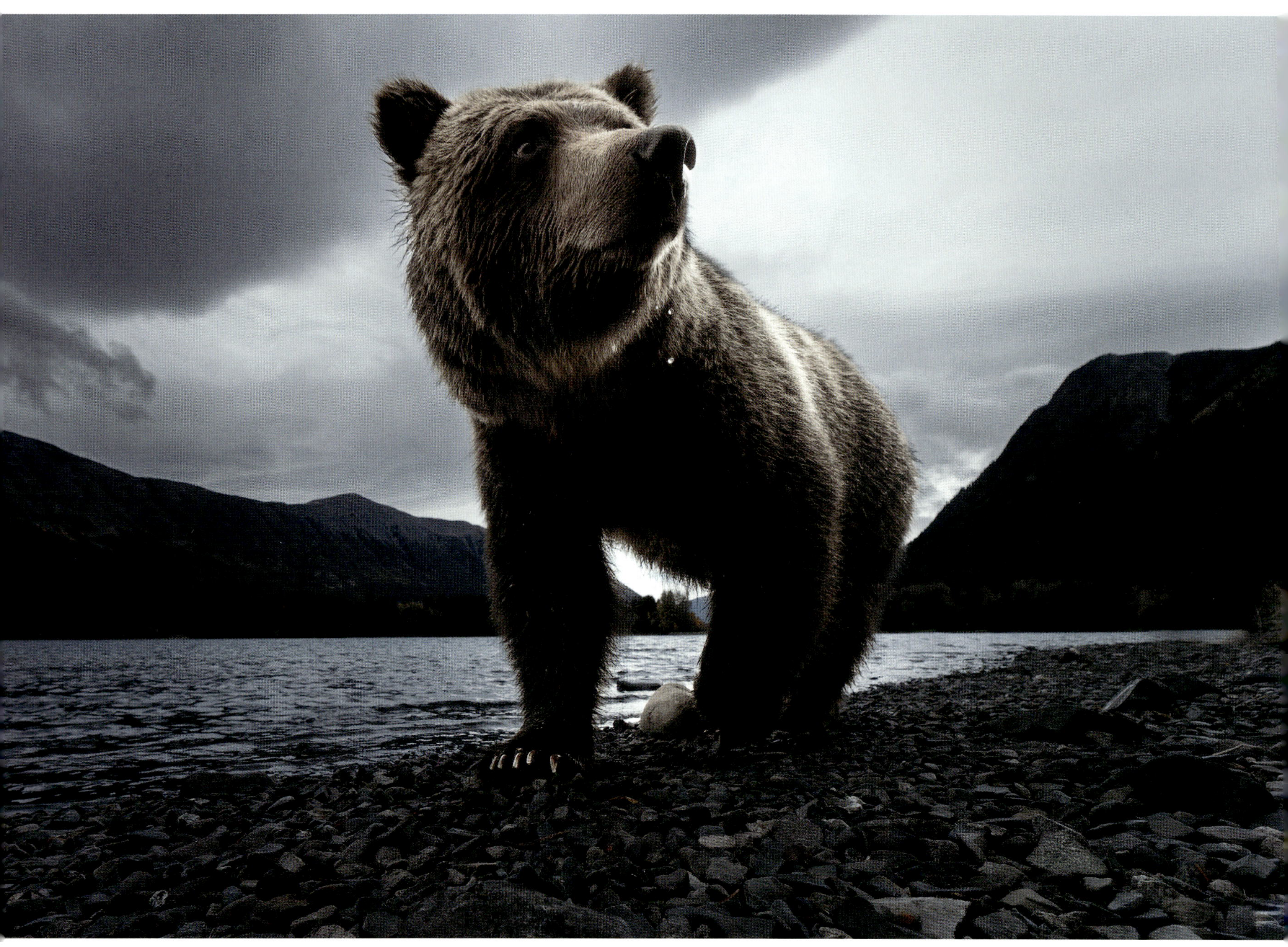

01

The Mind of the Photographer

The making of great photographs—images that are compelling and go beyond the obvious, not to mention those that have a feeling of being distinctly our own—goes well beyond the capabilities of our cameras. We know this. The making of photographs that do more than meet a minimum technical standard (perfectly sharp, for example) is the domain of the *mind*. This is a creative challenge, not a technical one, and once you've learned the basics of craft, that is where the rewards are the highest.

So why are conversations about creativity and the inner life of the photographer so unusual in the popular photography world? And when creativity *is* mentioned, why does it conjure up images of photographers swinging their cameras in the air like lunatics, shutters open in hopes of making something we've never seen before? Less fringe are the legitimate and powerful techniques like multiple exposures and intentional camera motion, but still, if creativity is limited only to photographers who embrace more impressionistic or abstract styles, then where does that leave the rest of us? What of the inner life and thought processes of those of us who want to make something beautiful or deeply personal and are stuck behind barriers of doubt or limited by our thinking?

Creativity is not synonymous with or limited to the more glaringly innovative; it is not the exclusive territory of those who identify as "artists." The mechanic who works on my truck is creative. He better be, because I've asked him to do some unusual things, forcing him to work through some interesting problems. Same with engineers and scientific researchers, teachers, and doctors. Anyone who has ever faced a problem or an obstacle and *thought* their way around it, often beginning with the humble question of "What if . . . ?" is creative. That problem might be visibly artistic, but for the photographer, it might *also* be technical or conceptual. For the photographer working with people, it might be a relational challenge. Working around that challenge and thinking differently about it when our usual approach doesn't seem to be paying off is what creativity is all about. Almost any question that begins with "How can I . . . ?" is one begging for a *creative* response that comes from the inside.

Not only is photography an opportunity for creative thinking, but it also requires creative *doing*. We *make* photographs. And every one of them is a chance to make unique decisions about what that photograph says, what it's about, and what it looks like. So unless you've put your brain into program mode, every photograph you make includes questions you need to answer about focal length, distance from subject, depth of field, focus, exposure, what you do with motion, how much you include or exclude in the frame, where you put the camera, and which moment you choose from among many to press the shutter. In the big picture, photography might be very technical, but *why* you do it and *how* you combine it all is creative.

Beyond the shutter itself and the pressing of buttons, you also make choices in the edit: which frame is the strongest and best accomplishes your purpose, or is most to your liking? Beyond the edit, you make creative choices about refining that image. Do you brighten the image or darken it? Do you add contrast or remove it? What do you do with colour and all the many choices you have with hue, saturation, and luminance? And what of presentation? Is this a single image printed large and placed on a wall, or is it part of a series or larger body of work that will find its best expression in a coffee table book? These are all creative decisions with no right or wrong answer. So long as you engage in this necessarily technical craft, these will also be technical choices, but this is not a one-or-the-other situation: it must be both.

The bookshelves that line my office are mostly filled with photography books. Not books *about* photography, but books of photographs. The masters are all there: Ernst Haas, Elliott Erwitt, Sally Mann, Saul Leiter, Josef Koudelka, Walker Evans, and Galen Rowell, among many others. They are joined by newer voices, and some I suspect you've not yet heard about. If you were visiting, I'd invite you to pull any of them from the shelf or pick one up from the coffee table. James Nachtwey's *Inferno* is there. Sam Abell, too. There are several volumes from Edward Burtynsky. And *Amaze*, by my dear friend Cristina Mittermeier. Open any of them and you'll see the results not only of what a camera can do but also of a human being's creative thinking as they engage the technical side of our craft to make something that is more than the sum of its parts.

Furthermore, you'll see undeniable variety in what they are exploring in those bodies of work, what they are saying about those subjects, and how they say it. The style (or voice) will differ from one to another, even among those who use the same camera and are equally skilled at spinning the dials and pressing the buttons. Why are they so different? Because they *think* differently—creatively—about how and why they wield the tools of their craft.

If you're familiar with my writing, then you know I am not dismissing the importance of craft and the time needed to make our skills feel instinctive. If this is your first time reading my work, then it will be helpful to

We do not need more of the same-old, same-old. We don't need conformity or consensus. What we need are minds that are more willing to engage in challenge and creativity.

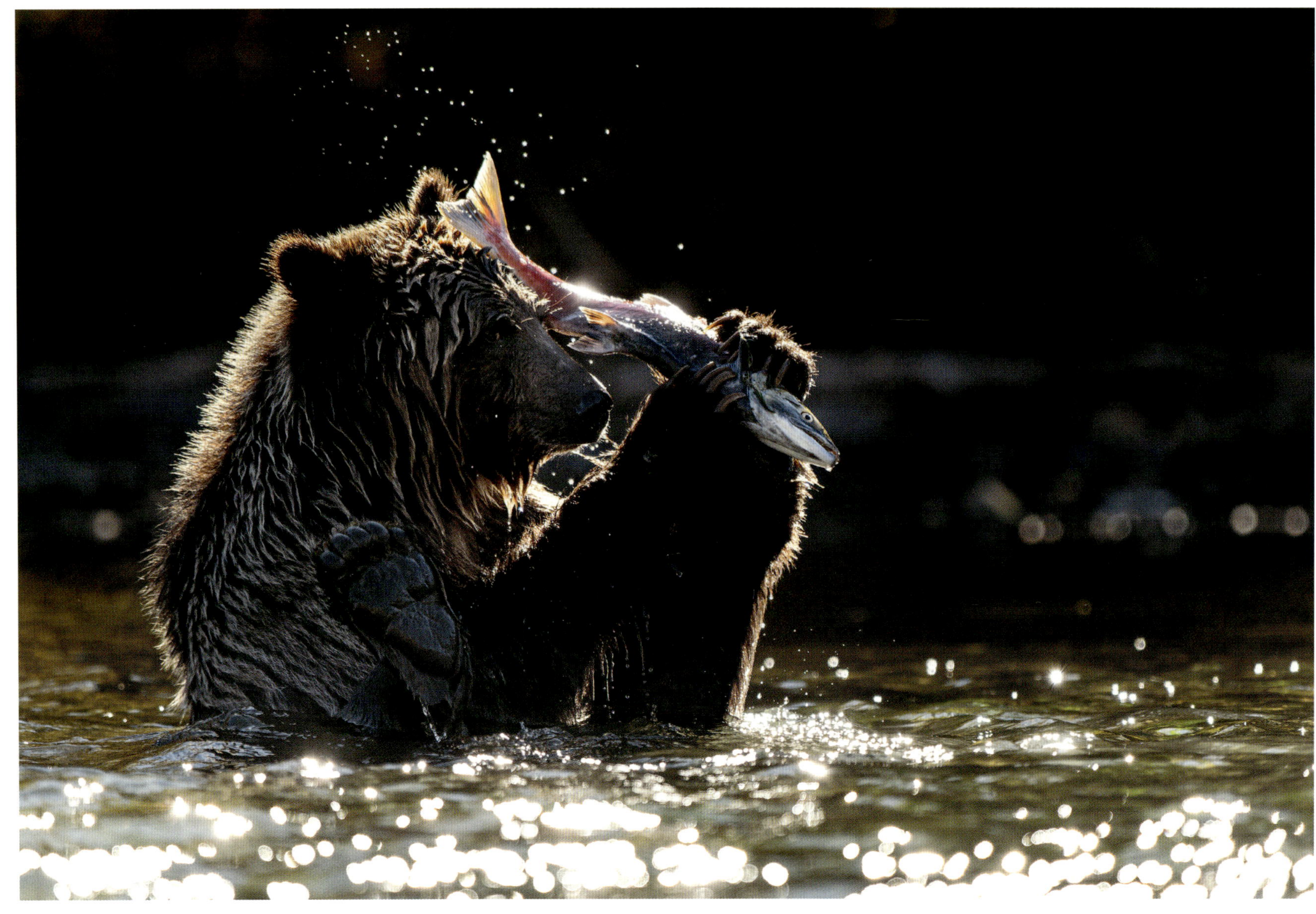

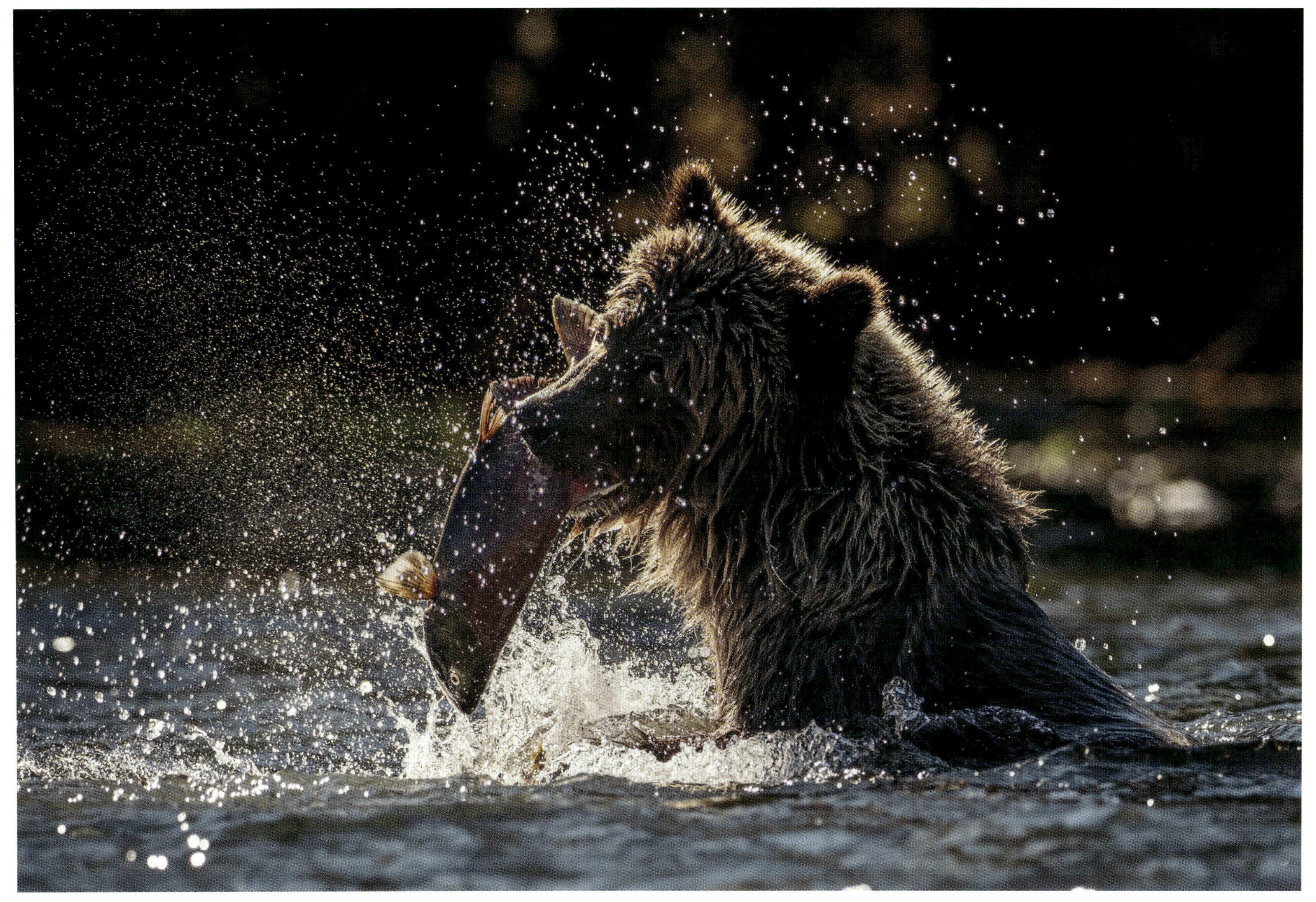

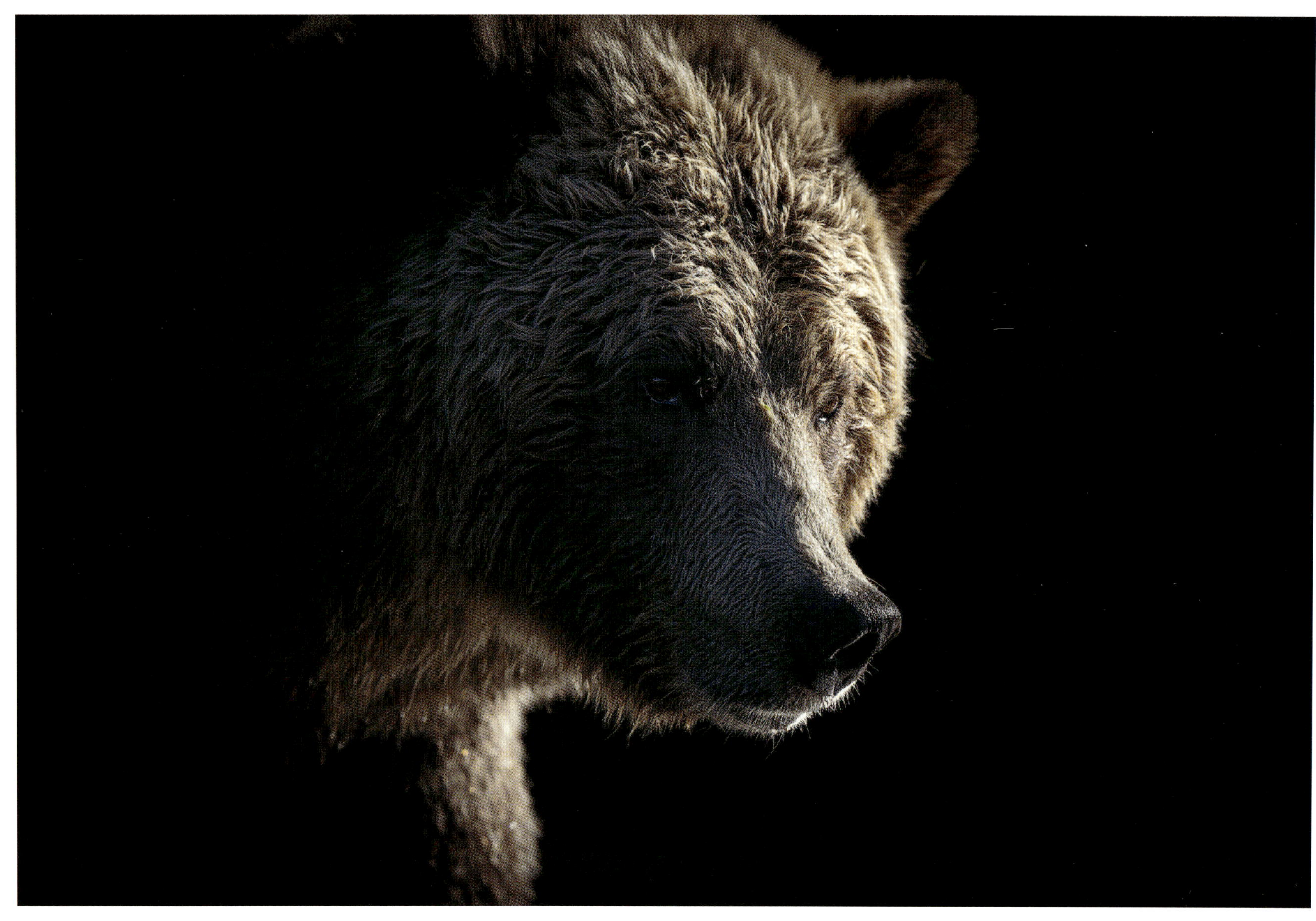

know that I hold those skills in the highest regard. *Ours is not a craft for the lazy or the negligent.* After all, we need techniques to be creative *with,* and every tool represents creative possibilities that others do not. But there will always be limits to those skills and constraints imposed by our tools and the contexts in which we work. There will always be problems to overcome.

See if this sounds familiar: you've gone out with your camera and a lens or two, and you see a scene that catches your attention. You put your camera to your eye and press the shutter, looking quickly at the LCD screen (if you're shooting digitally) only to find it doesn't look how you imagined it. You change the settings and try again. Nope. One more try with a different lens. Again, no. It just doesn't do the scene justice. What the hell is wrong with this piece of crap camera that you spent so much money on?

There's nothing wrong with it—it's probably better than all the cameras that made most of the best photographs in the 20th century put together. Barring a rare technical failure, what's not working is our approach: the way we're *thinking* about the tools we're using.

How we think matters, and this is a book about thinking. In some instances, it is a book of thoughts. In some, it's also about feelings because I can't see a way to separate the two; our emotional state can be as much a hindrance as it is a help in what we make. Specifically, *Light, Space & Time* is about

photographers as creative beings. We all know how our cameras work, but how does *creativity* work? How do *we* work? That's one of the questions explored on these pages. If you can be more comfortable with how your creativity works as a tool, then you can better engage it, be more comfortable and less frustrated with it, with yourself, and with the work you create.

Stephen Shore, whom I will mention again in the following pages, said, "It seems to me that a good photographer is a combination of two things: one is interesting perceptions and the other is an understanding of how the world is translated by a camera into a photograph." How we perceive the world is a matter of thinking creatively, as is how we think about what the camera does to translate that perception of the world into an image and how we combine the two.

This is neither a how-to nor a why-to book, as my others have been credited. I hope this one is not so easy to categorize as one thing or another. But if it could be something specific, perhaps it sits somewhere in between a celebration of the wonder of this craft and a manifesto defending its fundamental creative nature. No, wait—scratch that. This is better: a manifesto defending *your* fundamental creative nature. It's not that photography is creative (because much of it just isn't), but that *we* are creative. Or we can be. Whether we are or not, and whether our photography is part of that or not, depends on how willing we are to think differently about matters of craft, to perceive this world

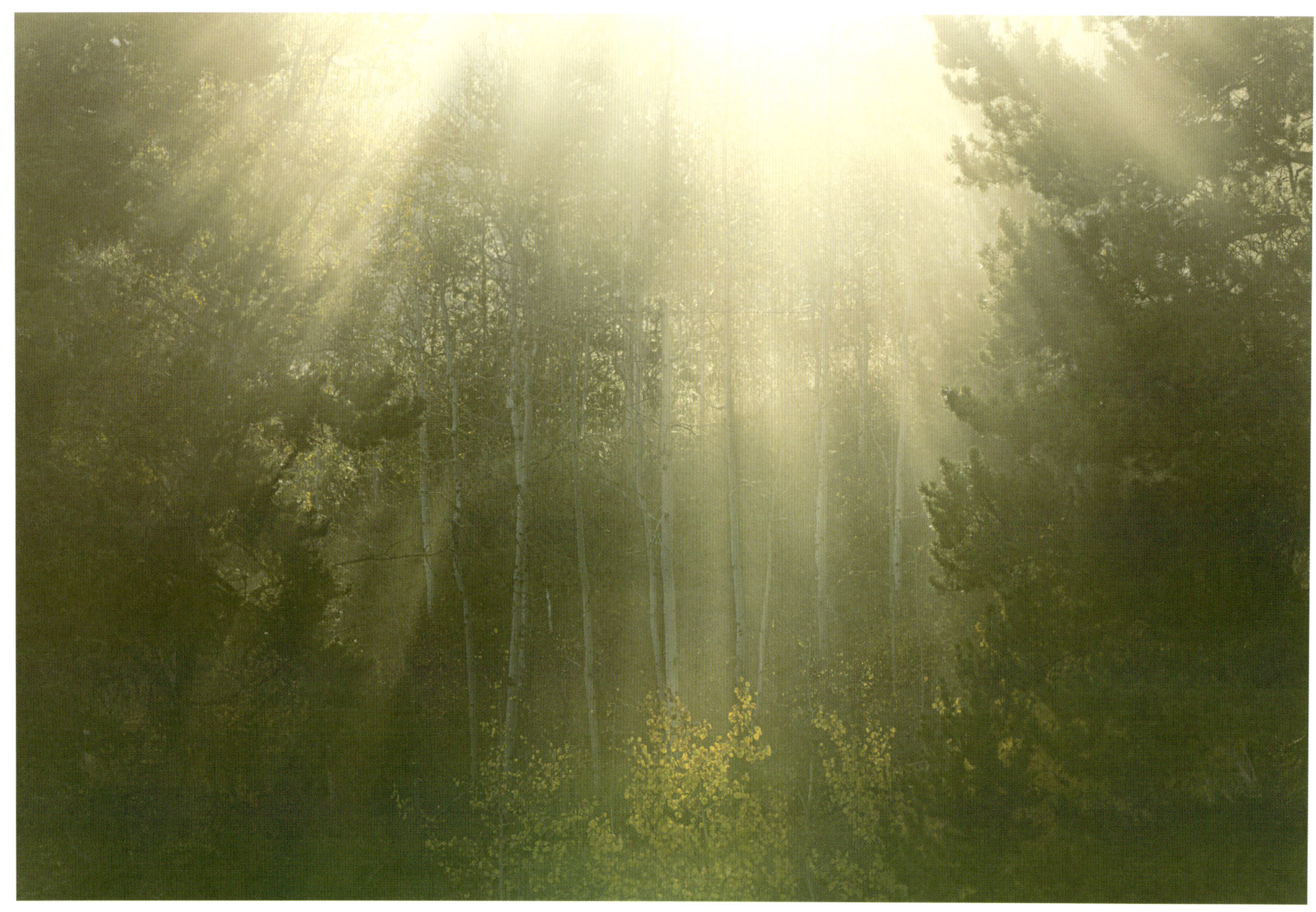

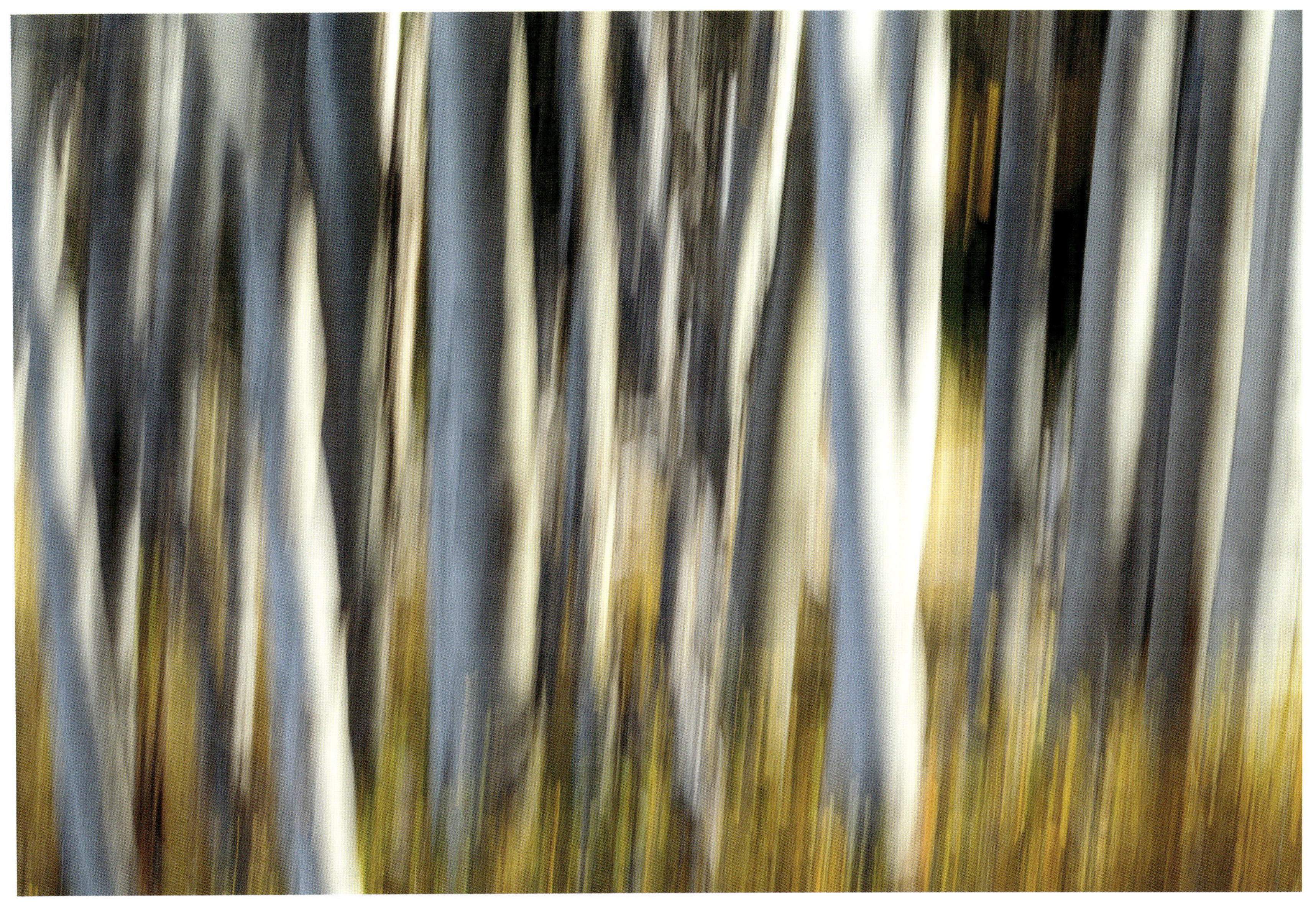

in new ways, and to use our tools with greater nuance and obliqueness of thought than the questions we too often ask: How *should* I be doing this? What lens *should* I be using? The *shoulds* and the *oughts* have no place in a craft with such rich creative possibilities.

What I want most for you is *freedom*. Freedom to find your own path. Freedom to find new ways, or maybe more comfortably embrace the ways of practicing this craft that are already uniquely yours. Freedom to think differently about the same tools and materials you've been using since you first picked up a camera. We do not need more of the same-old, same-old. We don't need conformity or consensus. What we need are minds that are more willing to engage in challenge and creativity.

I hope that *Light, Space & Time* gives you ideas, new frameworks for how you think about your decisions, and new ways to see and look. I hope it creates new sparks for you, raises new questions, and helps you find answers to others. Like a camera firmware upgrade that provides new functions and gets rid of bugs, I hope some of the ideas explored here do that for you. It's cheaper than buying new gear, and the results will be stronger.

Will this book make you a better photographer? Not a chance. But thinking differently about your craft and the photographs you make certainly will. Perceiving the world and the tools you use differently will make you a better photographer, assuming you're willing to do the hard work. That means figuring out what that means for you in practice and that you take advantage of the liberty to do so, unhindered by what you *ought* to do and free to pursue your whims and curiosity, to find your answers to "What if . . . ?" and "How do I . . . ?"

Or you could get a new camera. But unless the mind operating that camera shifts and grows, little will change. Faster focusing, perhaps, or better low-light performance. Those things matter to some, but as Ansel Adams reminds us, there is little value in a sharp photograph of a fuzzy concept, and the single most important part of the camera is the 12 inches behind it: your mind.

What goes on in your mind—and your emotions, wherever they are to be found—is the subject of the conversation we are about to have. I hope it gives you courage, quells doubts, stirs new ideas, and most of all, makes you aware that you're not alone in finding that the best of your work is hard-earned but full of joy.

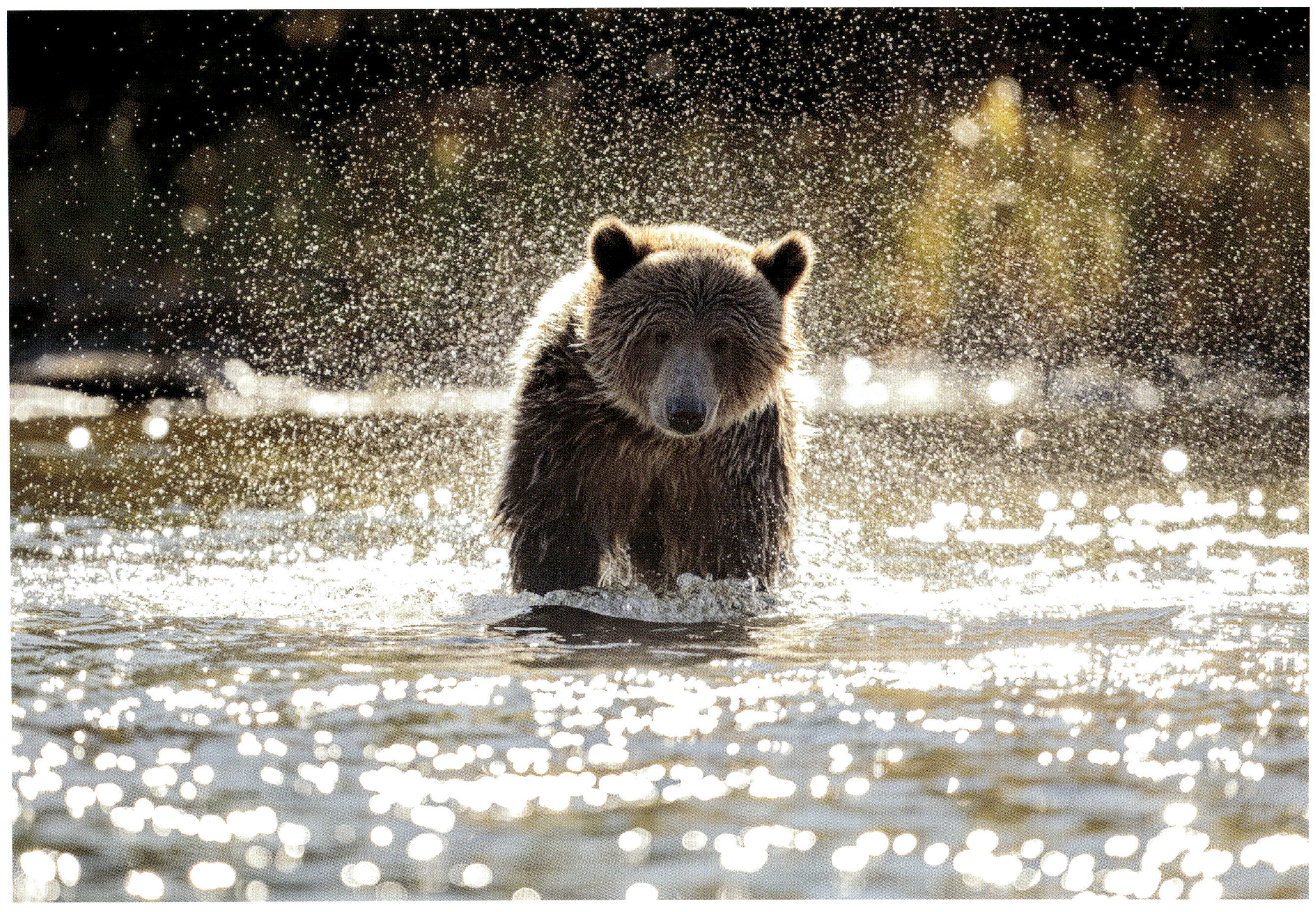

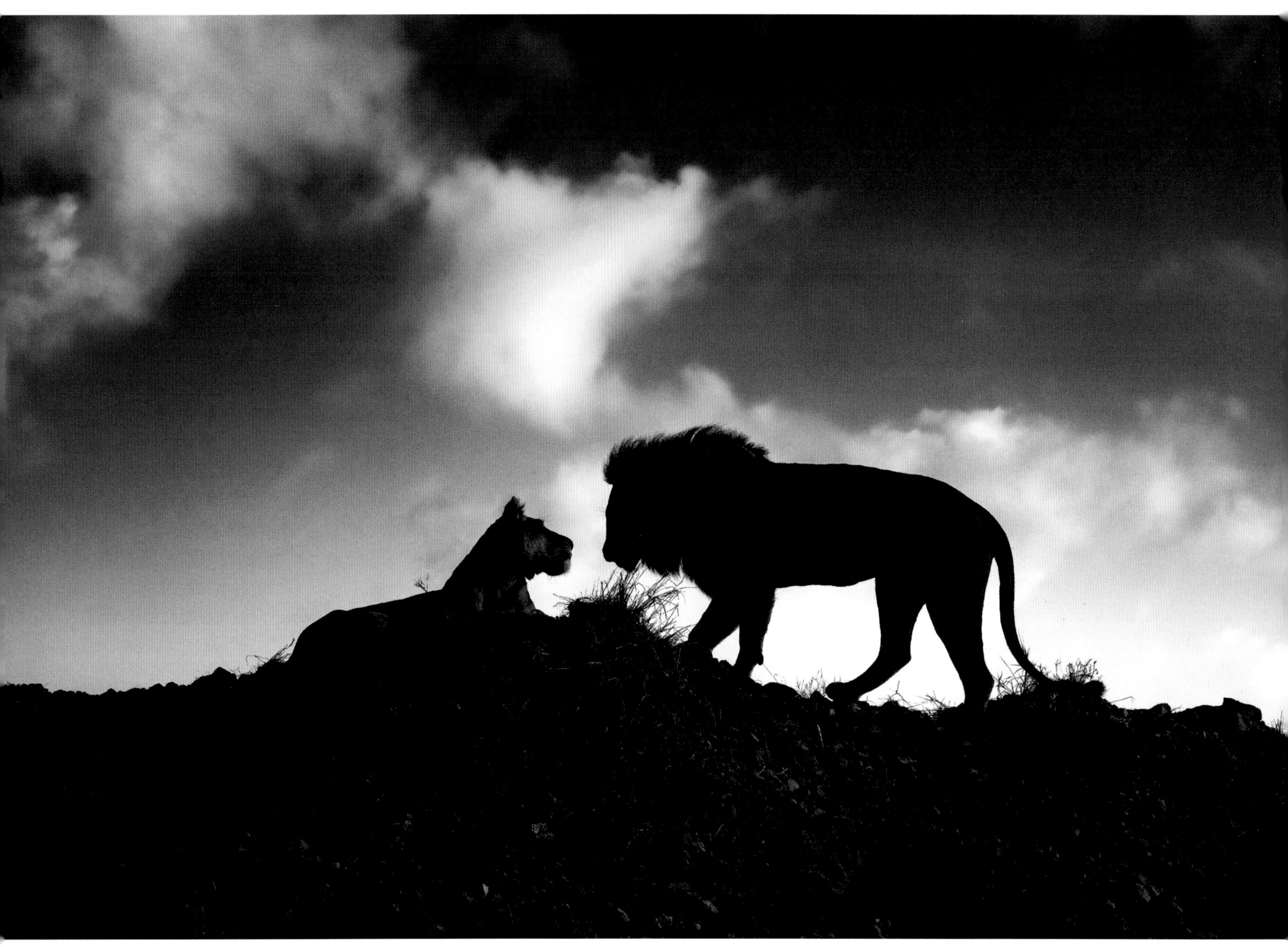

02
Light, Space, and Time

When I was 12, my mother enrolled me in the French immersion program at school. What little I had learned of the language to that point was useless when faced with all-French-all-the-time and a lexicon of real-world words I'd never had reason to learn. As the comedian Eddie Izzard once pointed out, *le singe est sur la branche* (the monkey is on the branch) is *very* hard to work into everyday conversations unless you travel to heavily wooded areas in France with your own monkey.

Meanwhile, words like *homework* are more useful to a kid in Grade 7 if he wants to stay out of trouble. It took me a week of daily rebukes to learn to stop listening for the words I was expecting (*here is your homework for tomorrow*) and hear something else entirely (*voici vos devoirs pour demain*). I got tripped up by a lot of other words as well. I know they say it's easier to learn a language when you're a kid, but I was hopelessly lost in a wilderness of unfamiliar words for a long time. Words that didn't even *sound* like words. The incomprehensible sentences I was beginning to mutter only testified to my slow and clumsy progress.

That first year of French immersion was confusing at the best of times—so many moving parts. Not just unfamiliar nouns but masculine or feminine ones with no apparent logic to help discern the difference. Verbs that felt like marbles in my mouth. Not only new words but new ways of *thinking*. Whatever progress I was going to make would have to take place in my *mind*.

Photography is also a mind game. The camera sees differently than you do, and the journey of mastering this craft is not so much in figuring out how to bend the camera to your will but in conforming *your* understanding to the unique ways in which the camera sees—and speaks about—light, space, and time. It's a way of *thinking*.

Photographers often talk about the need to "learn to see," but I wonder if it would be more helpful to finish that thought this way: photographers need to learn to see *as the camera sees*.

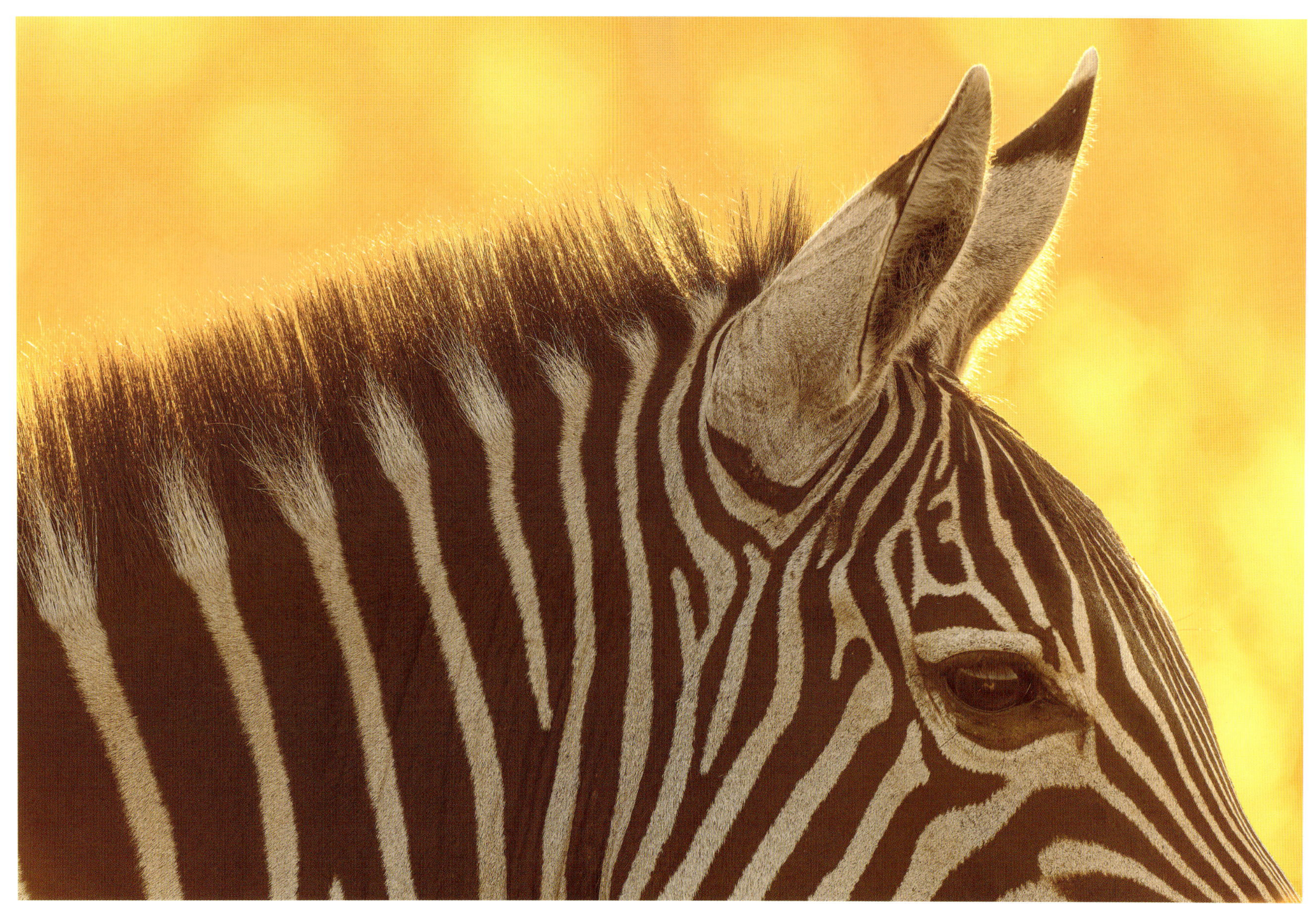

Highlight that last sentence. We need to understand, predict, imagine, and work with the unique way the camera sees light, space, and time. Or, more accurately, how it *expresses* those things because it's so wildly different from how we're even able to perceive these three raw materials on our own.

I think I learned photography backwards. I was given a camera and told how it *works*. I learned the technology that the camera uses to translate the world into a picture, but not the language itself—like giving a would-be painter a brush and showing them how to move their hands to push the bristles across the canvas. Necessary, but it does not a painter make; the language of painting lies elsewhere. How much stronger might that painter be if the earliest lessons were about colour and composition and the other aspects of that craft that elicit awe and engage the imagination, not just a curiosity about how to hold the brush?

Painters need to learn to think in the language of painting; musicians need to learn to think in the language of music. And photographers need to learn to think in the language of the camera to use that camera to translate what you see and feel into photographs that express that, and to stop looking at the results and asking why they don't look the way you hoped.

It doesn't *look* the way you hoped because you're not looking the way the camera does, nor are you thinking in the same language the camera speaks.

It doesn't look the way you might have hoped because you haven't learned to see or *imagine* light the way the camera does. You can't see it three stops over- or underexposed, but the camera can. Your eyes just can't do it without the camera. You see a different dynamic range, too. The camera sees light differently, and those differences will either be your technical obstacles or your creative possibilities, so how you think about them (or whether you think about them at all) matters deeply.

Time is perceived differently as well. Capable of seeing much faster (1/8000) and much slower (8 seconds, for example) than our eyes possibly can, the camera is a creative collaborator that has words for time that we don't have, similar to the way Inuit cultures have a greater number of words for snow than those of us living in more temperate climes. We don't have the capacity to perceive the differences, but that doesn't mean they aren't there. We don't see the blurred brushstrokes of elements moving through elapsed time, but the camera does.

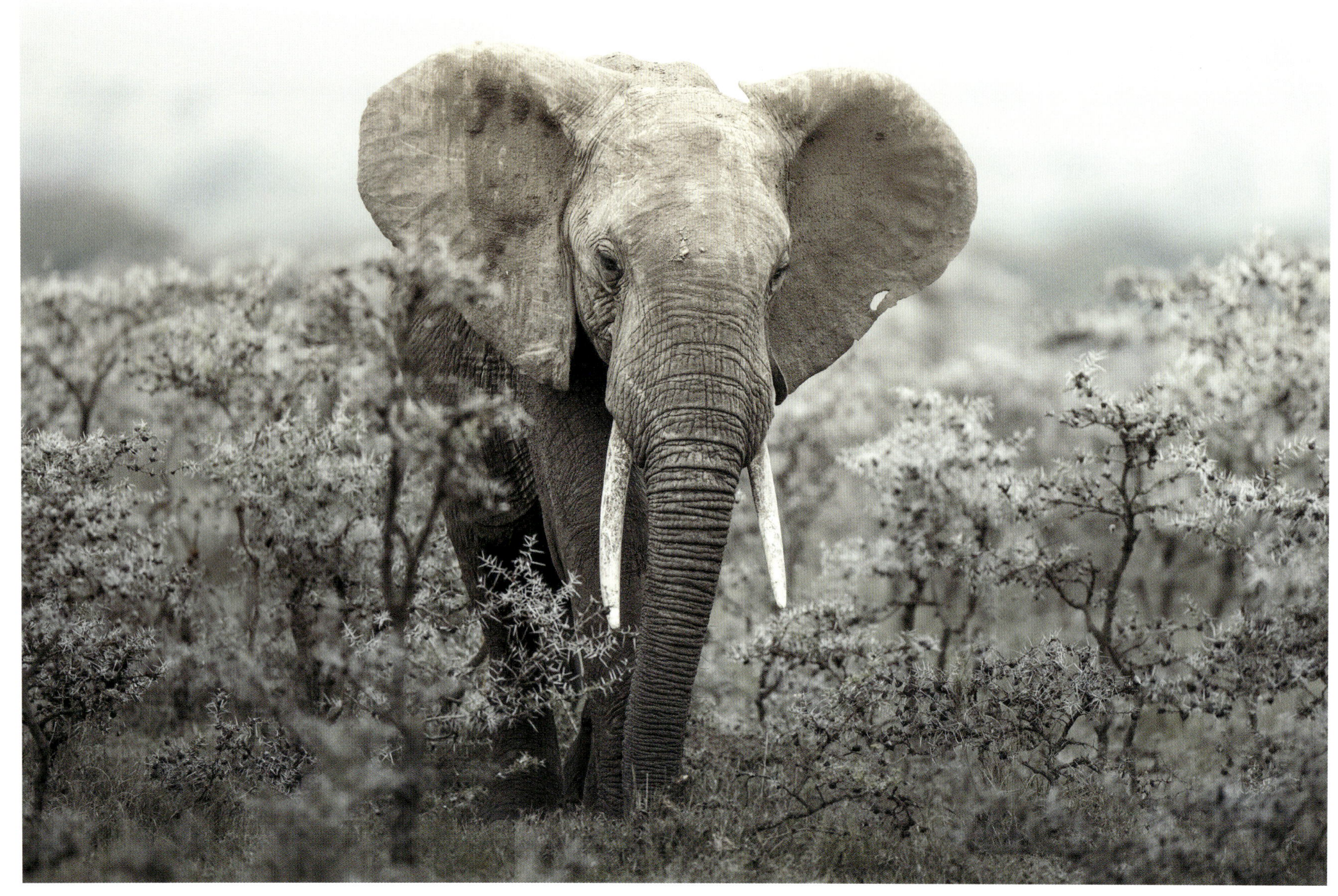

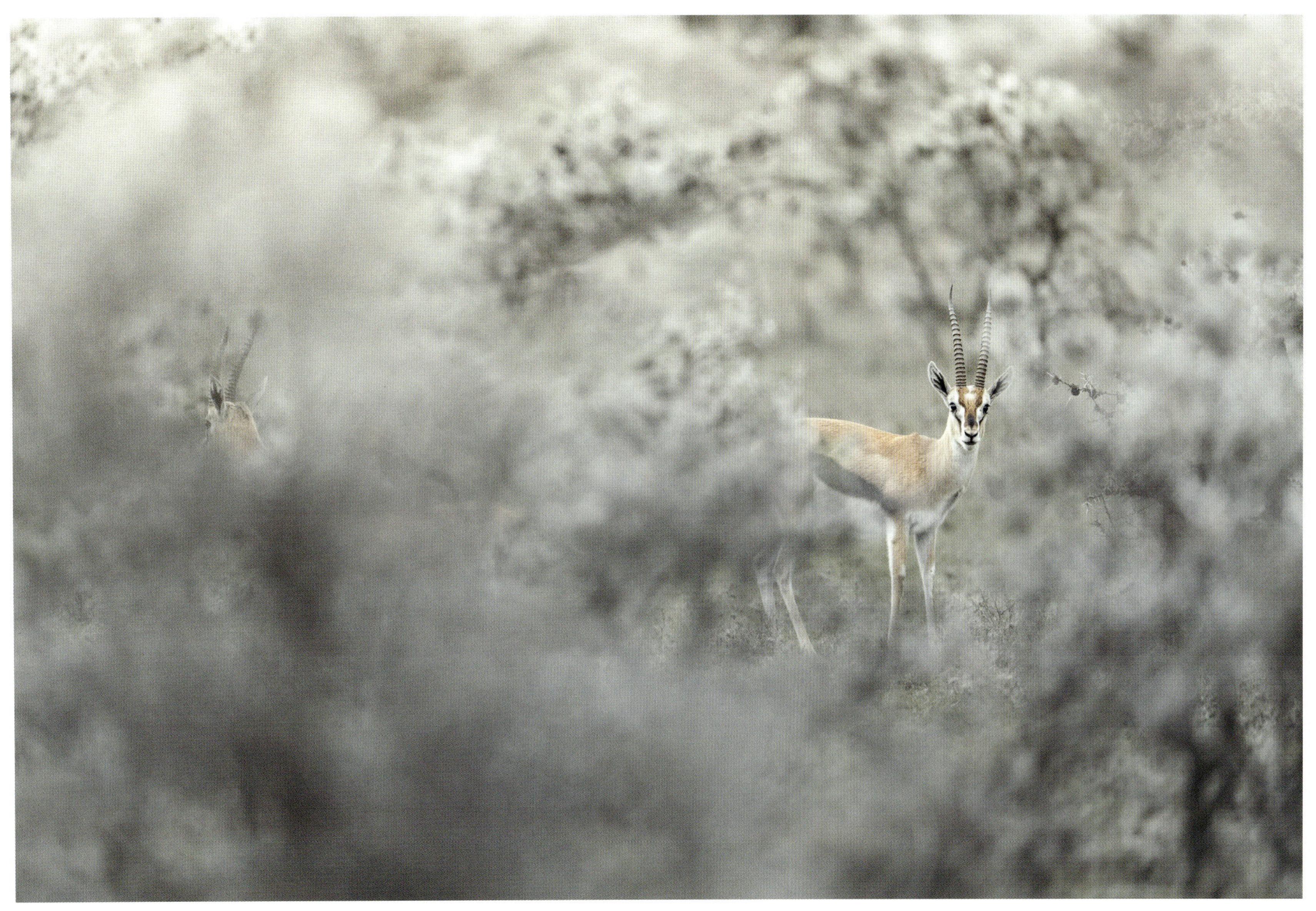

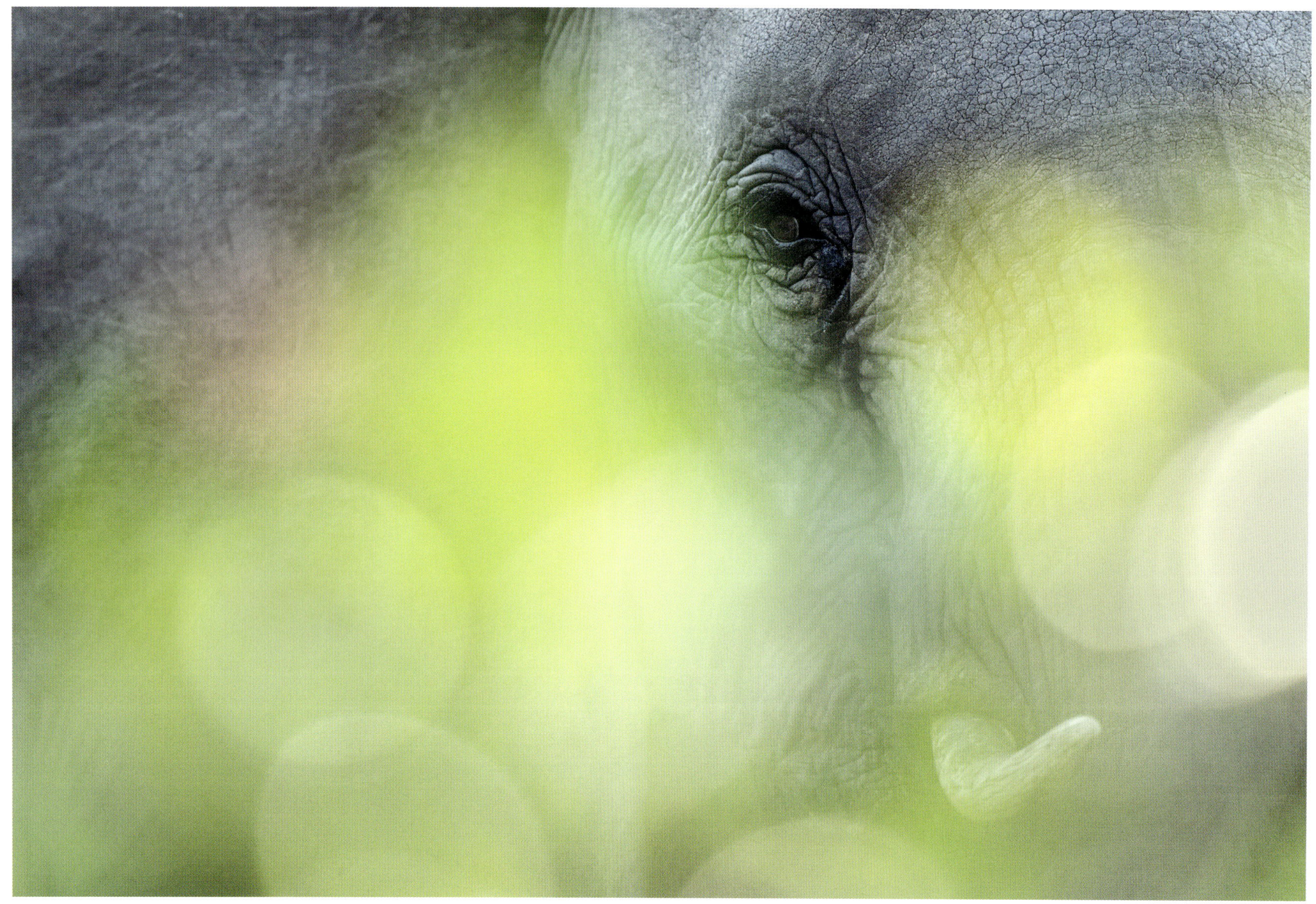

Photographers often talk about the need to "learn to see," but I wonder if it would be more helpful to finish that thought this way: photographers need to learn to see *as the camera sees.*

The camera can be not only your collaborator but also your teacher. If you're listening, it can give you new ways of seeing time and an expanded vocabulary you can use to speak photographically—more creatively and powerfully. Simply put, the camera has a much broader vocabulary than we do where time (as well as light and space) is concerned. We need to learn it.

Space is also seen much differently by the camera, and in far more ways than we can. Our different lenses allow fields of view and magnification we can only force ourselves to imagine otherwise. The illusion of compression of longer lenses? We don't naturally see that way. Or the effects of a shallow aperture that renders focused elements in space knife-sharp but makes a blur of unfocused space. We see with our eyes neither the magic bokeh of unfocused highlights nor the unmoving and unmovable relationship of elements in space once the shutter has closed and flattened that space forever into two dimensions. The camera sees through a frame, registering space not with binocular vision as most of us do but through a monocular lens. It's different, and we are the ones who need to learn and use those differences.

Our eyes can't see the way the camera does, but we can (and must) learn to both imagine and predict it. This can happen by making more photographs mind- fully and with an increased sensitivity to how the cam- era sees light, space, and time while at the same time not forcing it to conform to what your eyes see, which takes slowing down. After nearly 40 years, I still ask myself, "What are the possibilities I'm not seeing? How *else* can the camera see this?"

Other questions follow. How might the camera see and render light differently than is obvious to my eyes? And what about time? Will it render differently if I slow or increase the shutter speed? How might it see *space* differently if I use a different lens, aperture, or choice of focus? Am I willing to consider that my first instincts might need to bow to less obvious choices? This is a more inquisitive approach than I learned as a teenager. It inquires of the camera, "What is possible with this tool that isn't possible with my eyes alone?"

One of the best questions for the creative mind is often, "What am I missing?"

The photographer who only uses the camera in an attempt to faithfully reproduce what the more limited human eye can see is missing out on the much wider gamut of aesthetic possibility and creative expression made possible by the camera. Learning to see is not the same as learning to see *as the camera sees*. You begin to learn that by *thinking* about it, even obsessing over it.

Another way we can learn to see as the camera does is by looking at the *results* of how it sees by studying photographs themselves. How are light, space, and time rendered? How does the camera speak with or

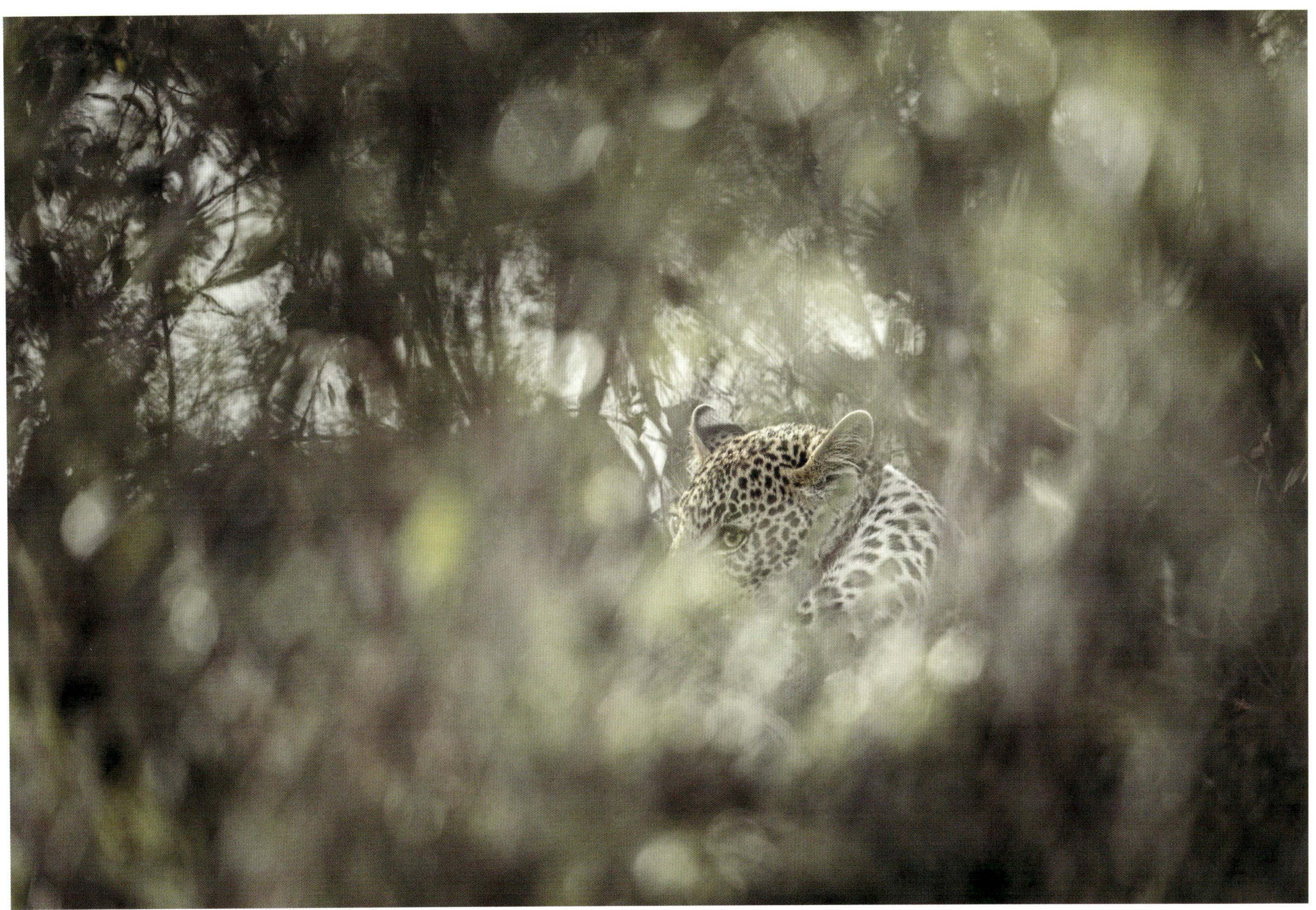

For every decision you make with the camera, what does that one choice do to light, space, or time?

about them in the final image? How do they make you feel? These are the kinds of questions a would-be poet needs to ask about words to learn a sensitivity to them and begin thinking in new ways, and it's how we need to think about our raw materials as well. It doesn't happen in isolation, but as we become more aware of the possibilities, of what can be done with the medium (the language, if you will) in which we work.

So what does this mean for you, the photographer? Practically, it means beginning to think about how the camera might be used to work with our three primary raw materials. For every decision you make with the camera, what does that one choice do to light, space, or time?

Using wide-angle lenses close to the subject translates space (and everything in that space) into a photograph differently than a long lens from farther away. The foreground gets much larger, and the background much smaller. Lines become more diagonal and exaggerated, increasing their energy. Closing the aperture also affects space in the sense that it translates areas of the scene in front of you into either sharp focus or soft out-of-focus areas of colour and tone. Even moving the camera and placing it somewhere else allows it to reorganize the frame spatially and change the relationship of one element to another in that frame. Choosing a slower shutter speed translates time, sometimes quite dramatically. Looking at a landscape and thinking,

"How could the camera see this differently in terms of light, space, and time?" might result in your choice to slow the shutter to blur clouds and water or a moving field of wheat. Taking in a scene on the streets and asking how the camera might see the light differently and then shooting into the light and underexposing by three stops might reduce the otherwise bright scene to nothing but silhouettes and shadows and more mood and mystery than you can see with your eye alone. None of this happens when staring at what's in front of you, camera in hand, and thinking, "Which lens should I use?" or "What settings are *correct*?"

All our choices are wrapped up in what the camera can do to light, space, and time. You can think in this way without *overthinking* it. Asking the questions gives you options by reminding you that there's a difference between what you see and what the camera can see if you'll let it. And if you do this long enough, you'll begin to anticipate how the camera sees and use it to make the photograph feel the way you want it to feel. Underexpose that backlit street scene enough times and you'll soon see the results in your mind; you'll begin to *imagine* them. That is the beginning of finding your answer to "How do I learn to see photographically?" Use a slower shutter for a while, and you'll slowly begin to see time the way the camera does, imagining the possibility every time you see an element in the frame moving through time: a person, an elephant, or storm-blown clouds.

Do that for long enough while paying attention to the results, and you'll begin to *think* differently about the possibilities. You'll see *combinations*, too: not only a slower shutter to give a sense of motion, but a change in the camera position and choice of lens to render space within the frame in stronger ways and take advantage of that sidelight that brings such wonderful depth and texture to the scene.

It is so often said that photography means "painting with light," but we've got a more extensive palette than that—one that allows us to blend not only light but also space and time. Thinking this way, rather than giving first consideration to the tools of aperture, shutter, and optics, allows your imagination to run in the direction of the photograph itself rather than the camera. It's to think creatively about the *effect*, about what the photograph might look and feel like, rather than thinking first about the tools themselves.

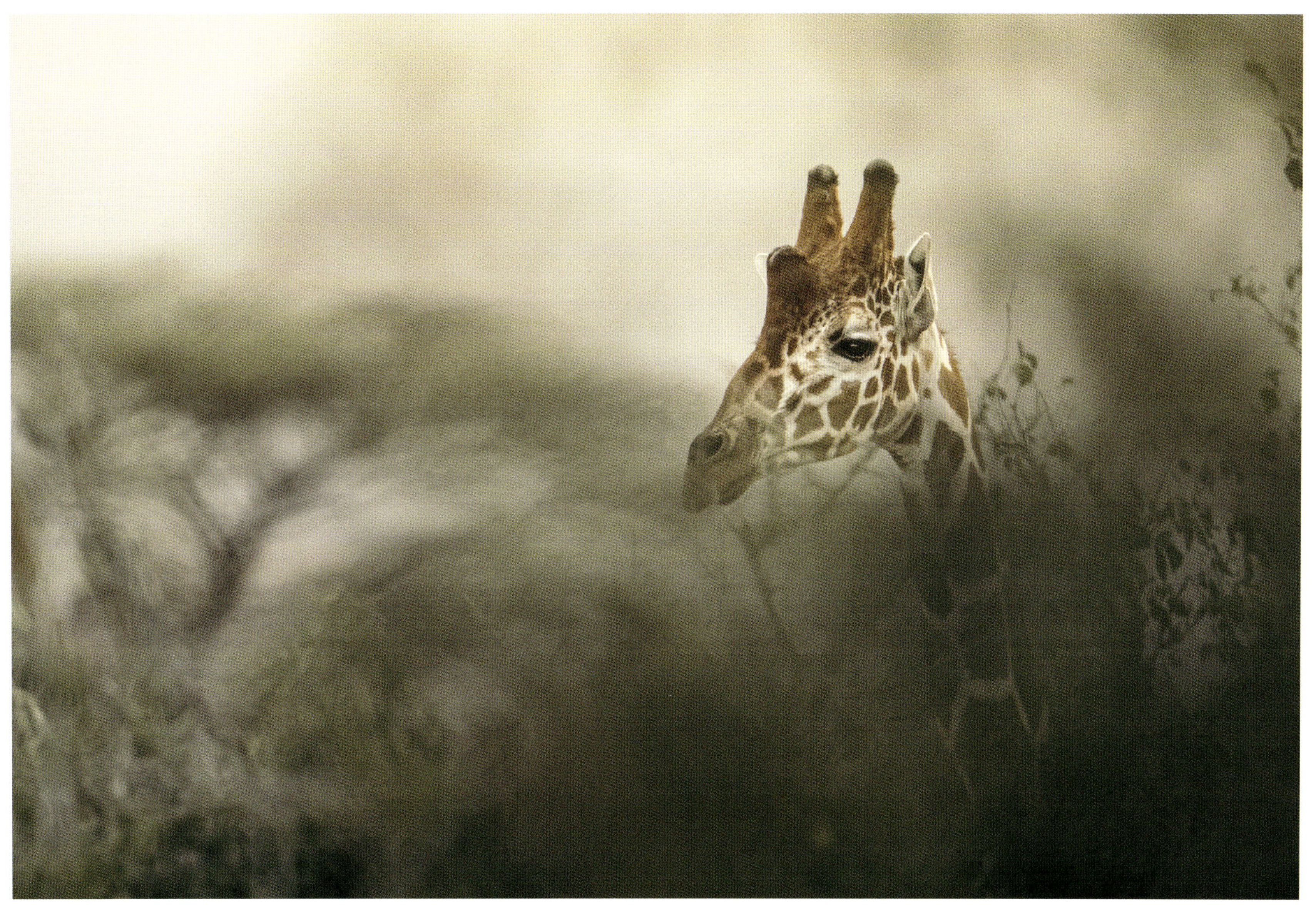

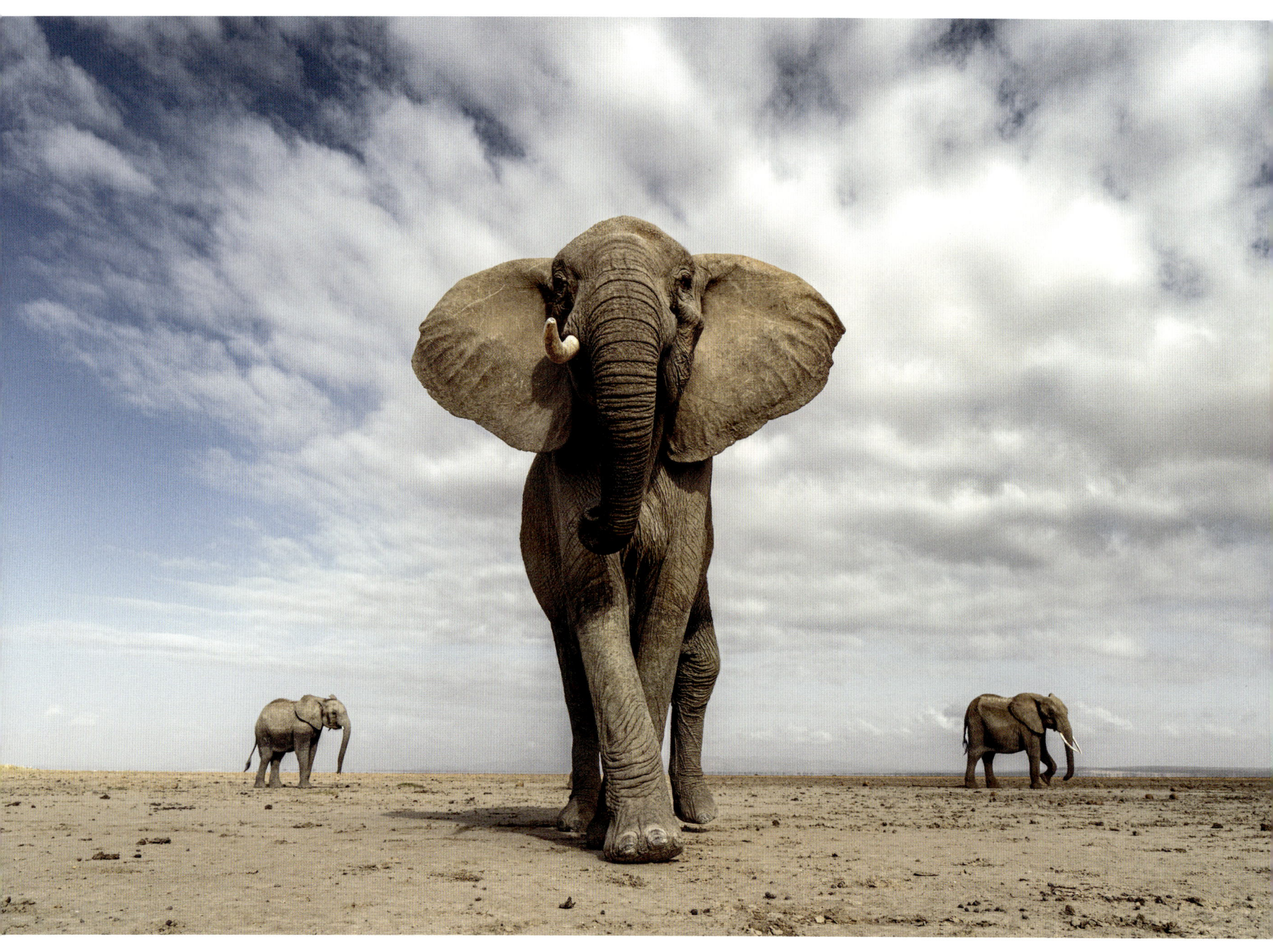

03

Interesting Perceptions

I previously quoted photographer Stephen Shore's belief that a good photographer combines interesting perceptions with an understanding of how the camera could translate the world into a photograph. I presume he specifically means a photograph that reflects those interesting perceptions. The latter is easy to understand, even if understanding how a camera sees the world is not as simple. But the former, the idea of interesting perceptions, is less clear. It's a little harder to pin down, and I think this is in part because it's just so damn subjective. Who am I to say your perceptions are interesting or not? For that matter, who am I to say the resulting photographs you make, even if you meet Shore's two conditions, are *good*?

The fundamental and unavoidable subjectivity of art is not a problem to be overcome but something to be celebrated. That you and I will find different things interesting is what prevents us from falling into the trap of sameness, which art of all kinds has long tried (with varying success rates) to avoid. It's not important that we agree on what is interesting so much as *that*

it is interesting, meaning it pulls your interest. It draws your curiosity, whatever "it" may be. As Shore contends, the photographers with the most to contribute are those who are interested in the world around them and, because of this interest, see that world from different angles. They think about what they see in interesting ways, and when they share that with their audience and the world around them, it is a glimpse into new ways of seeing the world.

Being more interested in the world around you affects the practice of your craft because that's how you get to new perspectives on what you photograph. It's how you get to new ideas about those subjects toward which you point your lens. You can't think more creatively about anything without being interested in it and giving it at least a second glance.

A well-worn trope in photography urges new photographers to "shoot what you love." The sentiment isn't wrong, but it's only part of the story. You might say I photograph wildlife because I love it, but I'm not sure

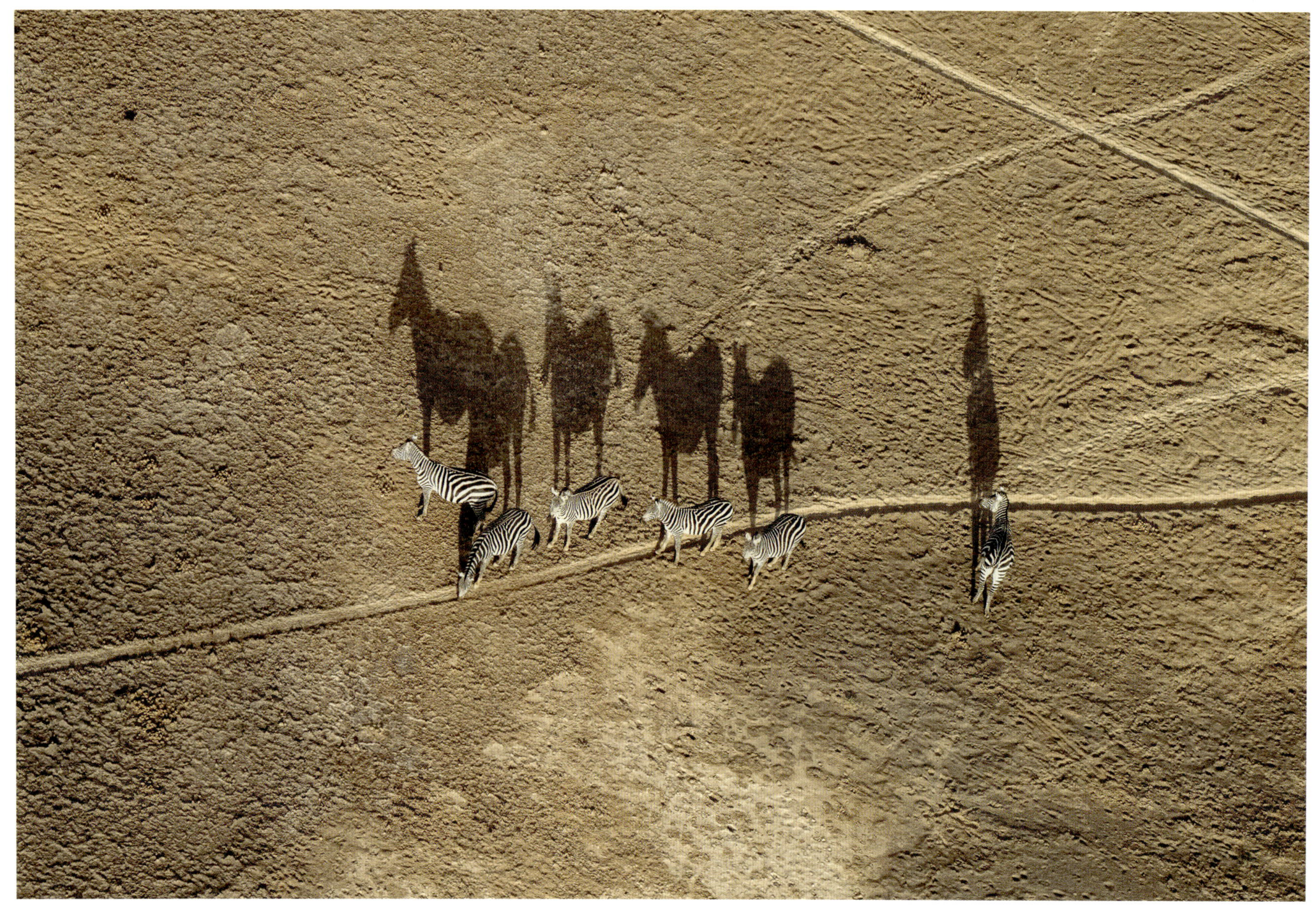

James Nachtwey photographs war and the horrors of human drama because he loves it. I don't know James Nachtwey so I won't presume to speak on his behalf, but he has said he's not a war photographer but an *anti*-war photographer. There is room (and need) for photographers who photograph what they don't love, even what angers them. Some will photograph what amuses or confuses them, but it must *interest* them. Something about the subject must call to something within them to keep them asking questions, looking deeper, and returning time and time again to the places, subjects, and themes they photograph. It must scratch some kind of itch. Perhaps that itch isn't love, but it must be curiosity or interest.

Only by being interested in what you photograph will you think about it long enough to see it from every angle, consider new approaches, and experiment with different combinations. This is the creative approach, and it alone is what gets you past the obvious, past the low-hanging fruit of what you have already done. I often hear the longing for more (or greater) creativity from photographers who say, "I wish I were more creative." There are many angles from which one could

approach finding that increase in creativity, but for now, I suggest it might be as simple as finding something in which you are truly interested. Not just *kind of* interested, but something closer to fascination. Something you think of when you don't have your camera in your hand. Something that distracts you when you should be doing other things. Find that subject or theme, and you'll have rich veins to mine.

It's been said that creativity is in connecting the dots. You combine, or mash up, the dots enough, especially if they're different, and some unlikely unions are bound to form. That's how new ideas are created. New ideas aren't so much new as they are a combination of older things. At its most basic, the math of creativity is something like A+B=C, though if you combine truly unusual pre-existing ideas, it's probably more like A+7=Green. Unexpected combinations come from thinking about things differently but also from thinking about different things—those that interest you. You can't force or fake interest, but you can nurture it.

Only by being interested in what you photograph will you think about it long enough to see it from every angle, consider new approaches, and experiment with different combinations.

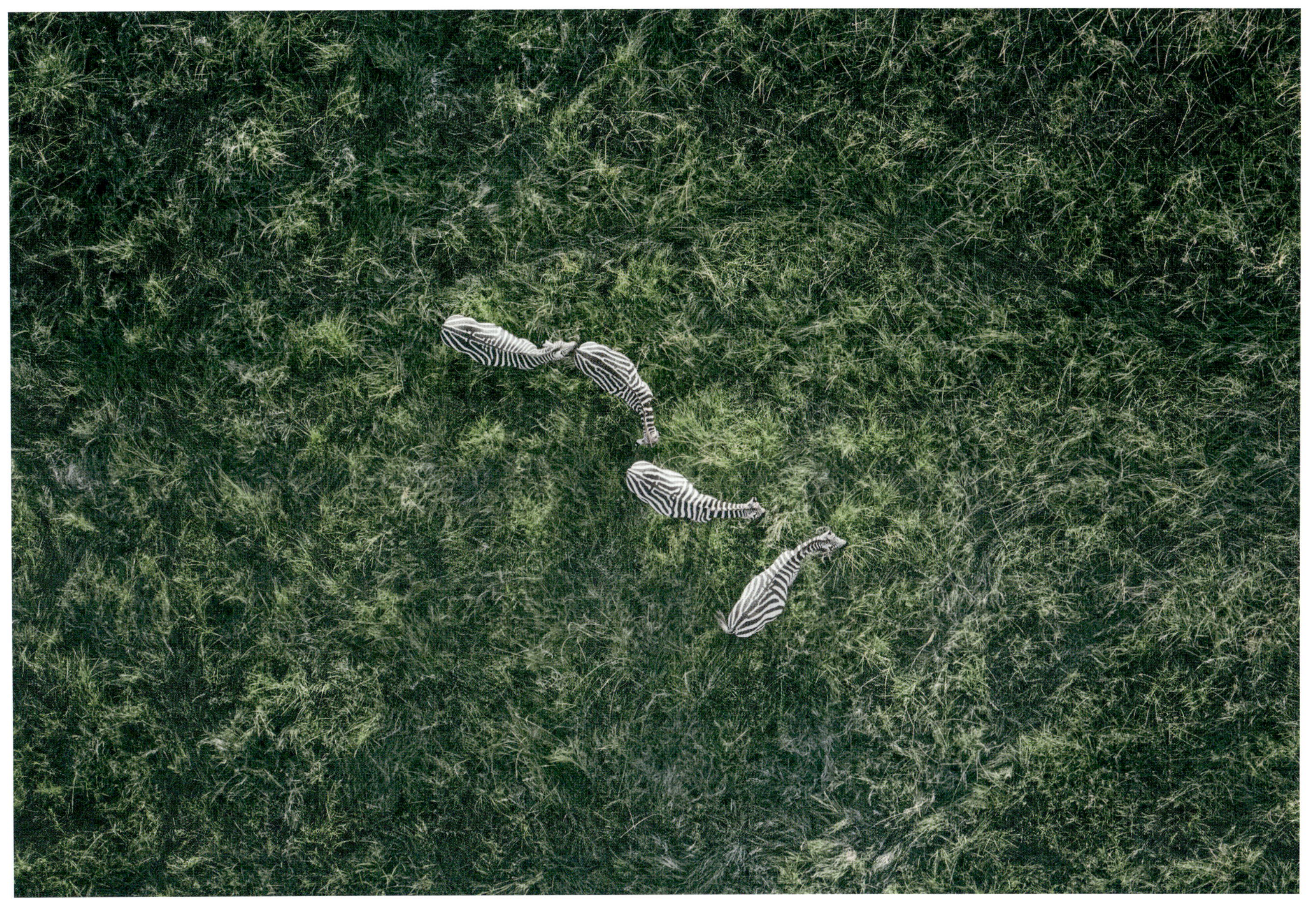

In 2001, Galen Rowell published *The Inner Game of Outdoor Photography.* The title hits the nail on the head, though I think *all* photography is an inner game, and its source (or perhaps the field on which the game is played) is your inner life. What do you think about? What do you read?

How do you absorb the thoughts, ideas, and new perspectives from others and the world around you into yourself? Many photographers are consumed with photography itself, creating a well devoid of new ideas, so efforts to draw from that well come up empty. Or maybe not empty, but I don't see how your fascination with the latest sensor technology might help you create more interesting photographs than, for example, a fascination with the paintings of Claude Monet. That might lead to a curiosity about his use of colour and the history of impressionism, which might further lead you somewhere interesting. And if it's interesting to you, there's a chance it'll be interesting to others. I'm not saying stop being interested in photography; everything you know about your tools is helpful. But beyond those tools, I hope you'll find something out there in the real world to captivate you. There has to be *something* that fascinates you.

We see the world through a lens of thought; seeing is not a task of the eyes alone but also of the mind. You look at what interests you and more readily perceive and recognize the things you think about more often. In 2010, I bought a Land Rover Defender. I was obsessed with it and almost immediately noticed how many people were driving Defenders, as though my purchase had kicked off a Canada-wide trend. It had not. I was just noticing them more. If we see (or recognize) what we know, it's probably worth both knowing more things and knowing more about them.

Let me try a more relevant example. A few years ago, I wanted to know how colours worked together and why, so I decided to study colour. I watched movies and made note of the different colour schemas and how they made me feel or drove the story forward. I looked at paintings by the early masters and at photographs from early colourists like Fred Herzog and Saul Leiter and more contemporary photographers like Alex Webb. I asked why they made the choices they did and how it affected my experience of their work, and how that work made me feel. I was *obsessed*, which is the nuclear version of *interested*. Driven by curiosity, a chunk of my inner life was preoccupied with colour for several months. The result? I started noticing colour schemas in the world around me and the scenes I was photographing. My sensitivity to colour grew; I understood colour in new ways and had new ideas about how I could make my work stronger. I'd watch a movie and think, "That's a *fantastic* complementary colour harmony!" My colour photography has changed not because my eyes suddenly started seeing in colour but because my mind now *thinks* about colour and is able to perceive it in new ways. More *interested* led to more *interesting*.

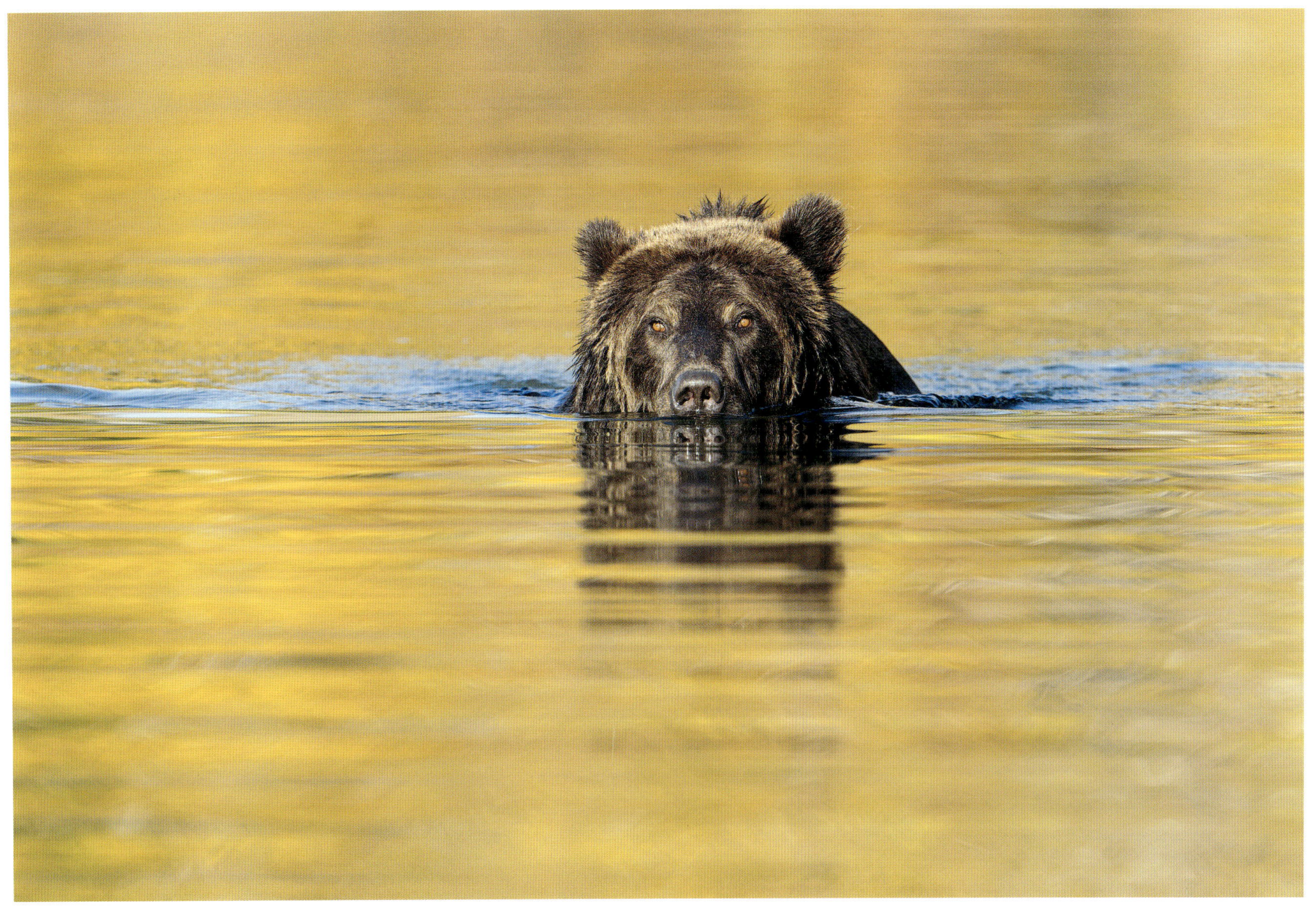

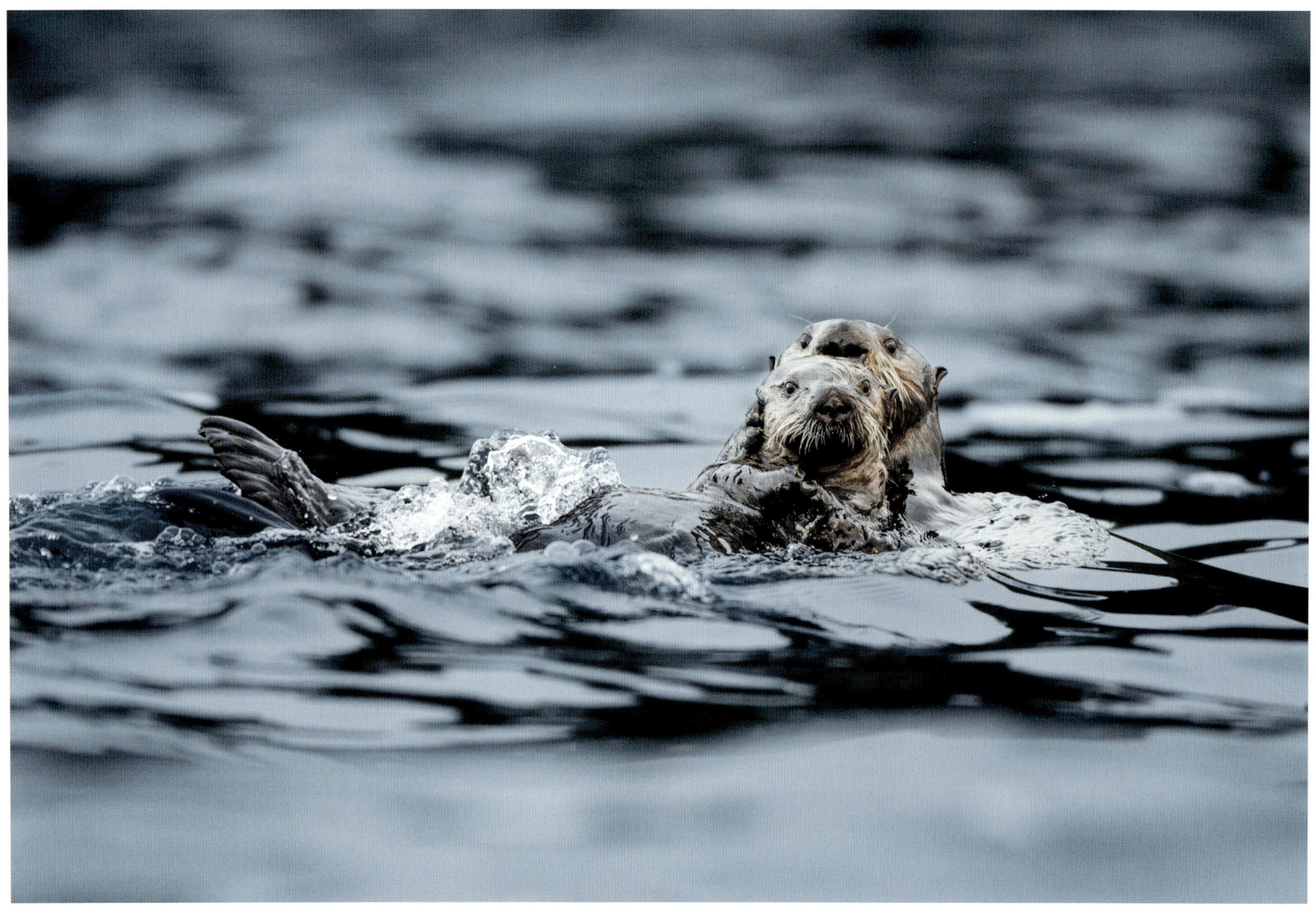

When a photographer's work resonates with someone and they remark that she "has a great eye," they don't mean it literally. They're saying, "That photographer perceives the world in a way that I don't." Maybe it's an "eye" for colour or great moments or composition. Or perhaps it's how they juxtapose elements in the frame in a way you or I might never have thought about. They don't have an eye for juxtaposition; they have a mind for it. They *think* about these things. Perception—how we see the world—is in the mind, not the eyes. You can't do much to improve your eyesight. Even with glasses and laser surgery, it only improves so much. But the mind? It's almost unlimited.

To have more interesting perceptions is to be more interested, not just in one thing but in many. That's how we gather not only the dots that creativity is concerned with connecting but also the dots we actually care about—dots we spend time thinking about. In my experience, that's how we get there: if you want to be more interesting, begin by being more interested. Want to be more creative? Be more curious.

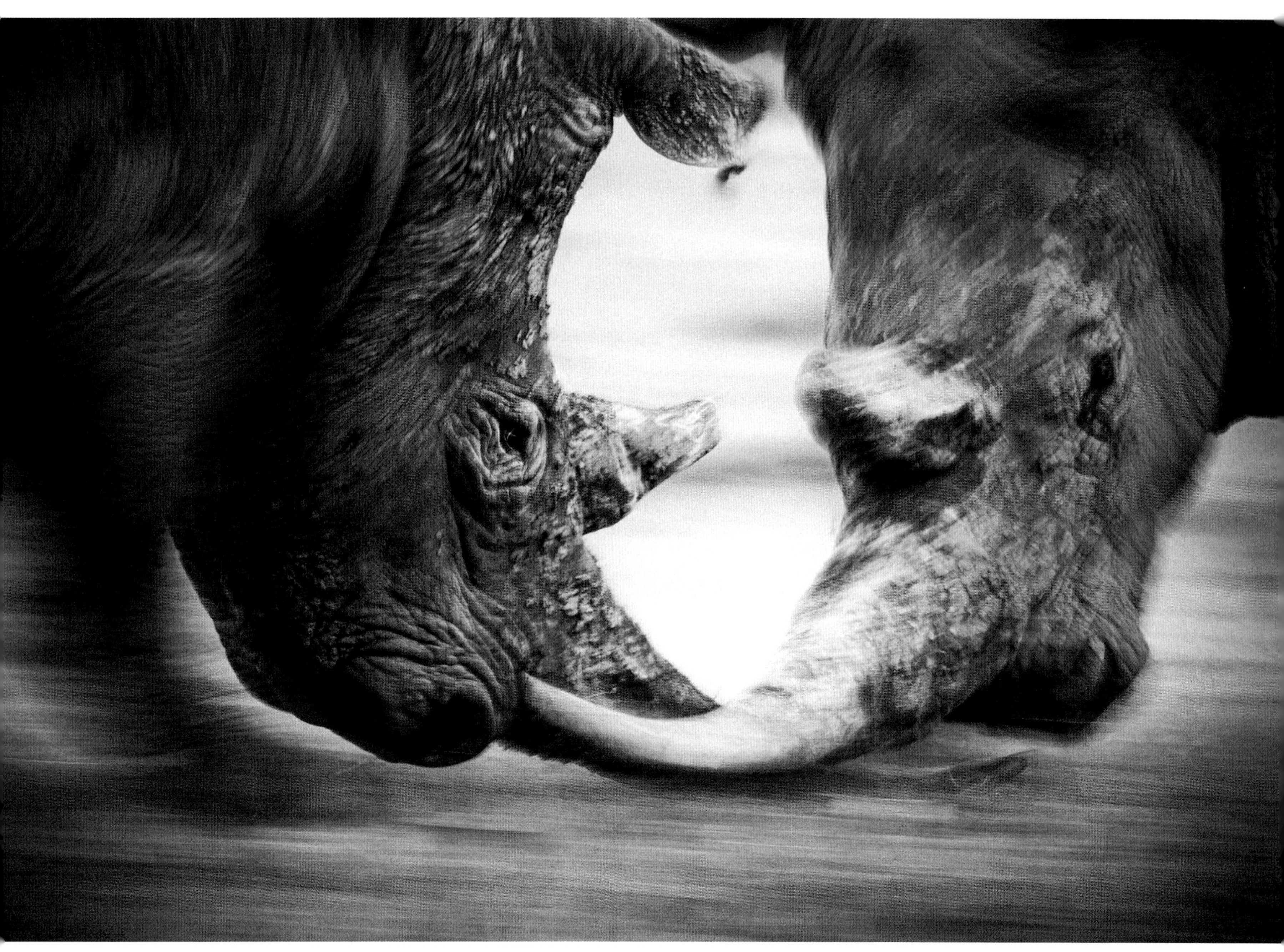

Repetition, Risk, and Reward

A more intentionally creative approach to photography is not only in the thinking. It must also be in the doing. If any single effort at making a photograph begins with thoughts like "What if I . . . ?" or "I wonder how I could . . . ?" then it's in the follow-through that we begin to look for the answers to those questions and to test them.

Years into your craft, you might have honed your imagination to the point that you can essentially answer those questions in your mind. As best I can tell, this is what pre-visualization means. But it's more likely that you need to make an actual photograph before you can know whether your approach works.

Wondering which lens to use to make an image feel the way you desire, it's possible to look at the scene and imagine what your 16mm lens might look like when placed a couple of feet from your foreground object, using f/8 and 1/500. But there's so much more that might be going on, and you might be depending on live subjects (a person or an animal, for example) to do something specific. You might also count on the light doing what you anticipate. To complicate it even more, you might want to use a slower shutter to capture the feeling of motion. Add complication to complication and it becomes impossible to solve your creative problem with thinking alone, especially in the early years when all the moving pieces required to make a photograph seem so wildly disconnected from each other; it's hard to imagine them together as a cohesive whole. In other words, you've got to do it to find out.

You've got to *try*.

Interesting perceptions don't usually lead immediately to interesting results but to interesting efforts, especially if you haven't previously been at this exact intersection of light, space, and time: different place, different moment, different things in the frame, different light illuminating it or casting it into shadow, and (probably) a different vision for the photograph you're trying to make from it all. Generally speaking, creativity is about *thinking* and *working* through what you haven't done before. If you've previously done the same thing in the same way, then the "what if" and "how can I" questions won't be there; you'll have already solved those problems. So unless you're satisfied with repeating what you've already done—what *Calvin and Hobbes* creator Bill Watterson calls "mowing the same patch of grass"—every photograph is a new and different thing. Even if, in the unlikely event that you are photographing similar subjects in similar light and circumstances, there's a good chance you've got an urge to approach it all differently this time.

A new approach resets your creative clock. I've been to Kenya dozens of times, but even in those moments when everything seems familiar and it would be the easiest thing in the world to do what I've done before, the thing that has always changed is the photographer in me. Since the last time I was there, my tastes have grown, becoming more refined. In the months since my last visit, I've probably learned something new about my craft or started playing with a new piece of gear that opens new possibilities I didn't once have. In other words, I've moved on, and that growth brings new questions. Or perhaps they're very similar questions, but I'm looking for different answers because the old answers no longer satisfy my new tastes.

I think one of the reasons photography (or any creative effort) is so hard is because repetition, while it's a great teacher, is low on reward. Every photographer I know is somewhat restless on the inside, wanting to do better than last time—usually meaning to do it differently. Maybe this time it's a photograph with fewer technical flaws, but also a stronger choice of moment. A more balanced composition. A more careful approach to

what you exclude or a more intentionally chosen point of view or perspective. Maybe it's a different feeling you are striving for or a different sense of story. No matter how much thought you give this, at some point, you're going to have to stop thinking and start doing, and trying something new brings an entirely different mental challenge: what if it doesn't work?

The missing piece between having more interesting ways of looking at the world and the knowledge of how the camera translates the world into a photograph is the speculative effort it takes to connect them. In a word, it's *risk*. Not every effort to make a photograph of the scene in front of you will match it to the image in your mind. If my hard drives have anything to say about it, then *most* of my efforts don't succeed, and it's not unreasonable to give yourself that same permission or freedom.

In the mash-up of all the choices you make to create a photograph, it's possible one will be brilliant, totally unexpected, and wildly compelling. All the others will be rubbish. You'll press the shutter and immediately wonder what you were thinking. Or not thinking. How did you miss that element in the background that is now so obvious you can look at nothing else? What in the world made you think 1/15 of a second was a good choice? And for the love of Dorothea Lange, why didn't you move slightly to the left or use a wider lens or pick a better moment?

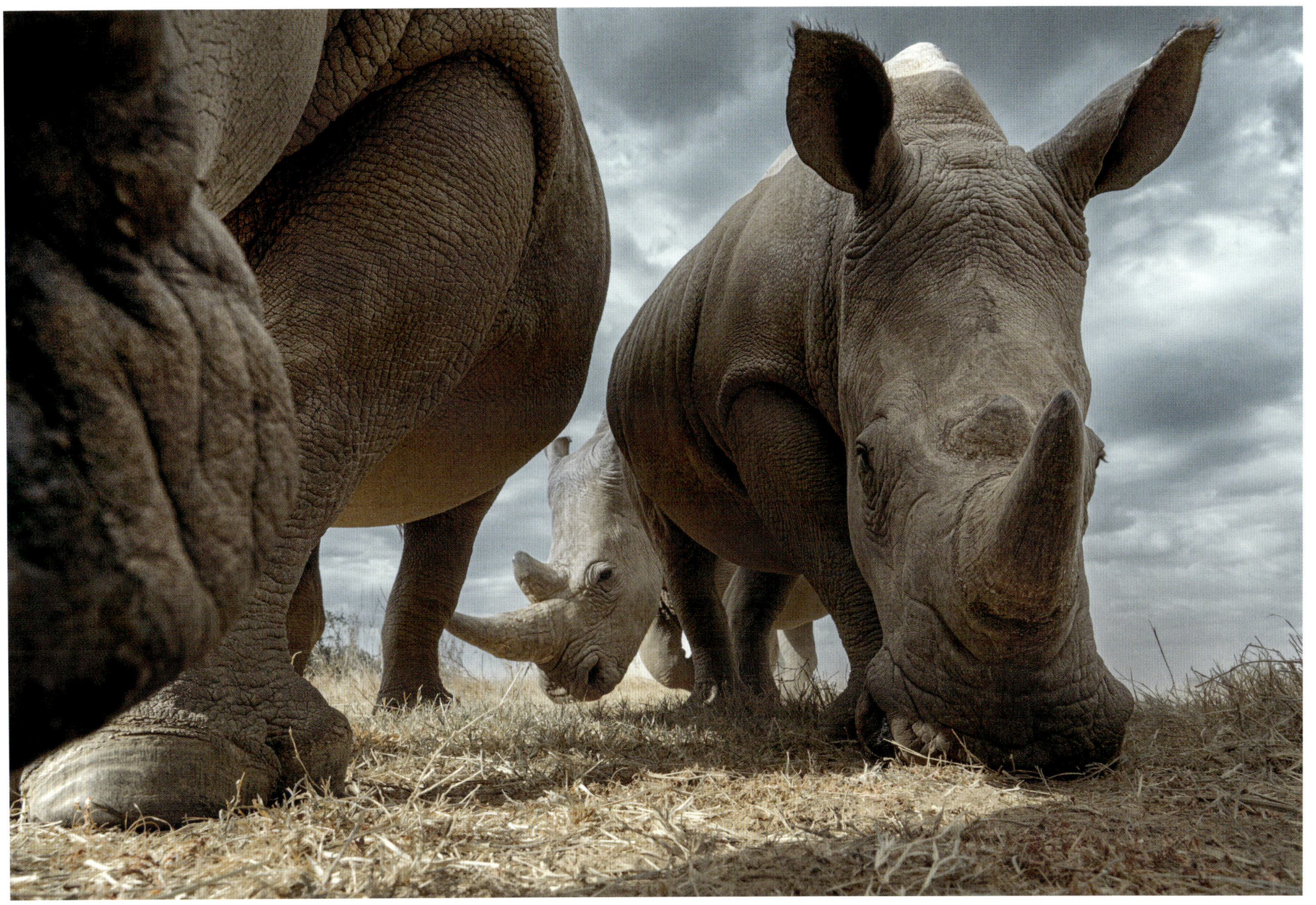

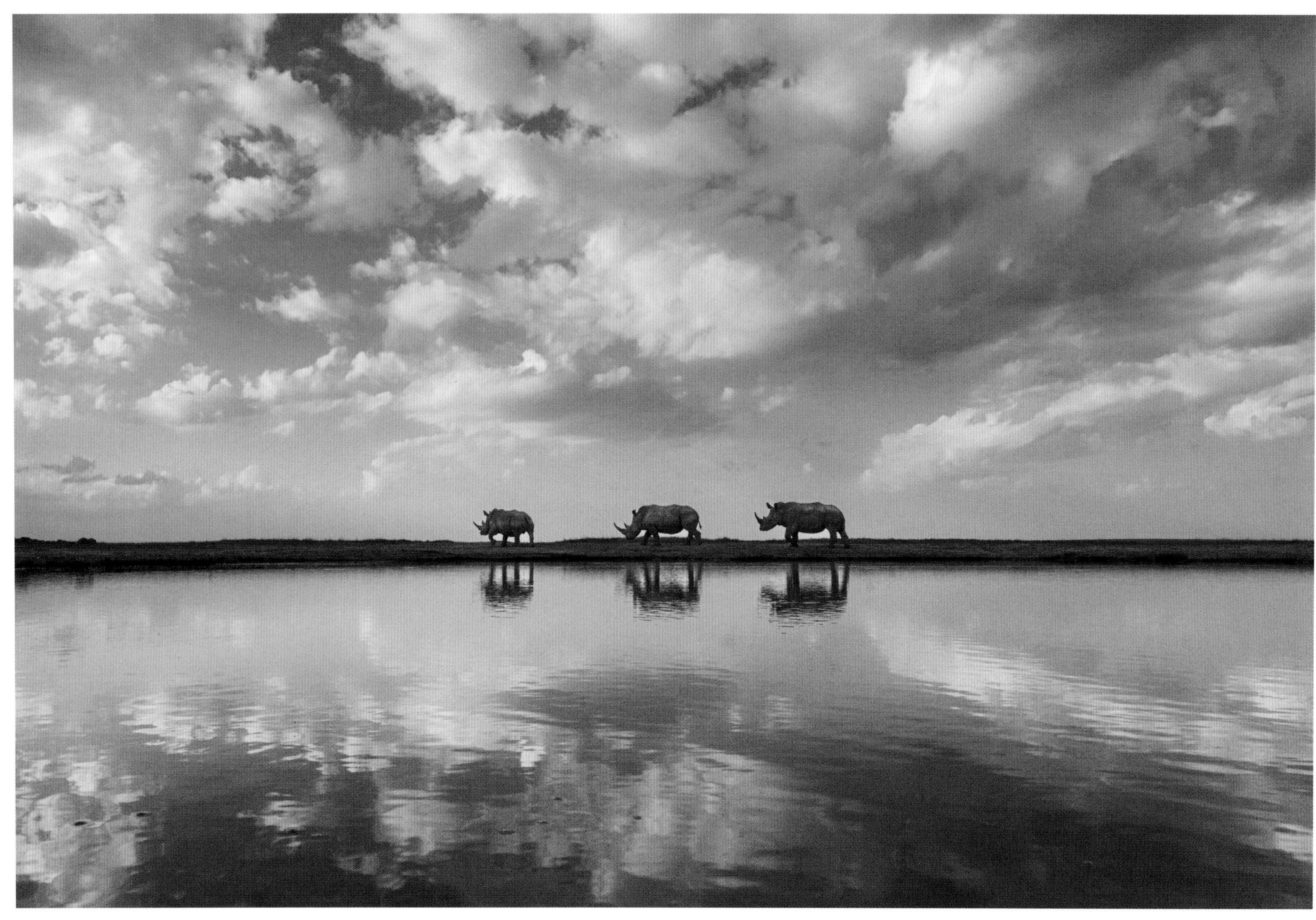

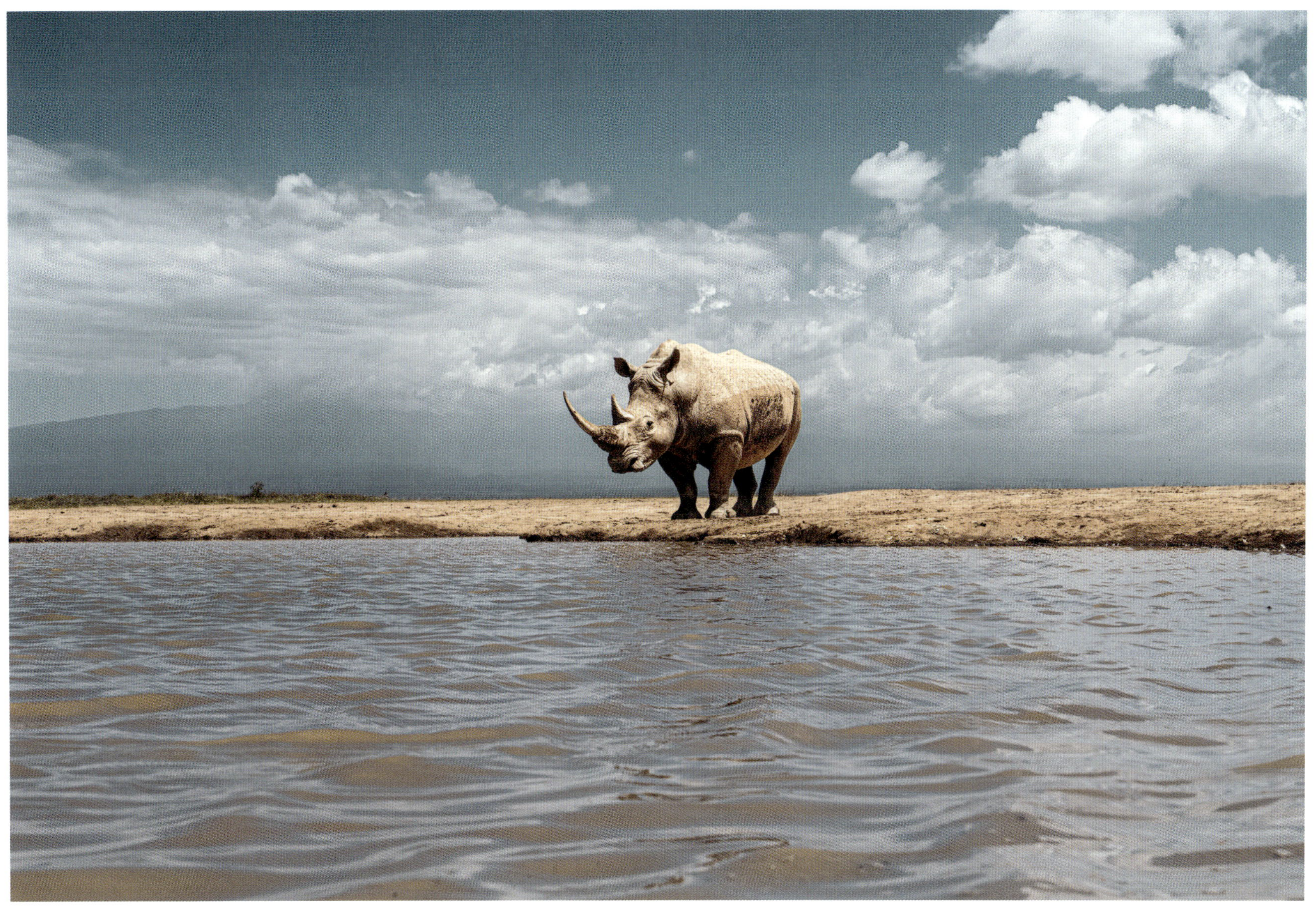

Those initial images will be disappointing. But once you set aside the self-recriminations, I hope you'll also see them as *necessary*. I call them sketch images, meaning they aren't the final photograph, but they help get you there. They are the multiple attempts to try something different and to answer those initial what-if questions. Even if you're not conscious of those questions, there's still this big one: can I make a strong photograph here in this moment from what I'm look-ing at? The answer probably won't be found in the first snapshot; you can't make one image and decide, "No, I can't do this; it just doesn't work." It's true that some-thing isn't working, but it's not the camera. It's you. You stopped too soon. You made one sketch image, decided it wasn't a masterpiece, and gave up.

It usually takes many sketches to make anything you might look at with pride, satisfaction, or whatever feeling you get when you finally pull it off, look at the resulting photograph, and call it "the one."

The creative process, varied as it is for all of us, is at least that: a process. We make iteration after iteration, slowly changing our approach until it all falls into place. With each change comes the risk that it might not work. It might even feel like a step backward. But does it mat-ter? Does it matter to you that you made 20 different attempts to get it right if you got there in the end? Will you look at that final photograph that gives you such satisfaction and bemoan the 20 or 100 sketch images that got you there? Probably not. You won't even think

about them. But isn't that challenge part of the joy of what we do? If it were as simple as point-and-shoot, would it be as rewarding?

I think there's a reason repetition lacks the kind of rewards that risk provides. We grow through challenge, and that's also where we find creative flow. Doing the same thing over and over again guarantees similar results and has no real payoff. There's no sense of "Will it work this time?" There's no sense of hope or antici-pation. You don't get that same feeling of overcoming or accomplishing something and making some new thing that no one has seen before. Of course, there's no frustration, either; it's same-old, same-old, and that's part of the appeal. It's easy. But if more interested pho-tographers create more interesting photographs, then I don't think it's unfair to wonder what kind of photo-graphs are made by bored photographers.

If you aren't trying new things, you aren't growing. If you aren't failing on the first try when you do those new things, there's a good chance you aren't learning. The only failure in creative efforts is to not try. When I teach international workshops and ask a student how it's going and they tell me it's not going well at all, I ask to see their photographs. They'll nervously hand me their camera, and as I scroll through their images, I'm not looking for the best work or for a frame I can turn into a lesson about aperture choices; I'm counting the sketch images and looking for the risk, the effort. I'm looking to see what they've *tried*. You can't make three

You can't make one image and decide, "No, I can't do this; it just doesn't work." It's true that something isn't working, but it's not the camera. It's you. You stopped too soon.

frames and know that "it's not working." So if you've only made three frames, I most certainly know it's *you* who's not working it.

But even when you *are*, when you've been at it for an hour, it's worth remembering how lucky so many of our best photographs really are. You can pound away at your shutter for 60 minutes and try different points of view, different focal lengths, and different shutter speeds but still not stumble into that all-important intersection of light, space, time, and all the many decisions that make for a compelling image until the 61st minute. If you make it to that 61st minute, you'll see it as sheer dumb luck. I seem to get luckier the longer I wait. I get luckier the more I press the shutter and try new things. I get luckier when I don't look at my initial sketch images and judge them too harshly.

And yet, sometimes I don't. But it can't be a coincidence that my luck increases when my willingness to step out of the comfort zone of the tried and true and take a few risks also increases. Conversely, my luck gets very thin when I do only what I've done before or think too highly of my first efforts, mistaking sketches for masterpieces and never sticking around long enough to make more sketches and take the chance at something even better.

I once traveled with a photographer whose motto seemed to be, "I got the shot." He'd see something, raise the camera, make quick work of the required technical choices, press the shutter, and announce, "I got the shot!" Respectfully, no. "The shot" doesn't exist, and thinking it does is the opposite of creative; it's lazy and complacent and prevents the thinking that wonders if there isn't a better "shot" that might be possible with different choices. Maybe a stronger moment. Perhaps one where you've changed position, and in doing so, you've allowed the light to come from the side rather than the front. Maybe you've crouched down, changing the composition or making all the lines in the frame slightly more energetic. It could be that after one more considered moment, you open that aperture to reduce the depth of field, and that's the choice that pulls it all together. And, frankly, it may be only after you've selected your best images from among many and seen the final frame, made a few nudges in the darkroom (traditional or otherwise), and printed that work that you can say with some truly well-deserved satisfaction that you "got the shot."

Is there no room for the intuitive? Are there no photographers with instincts so honed that they do get "the shot" on the first try? Of course, but intuition and instinct are trained, so if you're already at that point of grace in your craft, I suspect there are other books you're reading right now.

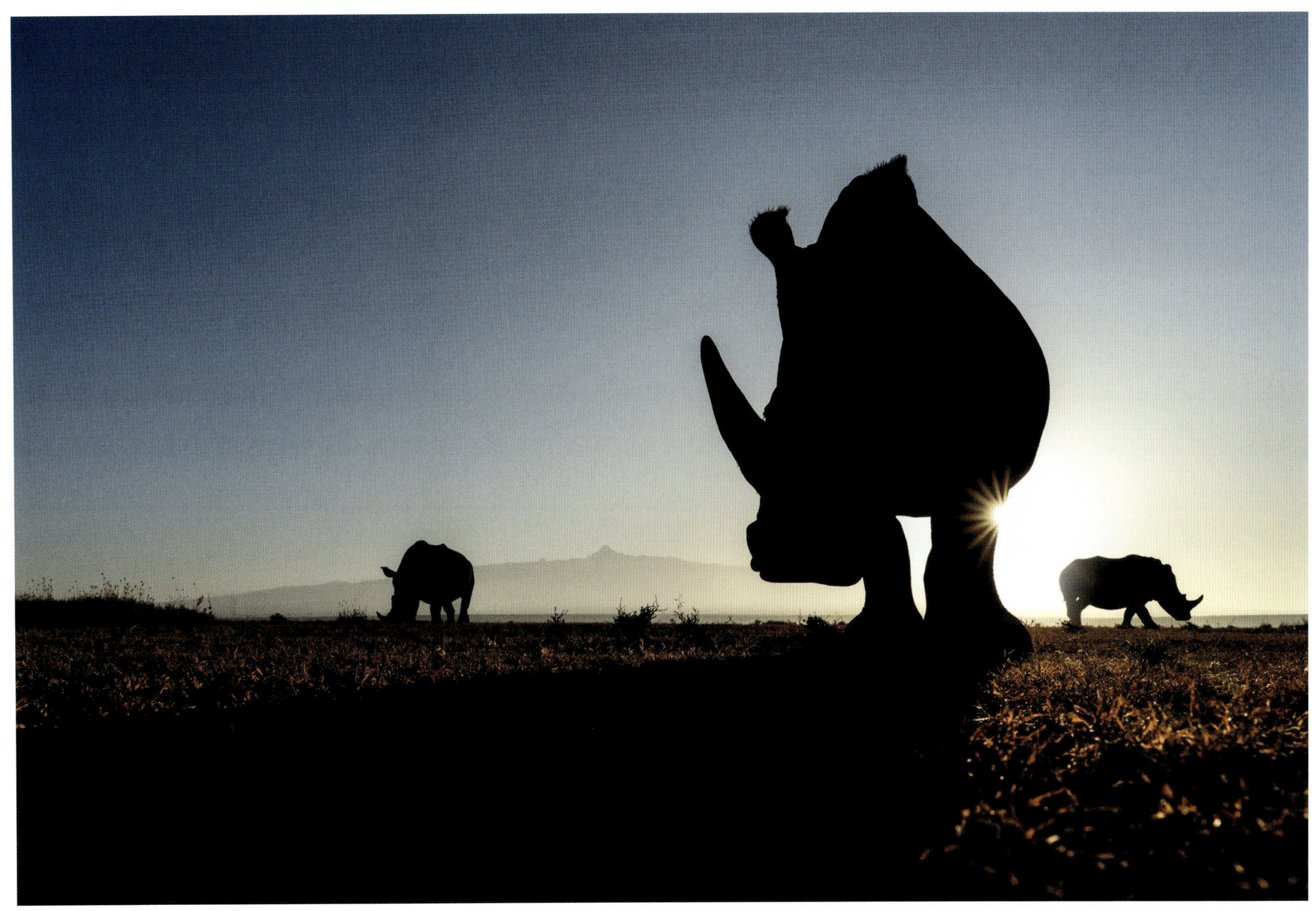

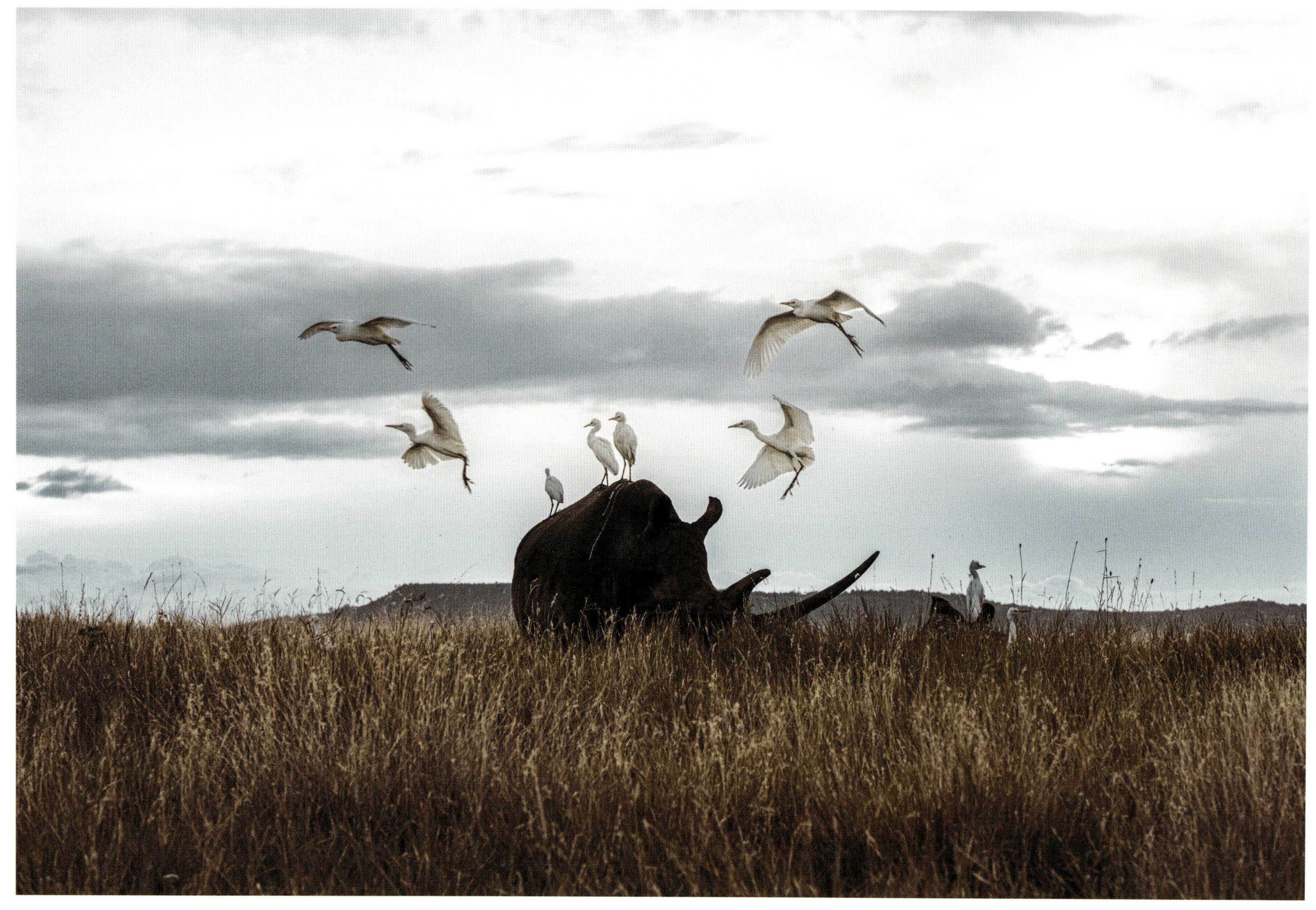

I seem to get luckier the longer I wait. I get luckier the more I press the shutter and try new things. I get luckier when I don't look at my initial sketch images and judge them too harshly.

I press the shutter a lot; my cameras are usually on a burst mode of some kind. For wildlife, this is just a matter of best practice, especially when the subjects are moving quickly. But even on the streets or in the quieter settings of a temple or mosque, I rarely shoot one frame at a time. A rate of three or four frames per second gives me a better chance at making one frame that does exactly what I was hoping for, that more perfectly (or more poetically) captures that beautiful intersection of moment and light and the scene in front of me. You can shoot in burst mode (and how lucky are we that we can now do that silently without the flapping of mirrors?) and still be very intentional about what you're doing. For me to do otherwise—to set my camera on single shot and hope my timing is impeccable—is not just too great a risk, but also the wrong risk.

Risk for the sake of risk has no intrinsic creative rewards. And what feels risky and uncomfortable to you will be different from what feels risky to me. It feels unacceptably risky to me to press the shutter once and move on without mining the scene for everything it has for as long as possible. It's too risky for me to take a quick approach by trusting my first instincts and not taking the time to see things that my first glance often misses, never mind the time necessary to wait for something unexpected to happen. That's a risk that has no real hope of paying off. It's not *that* we risk; it's *what* we risk.

Taking the chance that what you're about to try might not work or might not work immediately is a good (though uncomfortable) risk. Taking a chance that you'll miss the moment while you're experimenting with some new technique is probably a good risk. If you do miss that moment, you'll beat yourself up for a while, but it will lead to growth, if not to an image you've never made before. Risking that some new project doesn't lead where you expected but instead takes you down some unfamiliar paths that leave you with more questions than answers is the type of risk that has the promise of creating change and leading to more interesting (if not always predictable) photographs.

Repetition is easy because doing what you've done before, safe in the knowledge that it works, is comfortable. But that's not where growth happens. It's not where we learn and move forward. A more creative approach to making photographs will always involve risk, and that's where the reward is.

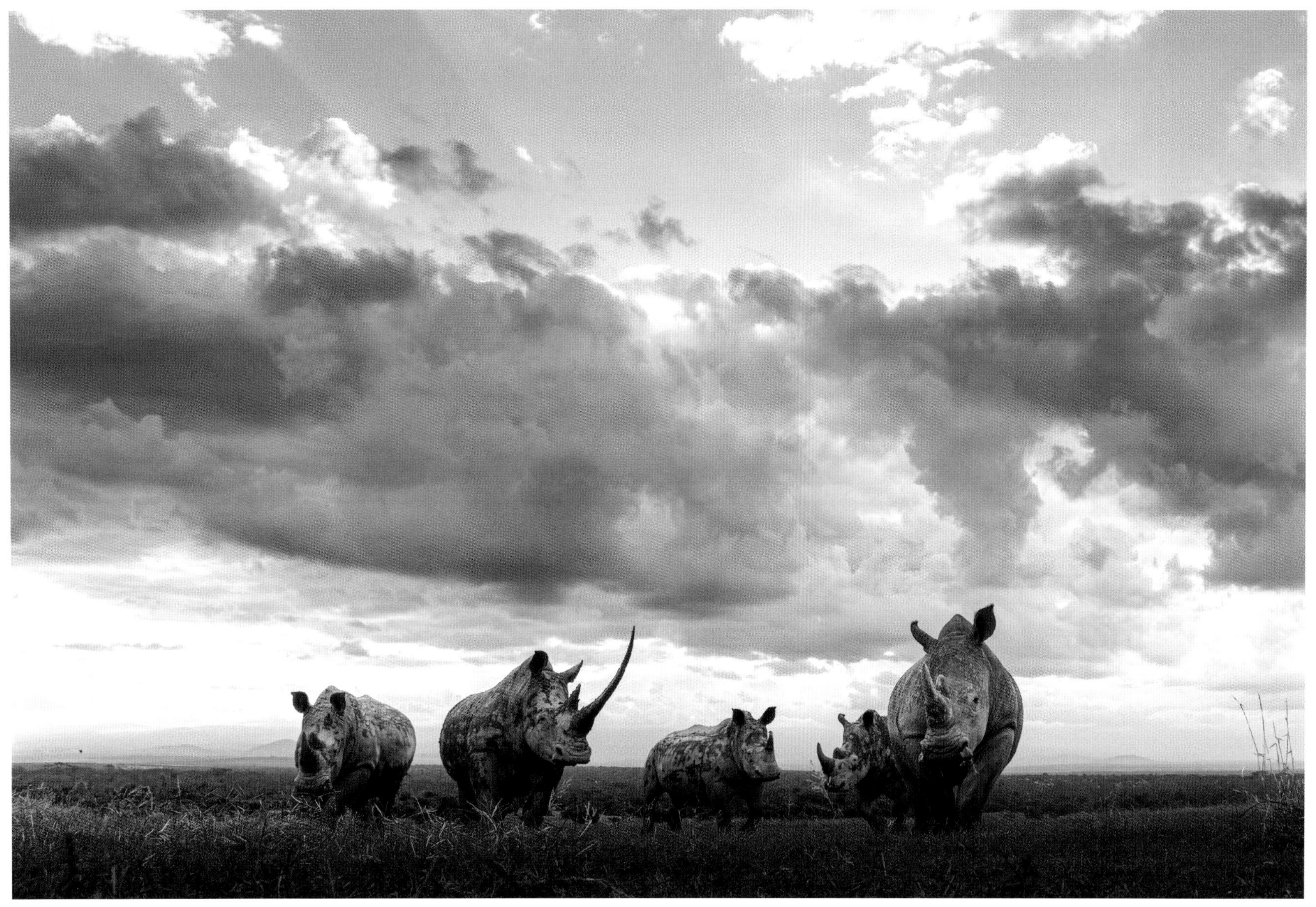

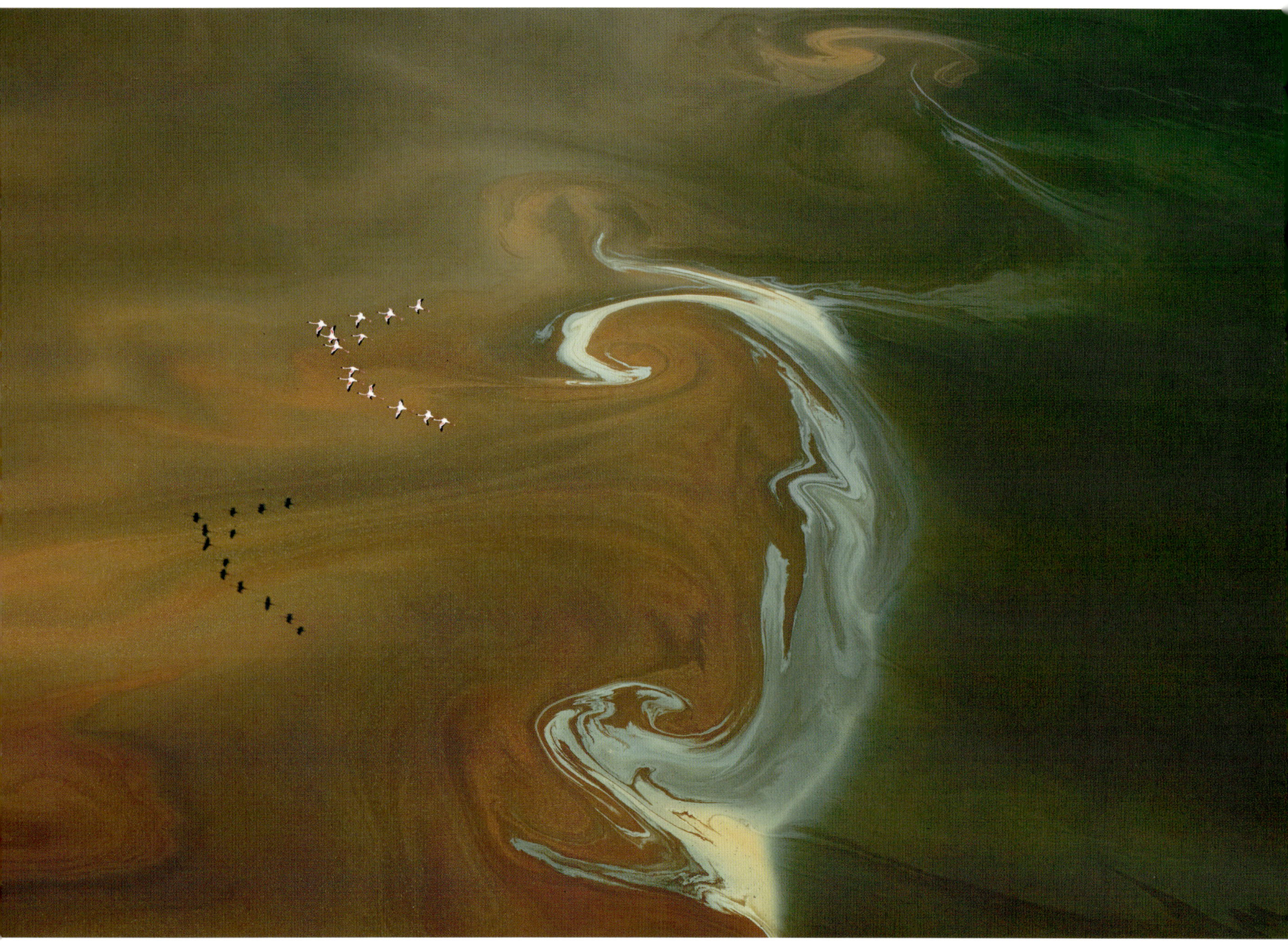

Reaction
and Response

Yes, it is *possible* to "get the shot" in one frame. It happens, but in my experience, it's so rare that it's more of a rounding error than a meaningful statistic. More importantly, if you expect it to be the norm and then fail to get the results you want immediately and give up because "it's just not working," then you'll have missed the more compelling photographs that almost always come at the end of the process, not the beginning.

And even when it *does* happen—when you experience something, put the camera to your eye, press the shutter, and are so satisfied with the results that you move on—I wonder what is being lost or missed by not digging a little deeper. Which subsequent or stronger moments might slip by unnoticed? Which alternate points of view or possible compositions might be ignored or never tried? Is it possible to miss what is better by settling for what seems good? And if you believe, as I do, that a valuable part of the creative process happens later when choosing that one final frame from among many, which raw materials were neglected or overlooked to make the most of that part of the process? It so often happens as I edit my work

that one frame, made only *fractions* of a second apart from a different frame, is so much better in what it expresses or emotes; I can't imagine being so sure of my timing that I would rely on making only one frame instead of four or five.

There is a danger in being so premature with our satisfaction that we don't chase something more by making sketch image after sketch image in that pursuit. There is no badge of honour reserved for those who shoot as few frames as possible, nor is there shame in making many.

The argument against making many frames in the pursuit of one final image is often about efficiency. "I don't want to have to go through a thousand images later on" feels a little like Michelangelo saying he doesn't want to chip off too much marble lest he have to sweep it up later. I'm as concerned about wasting time as anyone else, but editing is often a neglected part of the process; I'm not sure gathering *less* raw material and giving myself *fewer* chances to create the strongest photographs is a trade worth making. It doesn't take much time to look through a burst of five images and find the strongest frame. It's almost instinctive for me by now, and it can be so for you. One of two things will happen: either one frame will jump out at you as obviously more compelling, or they'll all be so similar there's no need to waste time choosing from among them. If it's the latter, then the many frames are a case of "no harm, no foul." Pick one and move on. But if it's the former, then the frames on either side of that stronger picture are a small price to pay to get there.

There is no shame in embracing the edit, meaning choosing your strongest images from among the many, many others as part of your creative process and, in doing so, making more frames from which to make those choices. Other disciplines enthusiastically embrace the idea of iterations. Writers make first drafts—often many of them—that they hope no one will ever see. The goal is not to get the perfect novel on the first try but to discover the bones, play with ideas, and see what emerges. They delete as many words as they keep (usually more), and no one ridicules them for the need to write and rewrite many times. It's part of how they honour their craft and the desire for the strongest final story. "There is no great writing," it is said, "only great rewriting."

Many painters sketch their ideas before putting paint on the canvas, filling notebooks with studies and versions of what might eventually become a painting. In our reluctance to do this ourselves and our worrying whether others think we're spraying and praying our

way to stronger images, have we missed an essential part of the creative process?

My memory cards and hard drives are my notebooks. Filled with sketch images, failed attempts, and a handful of good photographs (certainly photographs that satisfy me tremendously), it's a messy collection that few people, if anyone, will ever see. Messy hard drives are the necessary results of asking, "What if?" and then looking for the answers by pressing the shutter button, changing things up, and then pressing it again. And again. Sketching it out repeatedly until it goes very well, getting closer to the heart of the image I saw in my mind—closer to the reason I picked up the camera in the first place.

What I mean by "sketching" is making photographs—experimenting—just to see what things look like.

It doesn't often come together the first time. I sometimes need to move the camera to the left to shift the relationships of elements in the frame. Other times, I need to work through what must be included and what still needs to be excluded. And sometimes, I need to do all that and wait for a stronger moment or better light. I don't always show up with a clear vision of what my final photograph will look like. I have a sense of what I am attracted to, perhaps what the final image might *feel* like, but having vision and having *a* vision can be two different things. Sketching it out and playing with iterations can help to uncover both.

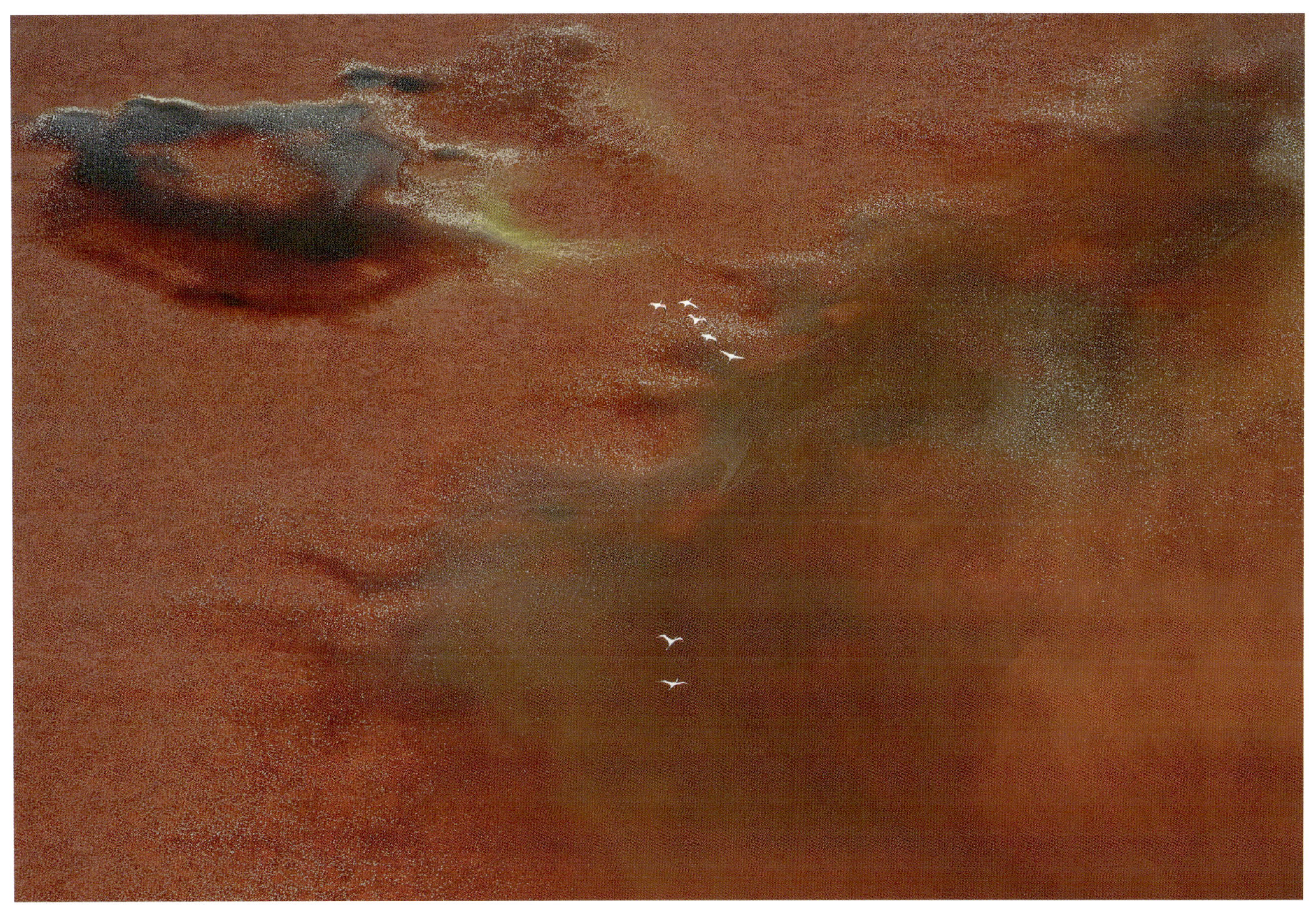

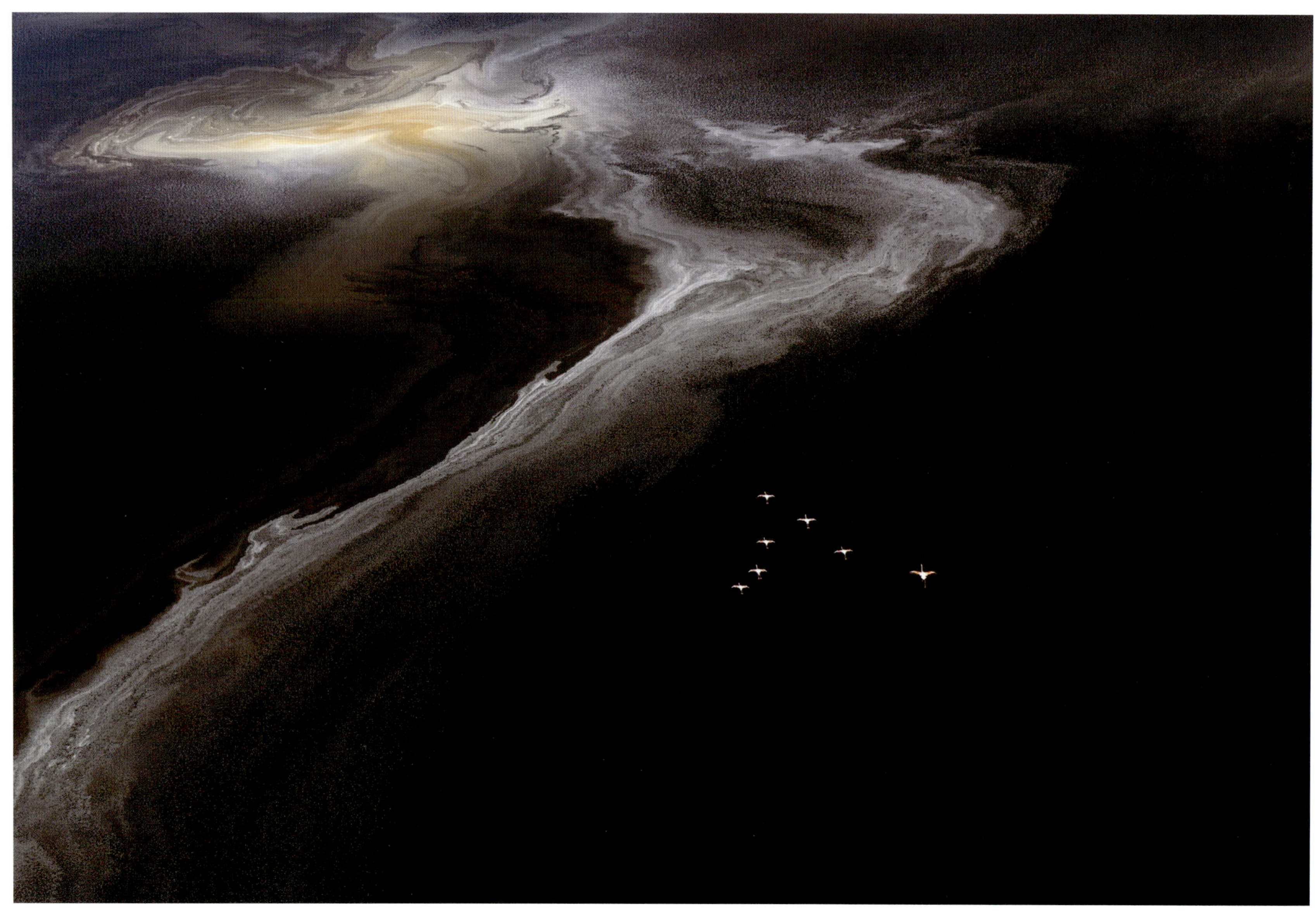

I have a sense of what I am attracted to, perhaps what the final image might *feel* like, but having vision and having *a* vision can be two different things. Sketching it out and playing with iterations can help to uncover both.

Someone once asked Pablo Picasso whether, when starting a painting, he knew what it would look like when he finished it. "No, of course not," he replied. "If I knew, I wouldn't bother doing it." I find it encouraging to hear things like this from an artist I would have assumed had a clearer view of the final outcome of his work at the outset.

Picasso's response implies that the act of painting was the way he discovered what the painting itself would become—that putting his brush to the canvas was an act of exploration before it was ever an act of expression of any specific idea. I believe he was also implying that the act of exploration was the very *reason* he painted to begin with. That should give hope to those of us who desire to make a photograph but don't specifically know where to begin and aren't exactly sure where we will end up.

When I arrive at a place or sit with a subject, it takes time to discover what that place or subject is all about. Even on the smallest scale, what is it in this specific moment that I want to express? I often don't know. You might not, either. My process, far from being tidy, looks something like this:

(click) Nope.

(click) Nope.

(click) Nope.

(click) Hmmm . . .

(click) Interesting, but what if I . . . ?

(click) Nope. But . . .

(click) Nope. Drat. Oh, but . . .

(click) Ooooh, hang on . . .

(click) This gives me an idea.

(click) That's closer . . .

(click) OMG. I love that.

(click, click, click)

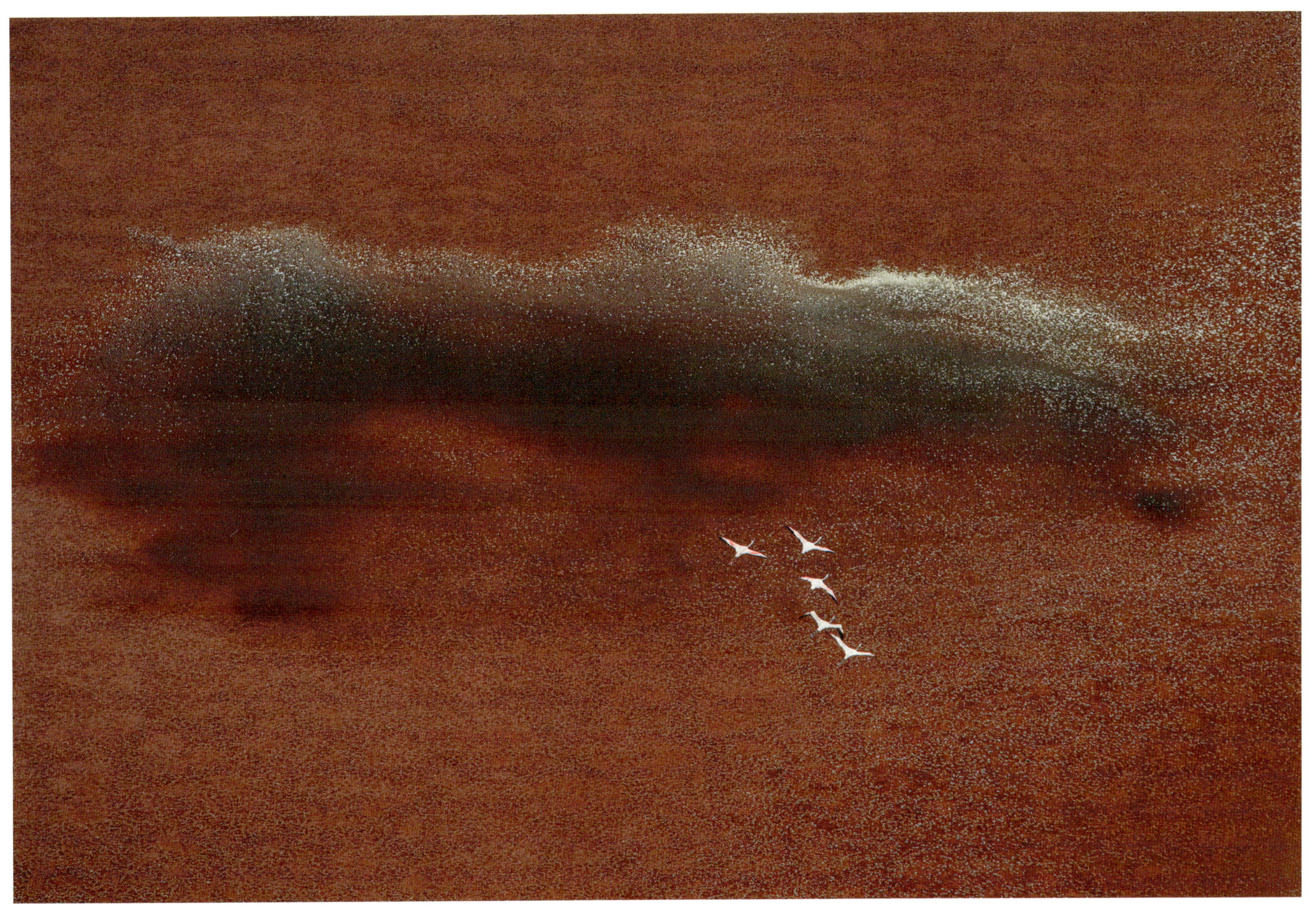

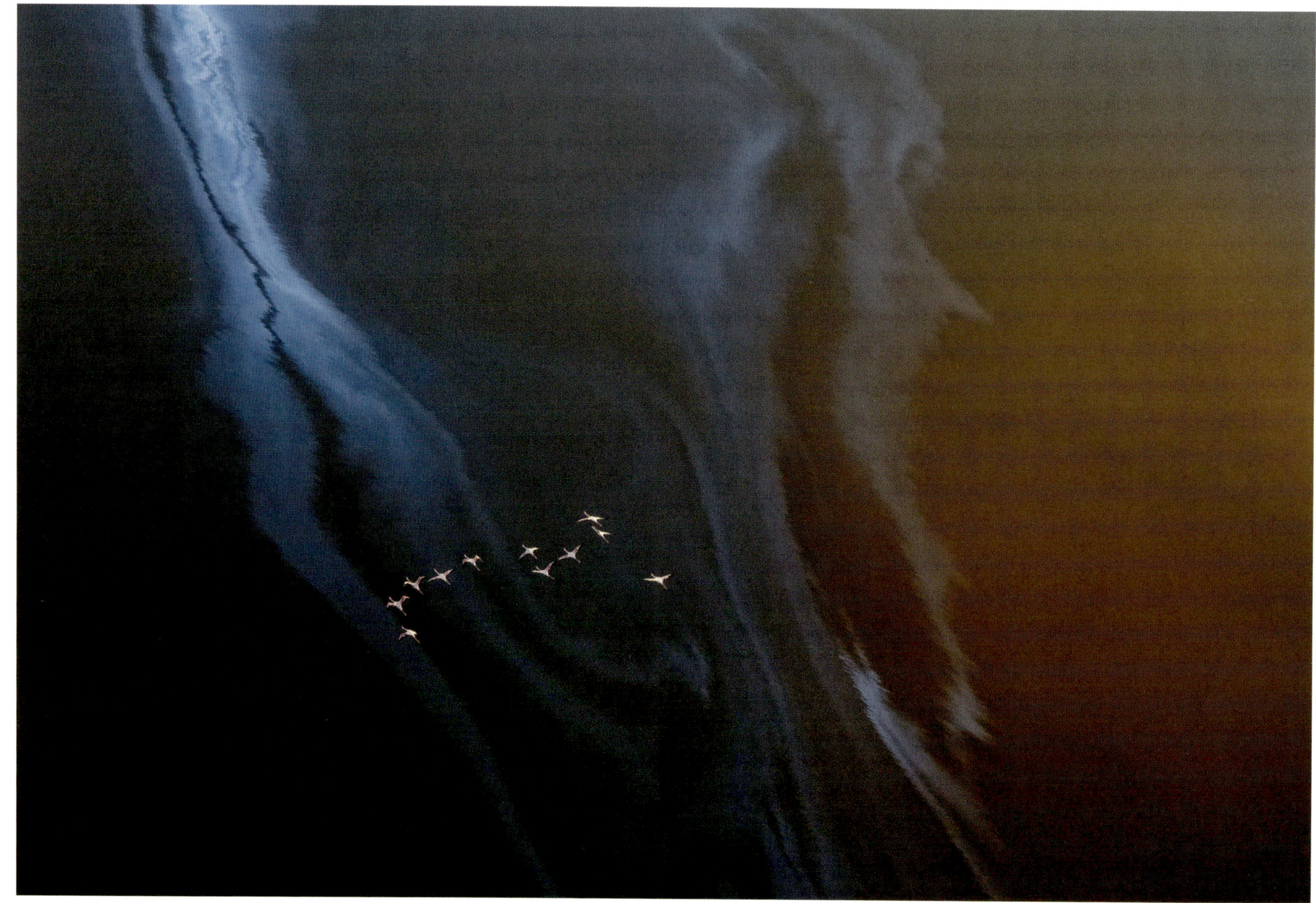

working, changing what's not, and trying new things to get closer. There is risk involved, of course, but also rewards. The best photographs don't just happen when the light is sublime and the moment is right; they happen when all your decisions about the camera craft work together at that intersection. It can take a few (if not many) attempts to get it all where you want it—not to get it correct, but to get it to *feel* right.

Iterations give us new ideas. These sketch images may not be where we're going, but they're so often how we get there, and in my experience it's the same with anyone engaged in creative efforts. Sir James Dyson, the inventor of the vacuum cleaner that bears his name, made over 5,000 versions of his cyclone vacuum before settling on a design that worked the way he had imagined. That's a lot of trial and error, but none were failed efforts. Each was a step forward, an evolution. An initial idea is helpful, but the real work is in the willingness to iterate, to not settle too quickly on what you think is the final image, and to keep exploring, keep digging, until you find it. Knowing that no single frame needs to be "the one" gives you the freedom to change things up and see what the next one might look like. With experience and a little luck, those subsequent frames look less like the first sketch images you made and increasingly more like the final photograph you're working toward.

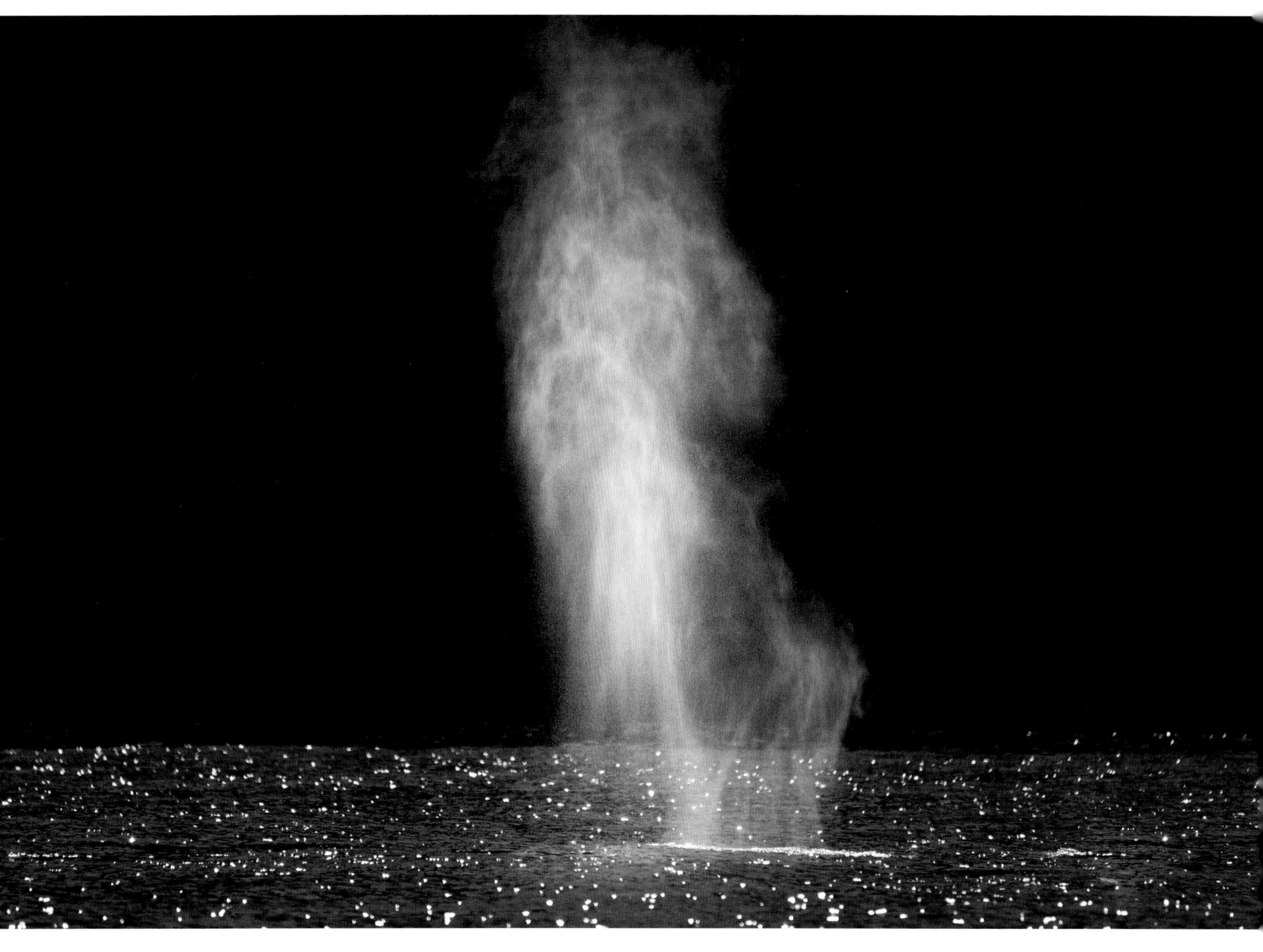

The Visual and the Visceral

"Don't tell me the moon is shining," urged Russian writer Anton Chekhov, "show me the glint of light on broken glass." His advice to those who hoped to be writers echoes the advice of American painter Robert Henri, who implored his students to "paint the flying spirit of the bird, rather than its feathers." Both exhortations are more directly expressed, if not less poetically, in the photographic advice to shoot what it feels like, not what it looks like.

The photograph can be many things as experienced by the viewer. It can be a document of record, an image that, in visual language, tells us the moon is shining: "Here is what the moon looks like." But it can be experienced as something so much more. A powerful photograph is more than visual; it is also *visceral*. We *feel* it. It can stir memories, latching onto the power of nostalgia for places and times long past. It can touch the near-infinite range of what our imaginations can conjure. Something as simple as a shift in colour can drop a line into our emotions and touch something deeper than what lies on the surface. Photographs can agitate us, calm us, remind us, arouse us, and stir in us every other emotion, including awe, curiosity, and fear.

We live on an image-rich planet. The abundance of photographs published daily is a testament to their power. If we didn't respond to photographs the way we do, we'd have given up and moved on to a different medium, like words, perhaps. Words aren't necessarily more or less powerful, but they wield that power much less quickly or immediately than a picture. "A picture is worth a thousand words" is only true in the sense that it is much faster and requires less attention on our part to feel the impact. Whether that picture or those words are worth anything at all is another matter.

Images have power—or they *can*. They are like the world around us: we see them with more than our eyes. We perceive photographs through our minds, and on the way through, they bump against all the memories we have, all our tastes and preferences, all the ideas we think about, and the values we hold. This is why beauty is so much in the eye of the beholder: for example, I perceive sharks differently than you might. Having had beautiful firsthand encounters with sharks, feeling the awe and wonder from touching their grace and power with my hands, I will see in the picture of a shark something very different than you if you were so haunted by scenes from the movie *Jaws* that you've never so much as put a toe into the ocean. The symbols are different for you than they are for me, but not necessarily less powerful. We feel them differently, but we do feel them.

A photograph of a shark is a good example of an image's potential to be visceral. You can feel it. And when that shark does not merely appear in an image but is shown carefully and intentionally—perhaps with a wide-angle lens that exaggerates the size of the head, a slower shutter that implies motion, or a carefully chosen moment that shows some teeth—the photographer has the chance not only to metaphorically say "the moon is shining" but also to "show you the glint of light on broken glass." But in this case, it's a shark. Whether that photograph is more or less visceral has to do with the choices we make when creating the photograph in the first place. A choice to frame it one way rather than another might make the image feel more claustrophobic. A choice to underexpose the image or darken it in post-production might make the image feel more threatening. The reverse choice to lighten it and present it in a softer colour palette of comforting pastel blues might make the image feel more serene. There's that word again: *feel*.

Images do not feel one way or the other only because of the subject matter. A photograph of an elephant can feel powerful and threatening with visible tension, or it can feel cute and welcoming. Different pictures of one actress can feel seductive, silly, elegant, or cold and unapproachable. Much of this comes down to what you choose to do at the intersection of light, space, and time. In other words, where you place the camera, which moment you choose, and what you do with the light. When I urge a more creative approach to photography, it's not an encouragement to get crazy but to get *intentional*. To create the photograph that feels the way *you* want it to feel.

One of the tools we underuse is luminosity, or how dark or light the photograph is. Whether using digital sensors, celluloid film, or other traditional processes, we've been taught to get the exposure "right," and are then left to ourselves to discover (or not) that exposure value can be a tool for so much more. Lightness and darkness, and the contrasts between them, are tools. The *correct* approach demands we get the exposure right, but the more *creative* approach asks us to consider the mood we're trying to create in the photograph in the first place. Lighter photographs *feel* lighter. Darker photographs *feel* darker. Part of making a more visceral photograph is more intentionally choosing the mood, and luminosity can be a big part of that.

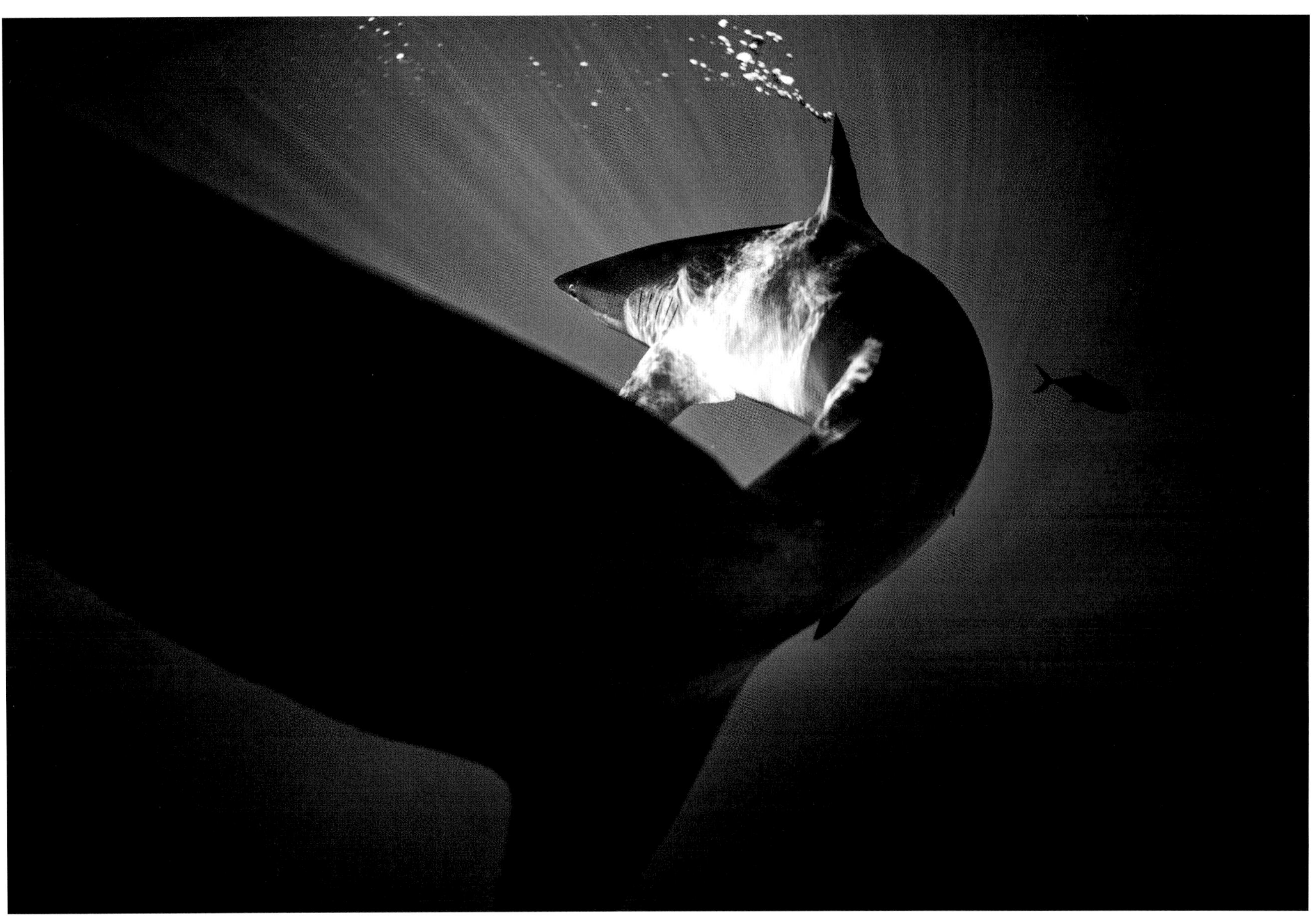

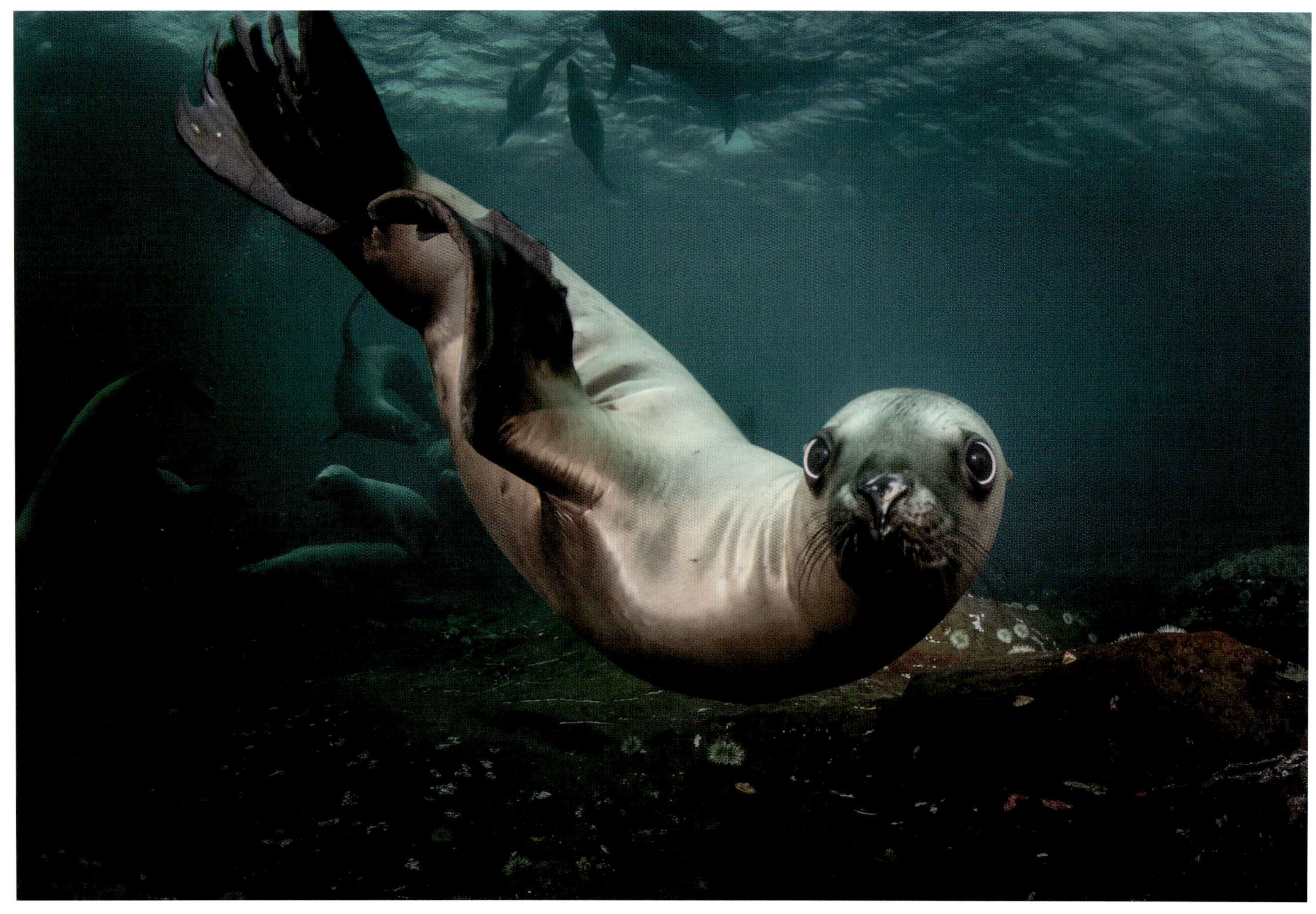

A photograph with a colour palette that contains yellows, oranges, and reds is considered warm. A photograph more dominant in greens, blues, and violets is considered cool. Those are visceral, *feeling* words, not visual words. We feel colours. We feel lines, too; they can be sharp, severe, sensual, energetic, and calm, among others. We feel texture. Even two-dimensional images we never touch can have a haptic quality. Our choices about whether and how we employ these more experiential possibilities will determine whether and how they are experienced in the images we create.

Photographers, especially newer photographers, are understandably concerned about the *quality* of their images. Is it a good photograph or a bad photograph? Is it clearly focused? Is it well-exposed? Is the horizon level? But there are other questions concerned about the *qualities* of an image, and they are equally important, if not more so. Quality (singular) is about getting the image correct. Qualities (plural) are about creative possibilities. So I want to suggest another question: what is the *experience* of the photograph? How do its qualities make you feel? Being concerned about the qualities of an image and being attentive to its quality are not two different questions; it is not an either/or consideration because they are connected. We ask one, then the other, and often it is only the answer to the second question, "How does this photograph make me feel?" that we can begin to find clues to the first one, "Is it any good?"

There is a feedback loop created when you ask how you feel about your decisions in matters of craft and what you see illuminated before you in time and space. It guides your choices about those initial quality questions. Maybe that straight horizon doesn't make you feel the emotions you want this image to evoke, and a more diagonal horizon line is the stronger choice. Maybe underexposing is the better choice. Maybe following the rule of thirds isn't serving you well in this case, and you feel stronger about a symmetrical composition. Maybe heeding the wisdom that suggests an 85mm focal length is the best portrait lens makes the image feel flatter than you want. Perhaps the advice to keep the sun behind you is exactly what prevents your photograph from having the kind of shadows that would otherwise give it depth or mystery. Sometimes (often, perhaps?), being correct sabotages being creative.

"What do you want your photograph to feel like?" is a question for every photographer who wants to elicit a more deeply human response to their photographs. I can think of no better way to learn this than by looking at the work you already respond to emotionally and asking *why*. If you want to make a photograph that feels mysterious, perhaps studying images that give you that same feeling and reverse-engineering that emotion, even guessing thoughtfully at the choices made to get there, will give you the clues you need.

Asking why or how a particular photograph feels mysterious provides the starting place for making your own images that feel this way. Is the photograph calm? Does it feel sensual? Does it make you laugh? Why? How? We make multitudes of combinations with the camera in hand, but there are only so many basic single choices.

What was included and what was excluded? If you want mystery, you'll hide things, perhaps excluded from the frame, perhaps obscured within the frame.

Which focal length was used? Every focal length behaves differently, often forcing us to use it differently. For example, how far your chosen lens is from your subject is incredibly important, which leads directly to the next question.

Where was the camera? Together with your chosen focal length, proximity to your subject can greatly impact the feeling of an image. But so can the movement from left to right. Placing a camera on the ground and pointing it up results in a photograph that feels much different than one made from a more conventional point of view. Moving alters the relationships of elements to each other. It changes the energy of lines. It creates different implications in the story. Moving can change the shape of things.

What was the light doing? Is it dark or light? Hard or soft? Warm or cool? Is it throwing shadows or creating reflections? If we're talking about feeling, there are few decisions you can make that shift the visceral qualities of a photograph more than light.

What was the exposure value? How much light did you let into the camera, resulting in lighter or darker images? Sometimes (often!) you've got to second-guess the camera and override its desire to get your exposure "right." So-called perfect exposures are often the enemy of mood. Being a slave to the histogram can get you to what is correct but not to what is creative or visceral.

What is the colour doing? Colour is a function of light, but it's worth its own consideration. What do the combinations of colour do to create a visual experience to which we respond emotionally? Which colours contrast? Which are more saturated? The colour photographer without a keen and growing sensitivity to colour and how we respond to it is working with an unnecessarily limited toolkit where emotions are concerned.

If you're looking at the images of others, consider asking *how* the photographer achieved that particular exposure value. What were the effects of shutter and aperture not only on the light (lighter or darker) but also on space and time? What's in focus? What has a sense of motion?

"What do you want your photograph to feel like?" is a question for every photographer who wants to elicit a more deeply human response to their photographs.

What does the choice of moment do to create story and feeling? Once frozen, not all moments are represented the same by the camera. The decision to press the shutter button at one moment rather than another has a significant effect on the later experience of the photograph.

Adding the choices you make in the darkroom to refine your pictures increases your options, but in some way, aren't those choices just opportunities to either amplify or diminish what you've already done with the camera? Regardless of how much or little work you prefer to do later in development, the following questions remain: What's the experience of looking at the resulting image? How will you, and others who respond to your photograph, think and feel about it? Where will the eye and the heart go? Can you be more creative and intentional in guiding them there?

Returning to the idea of interesting perceptions, surely that's more than just what we see or think and encompasses our emotions as well. Much has been made in recent years about the idea of emotional intelligence (also known as emotional quotient, or EQ), and I can't help but think that photographers would benefit from an awareness or sensitivity to their own emotions. In the same way that saying a photographer has a "great eye" implies a keenness in how they visually perceive the world, is there no equivalent to imply that a photographer has a good heart? That they perceive the world in different ways emotionally, perhaps in more astute or sensitive ways, and through their art have a means of bringing us there as well?

Don McCullin said, "Photography for me is not looking, it's feeling. If you can't feel what you're looking at, then you're never going to get others to feel anything when they look at your pictures." In making a case for emotional *sensitivity*, McCullin seems to suggest that before we even get to the tools and techniques of craft that might transform a photograph from the merely visual to the visceral—from what is only seen to what is deeply felt—we first need to have our own emotional point of view. To develop that, we need to open ourselves as fully as possible to the experiences in which we photograph, and that's not always easy when we're jumping ahead to thoughts of how we're going to capture that experience. But it's necessary, because you can't express what you haven't experienced; rather, you can more fully express what you have more fully experienced and explored.

Of the many challenges this craft puts to us, the challenge to be fully present and receptive is one of the hardest. To get past the camera and the lens, the buttons and dials, and even thoughts of composition, to first *feel* our way through a scene or an encounter is the start of making a photograph that others will respond to with their own feelings.

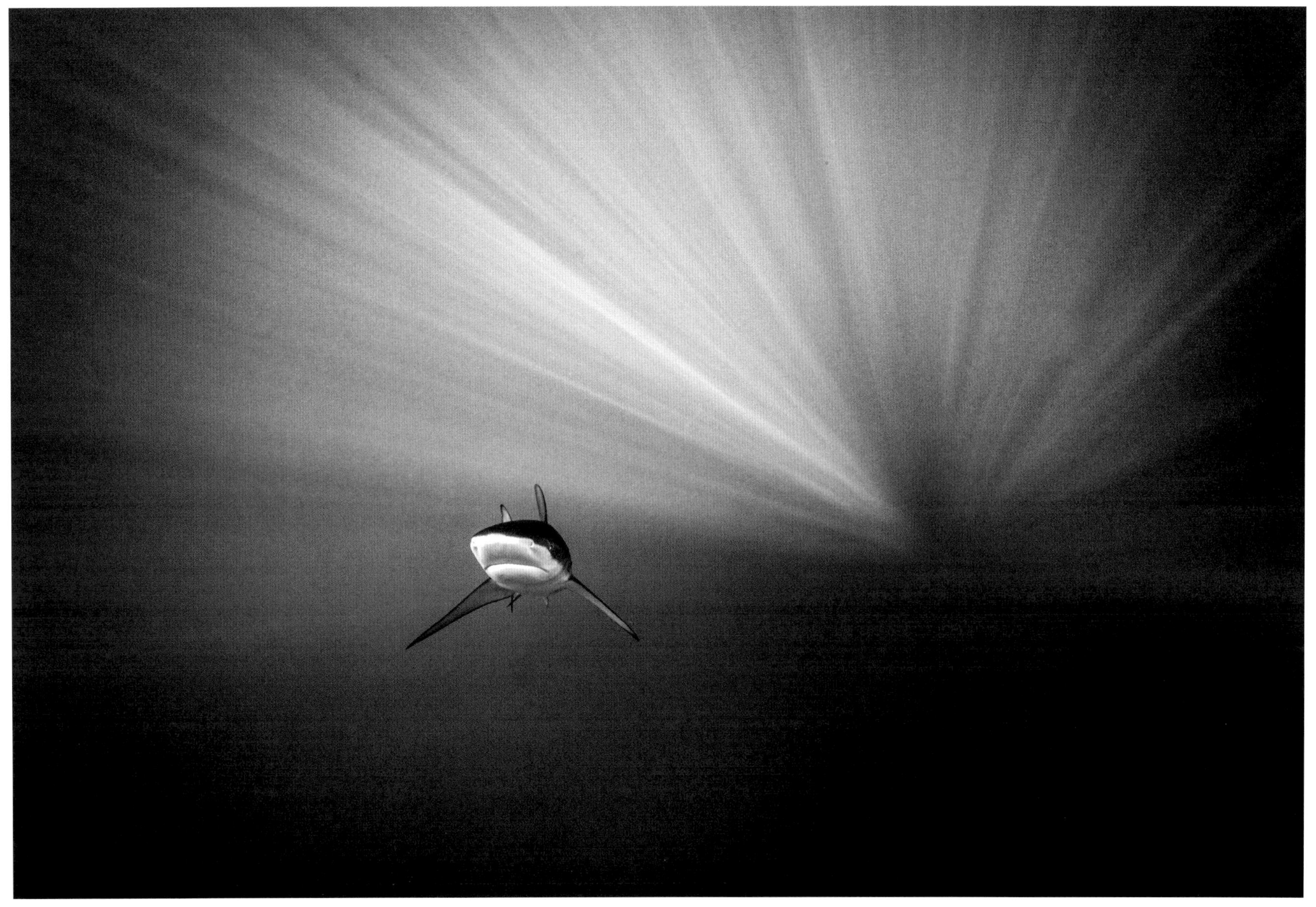

Which feelings others experience and whether or not those are the emotions you hope to arouse in the first place depends at least in part on the choices you make. But without mindfully considering those choices without first experiencing them and reacting to them, I'm not sure what's left to guide those decisions. In the absence of more meaningful starting points, it would be much more tempting to copy the work of others or blindly follow current visual trends.

The making of a photograph is a *response* to a thought or emotion. Whether the resulting image is rich in emotional resonance depends on first experiencing that rich emotional response. The photographer who feels wonder as a reaction to their subject and recognizes that feeling of awe will be better able to use that awe as a starting point to ask questions like "How might this feeling be best captured or expressed?" instead of "Which lens should I use?" Asking the former might get you to ask the latter and find your own answer, but asking the latter isn't likely to bring you back around to the former. It would be a mistake to pay more attention to your depth of field than to the depth of your feeling.

This might all be very counterintuitive if you view your craft as merely a matter of properly wielding your tools, of doing it "right." But I suspect it's a great relief—and a source of tremendous freedom—if you long to make what feels right to you and to do so in ways that also feel right. Feeling your way through this craft and the art you make with it is not only a path as legitimate as a more cerebral approach but might even be more effective if what you hope to do is not only "paint the feathers" but also give some deeper expression to the spirit of the flying bird.

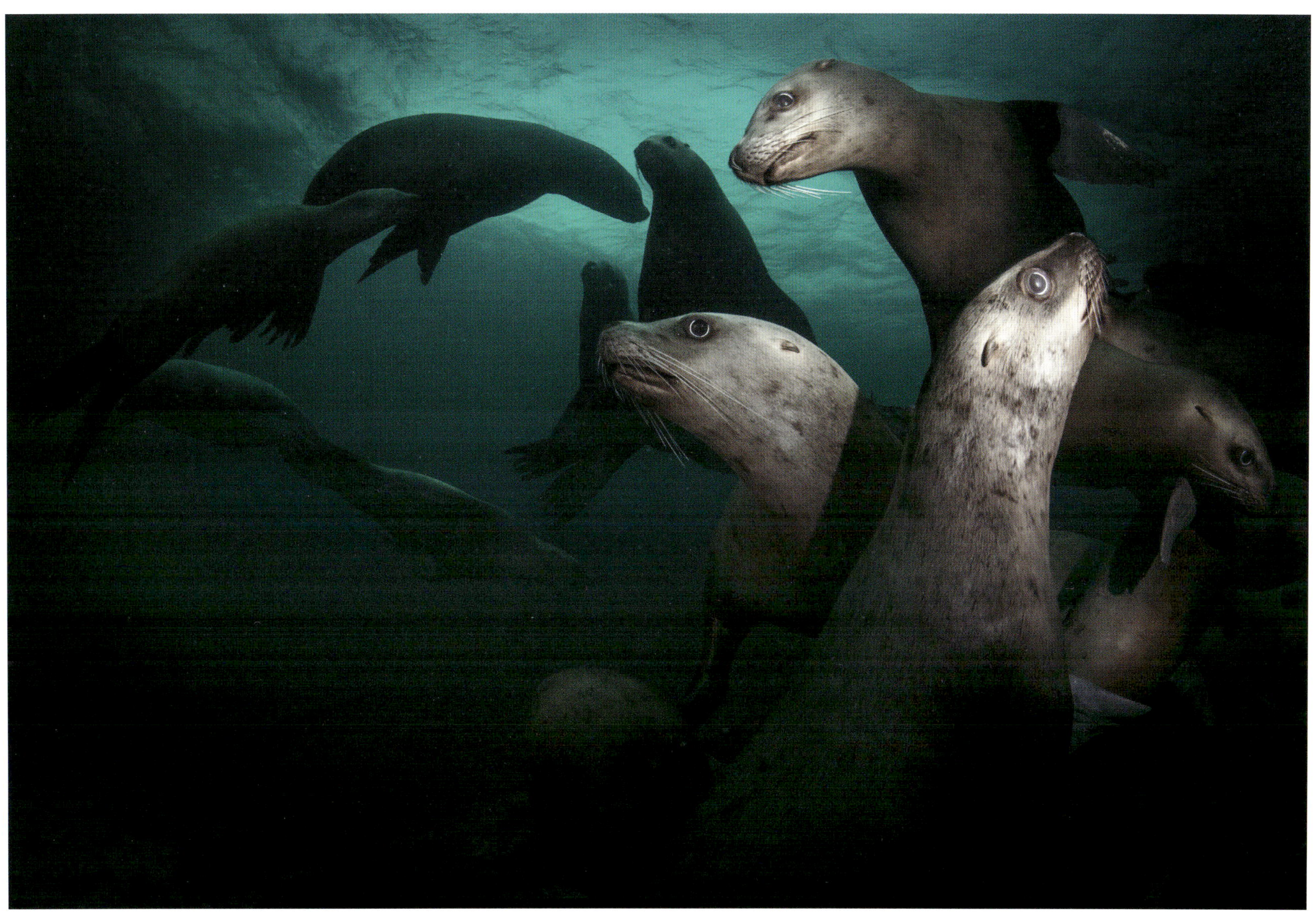

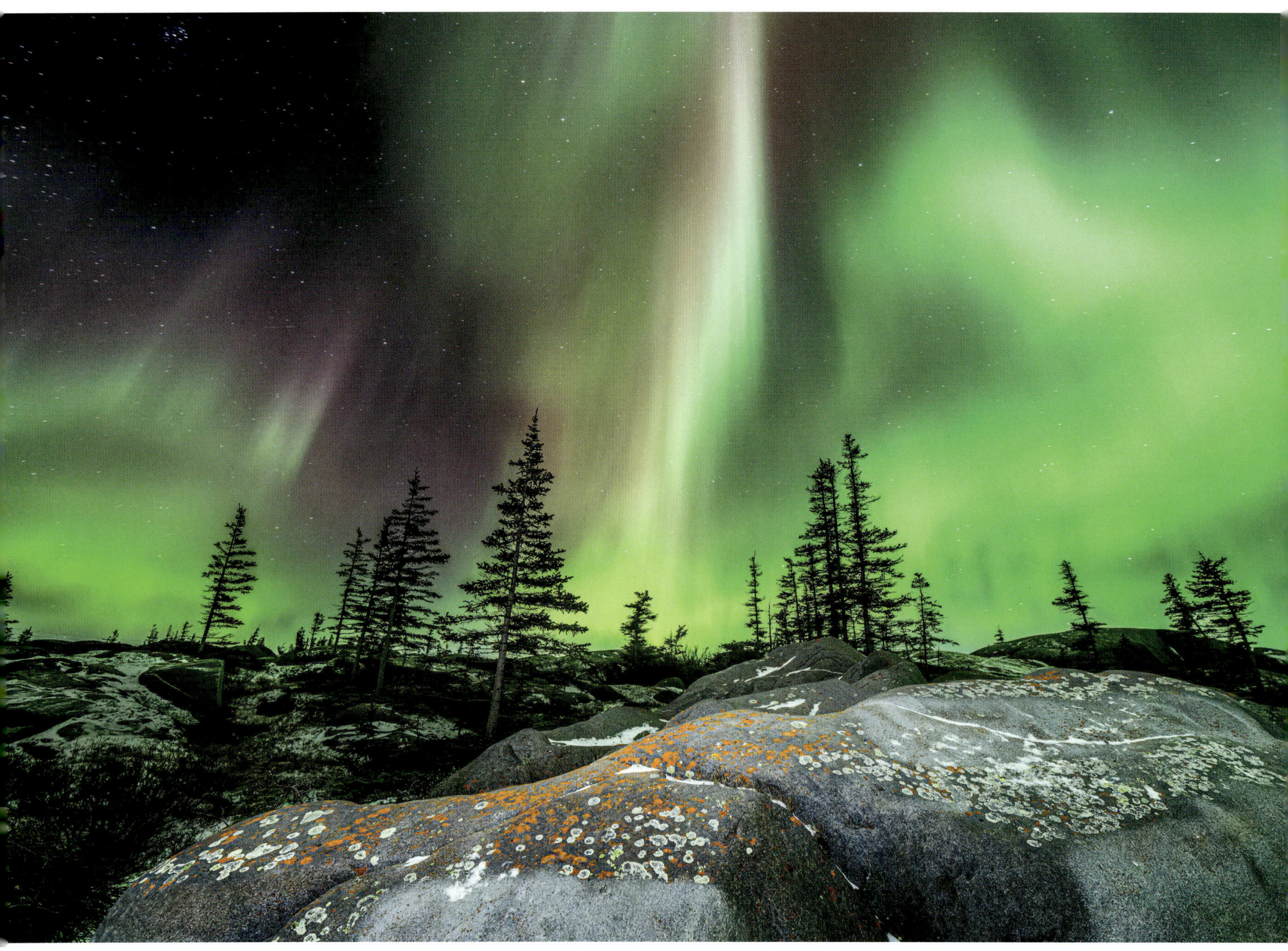

Art and
Artifice

The great jazz musician Miles Davis observed, "Sometimes, you have to play a long time to be able to play like yourself."

This is as true of photography as it is of music. You can be taught to use a camera, but not to use it *your* way. When you pick up a camera for the first time and say, "How do I make a photograph?" you can be taught how photographs are made, but not how *you* will make them. Miles Davis was being gentle; you *always* have to shoot for a long time to shoot like yourself. It is a discovery.

When you look at the work of the photographers you consider masters of their craft, you probably recognize their work even without a photo credit. It's unmistakably theirs. A portrait made by Yousuf Karsh is immediately distinguishable from one made by Richard Avedon. If you know their work at all, a photograph made by Sally Mann will never be mistaken for one made by Dorothea Lange (though I suspect this is much truer of their later work than their first exposures). Similarly, your early work will never be as truly yours as what you create after years of not only making photographs but also becoming you. Who you are at 45 will not be the same as who you were at 16, nor will your photographs.

What makes one photographer so different from another when we're all using versions of the same tools? Things haven't changed that much over the 200 or so years that this craft has been evolving, and where these tools have changed, it's not those advances that we point to and say, "Ahhh, so that's why Alex Webb's work looks so much different than Saul Leiter's!" Your favourite black and white photographer doesn't differ from your favourite colour photographer only because they chose to work without colour. That might be one of many elements, but it's never just one that accounts for the individuality of their work.

It takes so long to be able to shoot like yourself because it takes a very long time to *become* yourself, to accept who you find there, and to work from that rather than the expectations of others or those first influences that drew you to this medium in the first place. It takes as long to discover what is *not* "you" as it does to find out what is, and even then, it can be slippery because we evolve and change. And if we're truly making work that is authentic, then that work will evolve, too.

The metaphor of *voice* is a helpful one, though it can be confusing when we're talking about a medium that is so entirely visual. The phone rings, and hearing only a few words, you recognize the voice and know exactly who it is. I recently heard one guitar lick in a song I don't recall ever hearing before and said to my wife, "That's got to be Eddie Van Halen." And it was. I recognized his "voice" in the unique sound of his guitar. Even using that same guitar, no one else would sound like Eddie. You could try hard to do so, but at the same time, you'd be giving up the chance to play like yourself. Imitators abound, but as they get closer and closer to sounding like others, they get farther and farther from the chance to find their own voice.

Imitation is necessary at the beginning. Writers do it as they learn different ways of writing. Go to any art museum in the world, and you'll see hopeful young artists sketching the work of the masters. Young guitar players learn to play in the style of the musicians they adore. By "trying on" the techniques of the greats, they learn it all. But they don't *stay* there. It's simply a way to learn what's possible, but it's not a way to discover their voice. Imitation is one step on the path to discovery, but it is not the path itself—and it is certainly not the destination.

The reason one photographer might have such a recognizable voice while another does not is that the former makes choices consistent with exactly who they know themselves to be. That takes courage, and there is no setting for that on a camera. Art doesn't come from the artifice—the tools, the tricks, the techniques—but from something more: it comes from you and the choices you make.

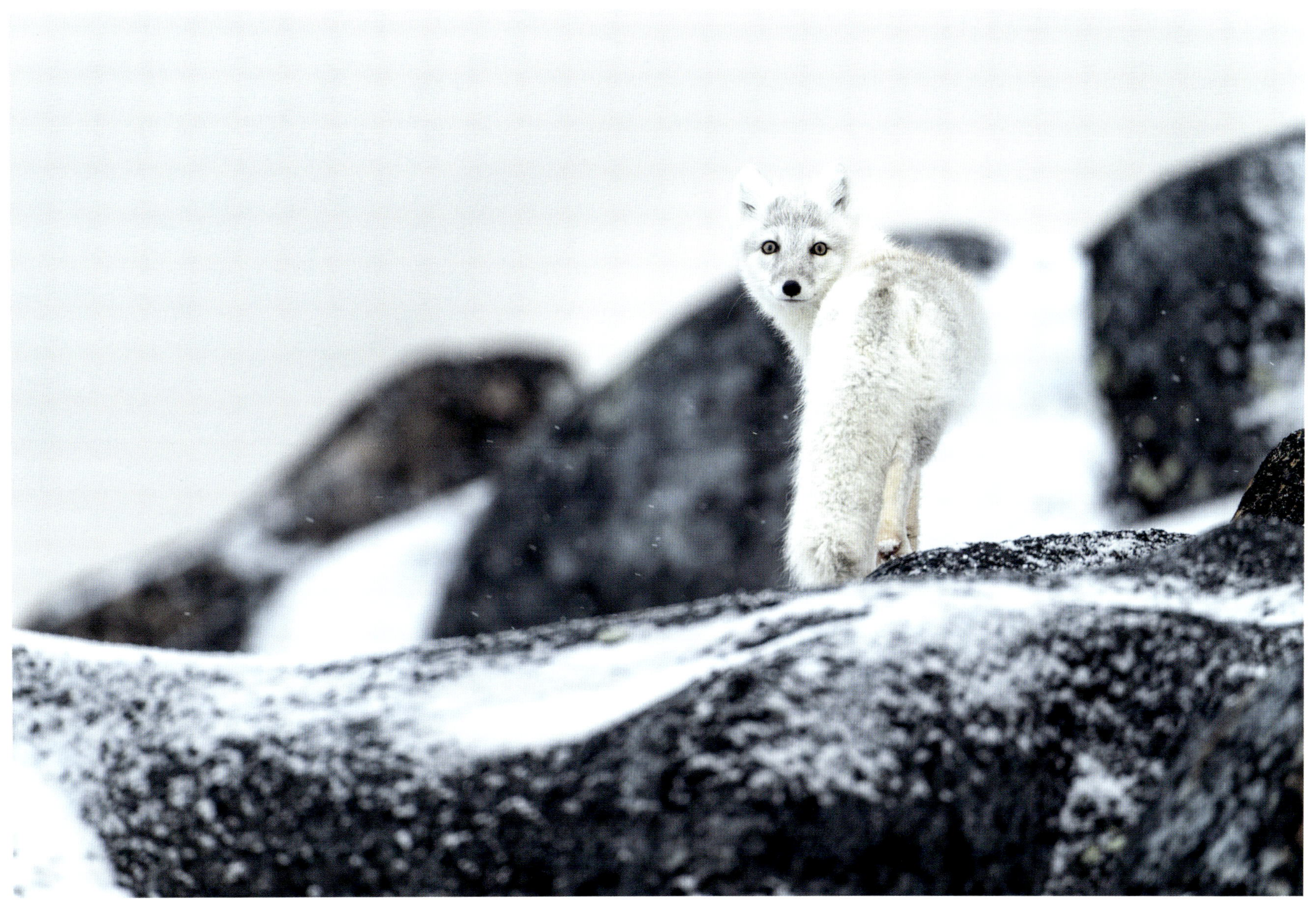

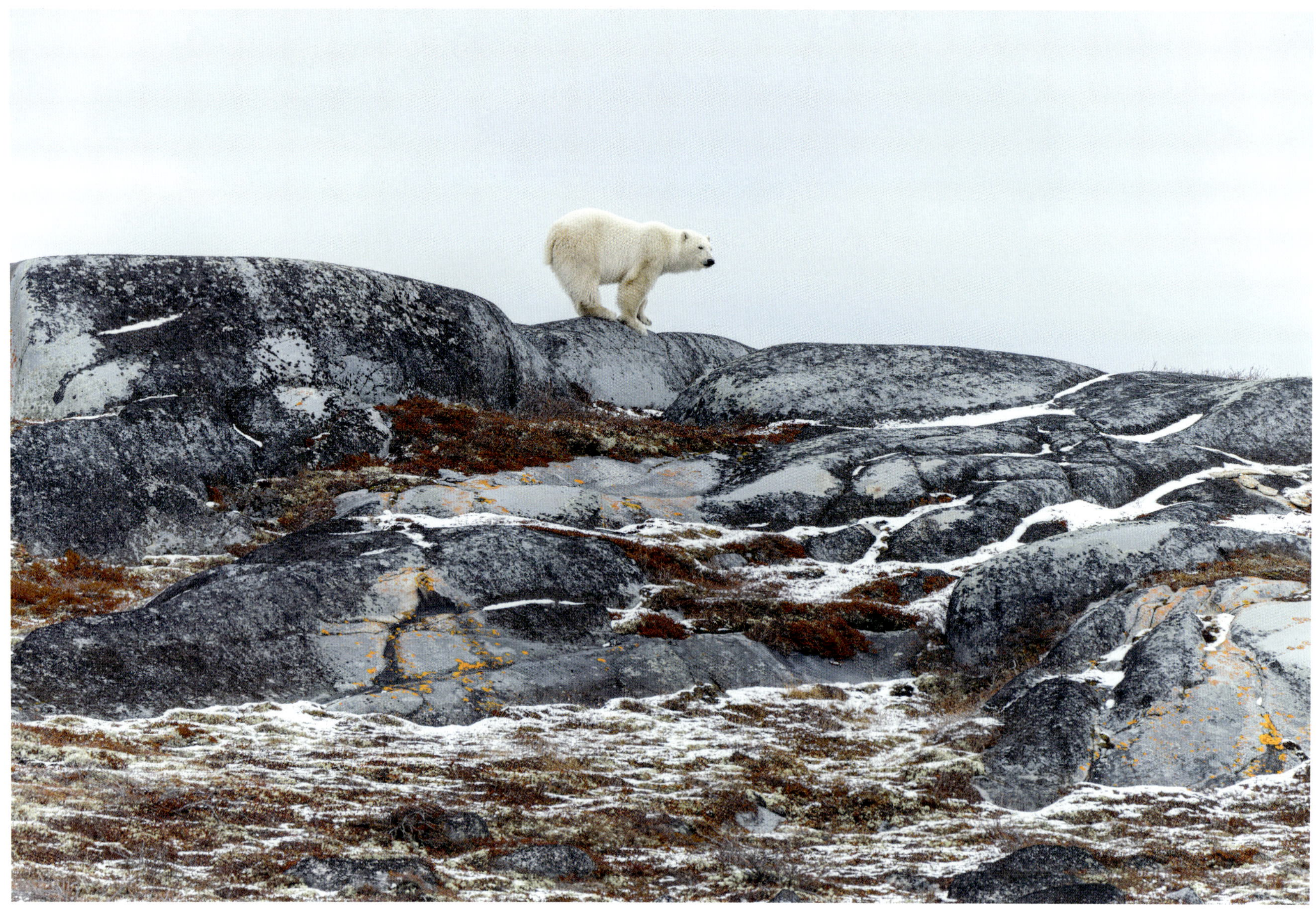

Art doesn't come from the artifice—the tools, the tricks, the techniques—but from something more: it comes from you and the choices you make.

Photographically speaking, voice is found in decisions that come from your tastes and preferences and having the courage to embrace them once you know what those are (and remembering Miles Davis's words about how long this takes) and reject everything else. Imitation is helpful because it lets you try on many styles and experiment with many tools and techniques, but it's important to remember you aren't looking only for what *fits* but for what is truly *you*. And that will be as much its own *combination* of different elements as the voices of the artists you imitated as you learned.

Great filmmakers all use similar tools, but what they do with those tools and the stories they choose to tell are different. You won't mistake a film by Steven Spielberg for one by Wes Anderson; they choose to make films about different things, preferring different camera angles, compositions, styles of production design, colour, and music. All of these choices come from an intersection between their personal tastes and preferences and the discovery of what they find effective. That is where they've found, or perhaps chosen, their respective voices.

What they do not do in search of that voice is ask what *you* want to look at. Their choices come from their tastes, not yours. And the more aligned those choices are to their particular tastes, and the more they choose to explore those and reject anything that isn't "them," the closer they get to having a distinct and recognizable voice. An *authentic* voice. They don't just use what they've found to fit them, but what's also truly them, in the same way that I could try on a pair of rhinestone-studded jeans that fit like a glove, but they wouldn't be *me*.

The hardest work for you as a photographer concerned with shooting like yourself is making the choice to say yes to tools and techniques that resonate with you, to say yes to subjects and themes that draw your strongest curiosity, and to say no to anything that doesn't feel right. That doesn't mean rejecting one technique or subject matter outright before really trying it on. That's often where the real creative work is—not in deciding if something is a fit for you, but in figuring out *how* it might be a fit and *how* you could make it your own. That's the discovery. Others make it look so easy, but that's because we don't see the hard-fought process of their creativity but rather the end product, polished in private for years, often with great difficulty and frequent—though unseen—failure.

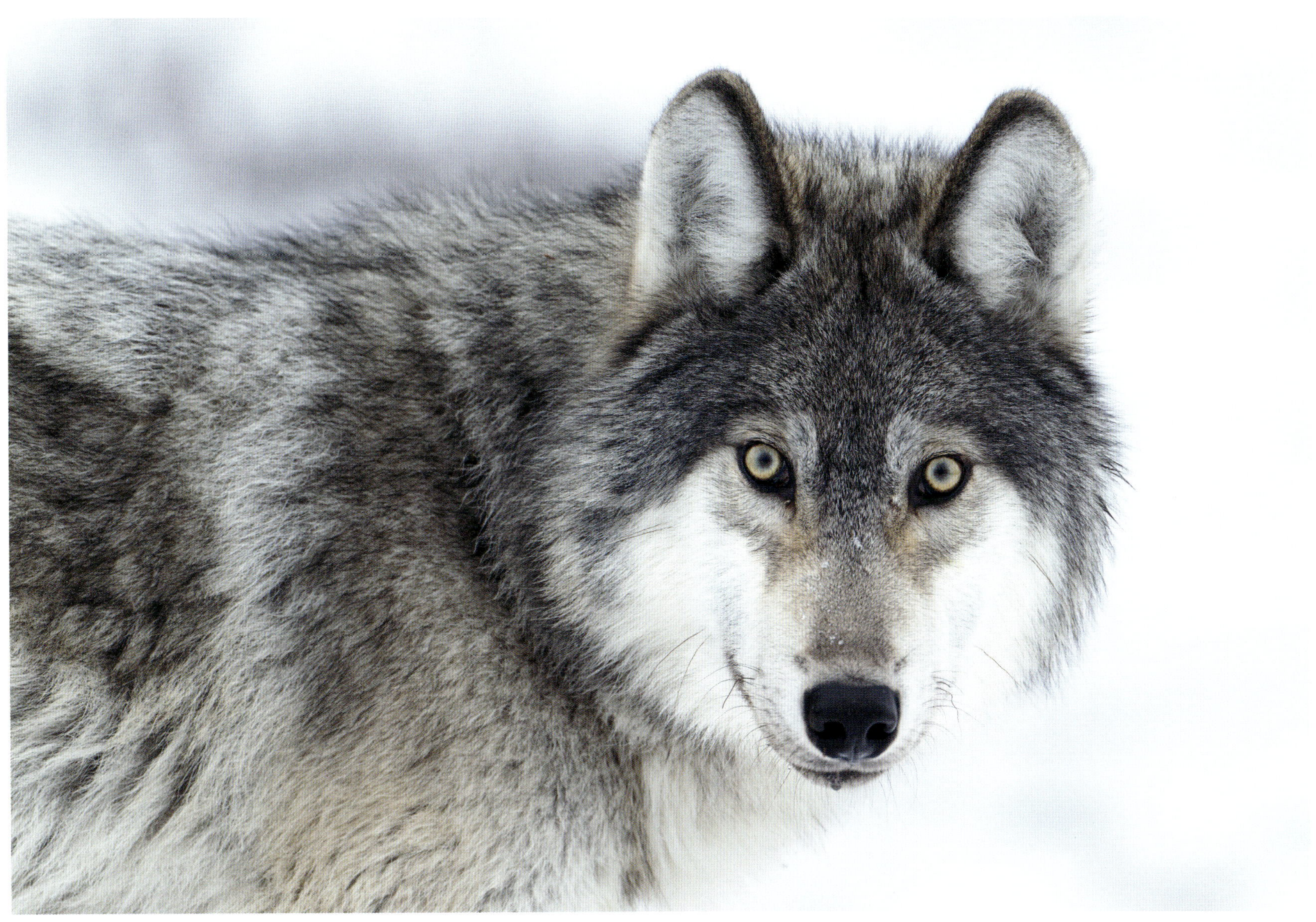

The creative process is necessarily messy, full of detours, and rife with options where tools and techniques are concerned. You could spend a lifetime tinkering with every possible subject or idea. Your voice will emerge when you start making choices about remixing the things that are *most* aligned with your whims and curiosities, your passions, and the things you most value, made more challenging because those things change with time. You can't rely on what you've done in the past. Art isn't made looking backwards.

To recognize an artist in their work does not mean that the artist or the work is unchanging, but they change with each other. You recognize an artist through their work and identify the work as theirs because you know the artist; one changes as the other does. It flows in new directions but seldom bounces wildly. Most people don't change so dramatically that their work becomes unrecognizable. We just don't work that way. A leopard's spots do change as they grow, but they remain spots; they don't change into stripes.

In the last few years, my work has shifted from being primarily focused on human subjects and stories to those found in the wild. It has also shifted mainly from monochrome back to colour. But the way I use my camera, the optics that I prefer, and my tastes for juxtaposition and photographs that feel immersive or intimate and have a sense of visual depth haven't changed. Although my voice keeps evolving, it has remained consistent with who I am even though the ideas I photograph have shifted with my interests. The choices I am making now still happen at the intersection of my tastes and preferences and what I feel is effective in picture-making. Those haven't so much changed as they have grown.

All artists grow, including you. So does your skill, the things you find interesting, the way you see the world, and the ways you choose to allow the camera to translate those perceptions. Voice, as a metaphor, will also grow with time. As it does in real life, it might get deeper or more mellow. The opinions you express might become more graceful or impassioned, but there's a consistency that comes from the unalterable fact that you're still fundamentally you.

The creative process is necessarily messy, full of detours, and rife with options where tools and techniques are concerned.

How this works out visually depends on how aware you are of your tastes and preferences and how willing you are to work within those rather than being seduced by trends or the tyranny of the new. How many photographers move from one visual trend or "look" to another, not because that look might be in harmony with who they are and what they're trying to say, but with what's current? That's not growth; it's a detour. And while they might find something of value in that detour to learn and use, I wonder how often it results in getting closer to something that is merely *different* rather than something that is *true* to the artist.

What do you *like*? You have preferences. You have images that resonate with you and those that don't. There are subjects or themes you could photograph all day long and some that just aren't you. There are colour palettes you are attracted to and those you find distasteful. And there are ways of working that feel right and fit you perfectly and ways of working that do not. Some photographers love complexity; some prefer simplicity. Some are real sticklers when it comes to symmetry. I don't love brightly saturated greens or working with artificial light, but I love images with depth. What we choose to do with all these tastes and how we bring them all together effectively and in harmony with the ideas and subjects we photograph is *voice*.

It takes courage to choose to explore the intersection of all these tastes and preferences. The more there are and the more divergent they are from what others might be doing, the harder it is. There's risk involved. What if people don't like it? But this is where your voice will be not only its most authentic, but also its most individual. The goal isn't to be different but to be truly you. This is only one sense in which people use the word *creative*. Not just that you make things, but that you make things only *you* could in your own unique way.

Your voice lies in the unlikely combination of all the things you ever imitated, but it is more than that. Voice is rooted in how you perceive the world, what you like to look at, and the ways you choose to do your photographic work. Miles Davis took a long time to learn to play like himself, but it was not accidental. He chose to do what felt most Miles-like and abandon what didn't. It's no more complicated than that for any of us. But there's a big difference between recognizing that instinctively "right" feeling in your gut (whether you need to try it on for size first or not) and having the courage to do what feels right and leave the rest for everyone else.

What we choose to do with all these tastes and how we bring them all together effectively and in harmony with the ideas and subjects we photograph is *voice*.

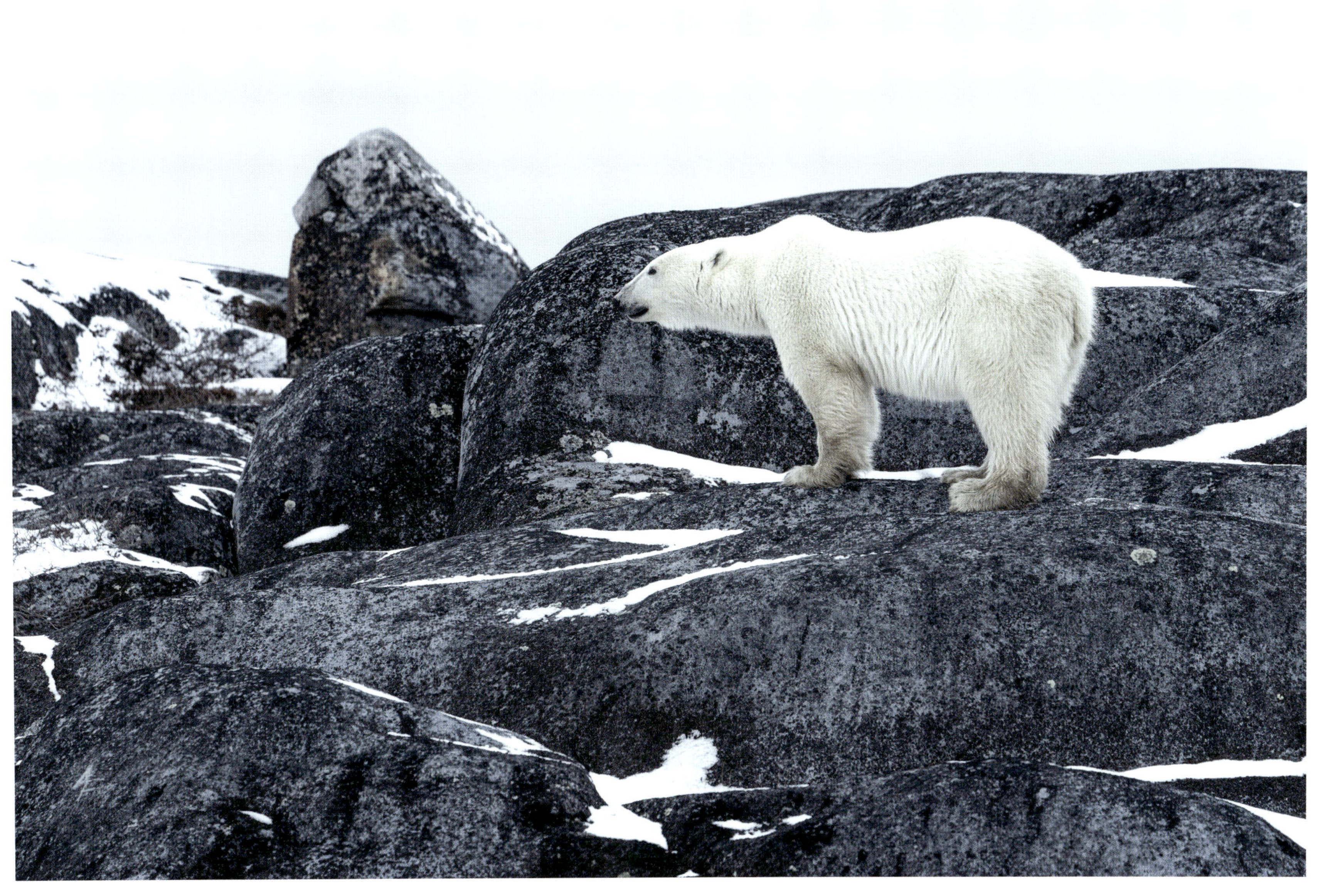

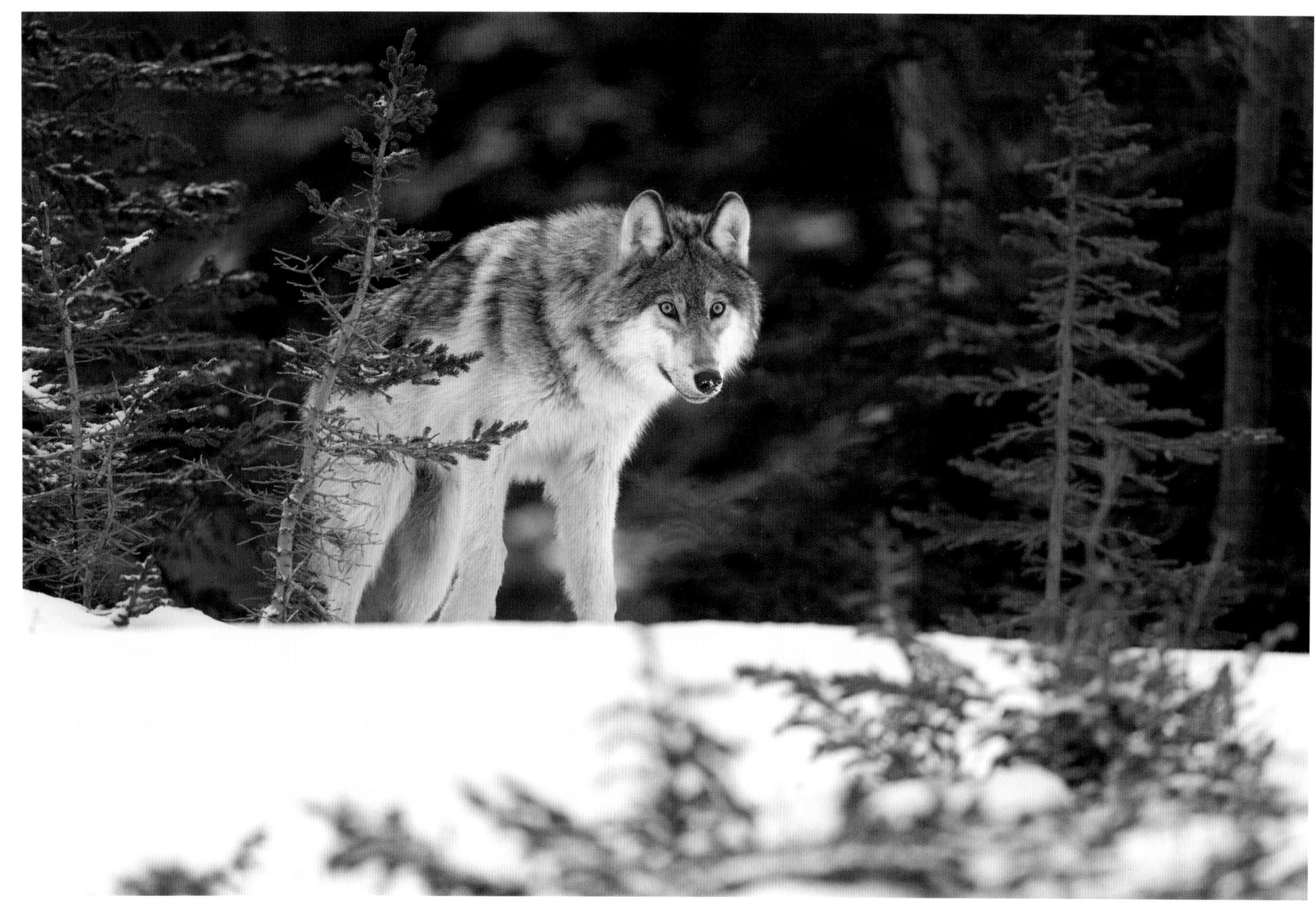

There is tremendous freedom in pursuing what feels right to you. It allows you to go deeper on fewer things and do better. It allows you to get great at something deeply meaningful to you rather than being merely good at many trivial things. But more importantly, it allows you to explore both your art and yourself, which is where art of the most authentic kind comes from. I suspect that the most frustrated photographers are those who are trying to work in ways that are incongruent with who they are. Without the drive of genuine curiosity or passion, they will never get to the kind of perceptions about the world they explore that would make those perceptions interesting. Without going deeper, they never get to their own ideas and opinions or their individual ways of expressing them.

You can't be faithful to the art without first being faithful to the artist from whom it comes. Without that, all we're left with is artifice.

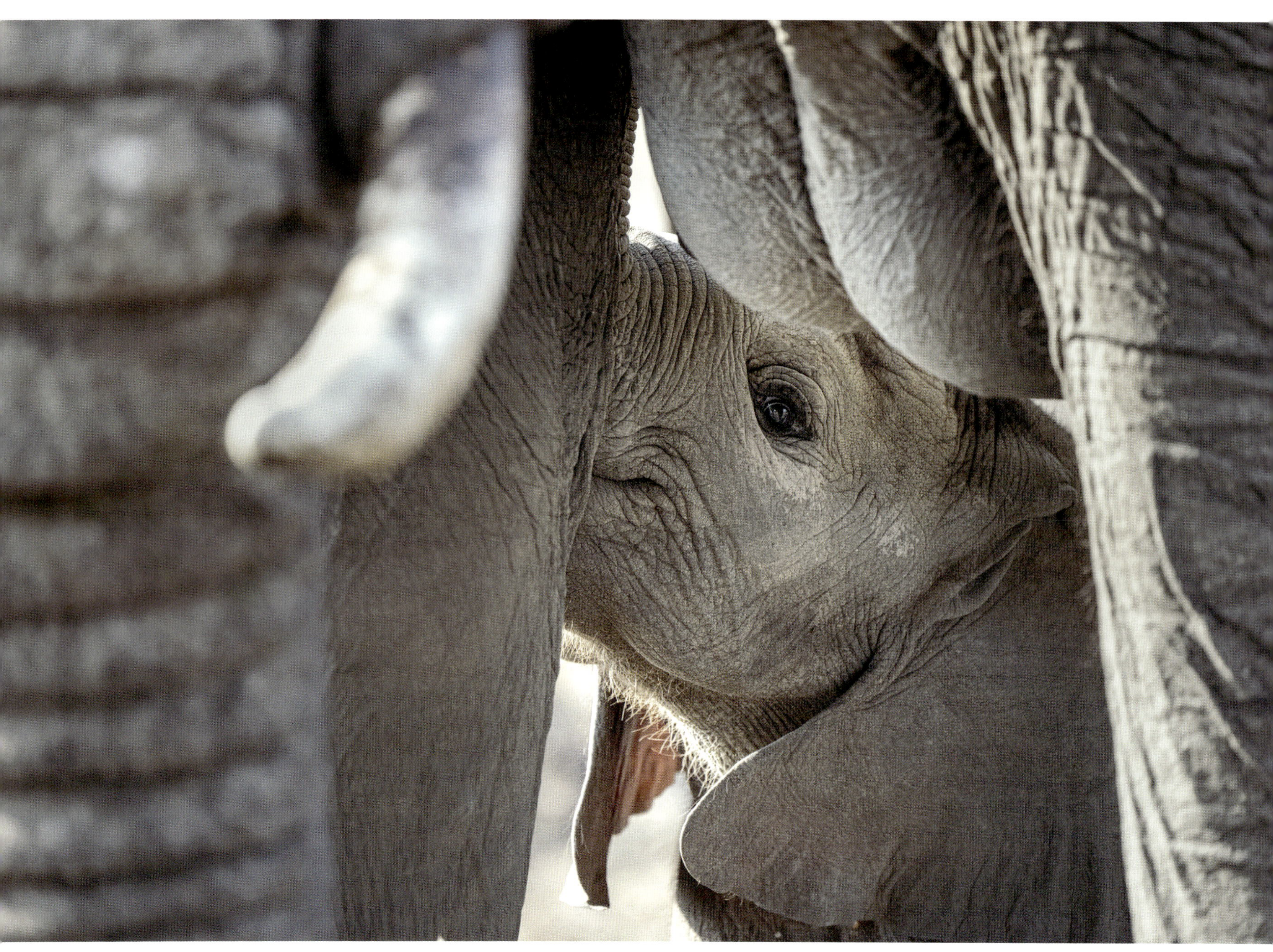

The Seduction of Subject

In looking from the outside in at my evolution as a photographer, I have made what might appear to be some big changes—from travel to humanitarian to landscape to underwater to wildlife photographer. I've been called a street photographer as well. Each time the moniker changed, I felt a sense of unease, both about the expectations of others concerning my work and the work itself. It has taken me years, but I am now comfortable being called a wildlife photographer.

Still, the labels worry me. They create expectations and, if we're not careful, limit our thinking when it should probably have more freedom to roam where it will. When we allow those labels to suggest how things should be done or how, for example, a landscape photographer should think about approaching a scene, we think less creatively than we would if we asked better questions. Questions that are less related to specific subjects or genres and have more to do with photographs themselves. Line, shape, and colour (or tone if your medium is monochromatic). Balance and tension. Depth. Story. Those kinds of things. What's in the frame might not be the point.

It is true that with every genre, there are ways of thinking that might strengthen your work. The photographer who understands the behaviour of a rhinoceros is in a much better position to anticipate a moment that will make for a stronger composition. The photographer who has made hundreds or thousands of portraits will have ideas about working with people that others might not. The photographer who has been photographing flowers for 20 years has a much more intimate understanding not only of what is possible but also of their own tastes and preferences. A specialist in any genre has the advantage of having thought (and shot) their way past the low-hanging fruit that newcomers to that genre have yet to contend with if they want to get to the place where they are making photographs of a particular subject with insight and sensitivity.

What a beginner brings to new subjects is a curiosity that has yet to be dulled by familiarity or convention and an openness of thinking that is unblemished by assumption.

But specialist thinking can trap us when we get to a point where we begin to believe we've got it figured out and stop approaching our subjects with a beginner's mind. What a beginner brings to new subjects is a curiosity that has yet to be dulled by familiarity or convention and an openness of thinking that is unblemished by assumption. "What if?" more naturally springs to mind because they haven't answered it hundreds of times before they stop asking the question at all. It's easier to come to things from a fresh angle when you haven't tried them all before and made up your mind about what works and what doesn't.

"I've always done it this way" is dangerous thinking to the photographer who hopes to approach their work with fresh ideas and evolving creativity. That kind of thinking can blind you, especially when it's subconscious and you're unaware of the mental rut you may have carved out for yourself. I'm very interested in hearing how a wildlife photographer thinks about and approaches their work with elephants, but I'm also keenly interested in how a portrait photographer would think about photographing those same elephants. What would a photographer who normally identifies as an abstract or impressionist photographer bring to the same scene? It's a fascinating question because each photographer would see the world through a lens of possibility the other wouldn't be trained to consider. To return to this idea, isn't it possible that a wedding photographer might be more likely to have interesting perceptions about a group of lions than the photographer who's more familiar with those lions? And how would that wildlife photographer approach a wedding? They would certainly see it differently.

The lines between genres are more porous than our keenness for labeling them might suggest. I wonder if we've outlived the usefulness of defining our work by the things we photograph, by what we choose to put in the frame. Increasingly, I've been thinking about my true subject as *otherness*. In some ways, it's wonder, or perhaps it's encounters. Those are certainly closer to describing what I'm really photographing than, say, wildlife. Admittedly, if you had just met me and I told you I photographed "wonder," you'd probably roll your eyes and move on because it sounds nebulous and pretentious. Perhaps, but it's closer to the truth. And it gets me away from the labels that increasingly feel unhelpful and distracting, especially to me. What *is* common in all the photographs I've made is that they explore encounters with other cultures and species, and they're driven by wonder. The true subject of my photographs—what my photographs are *about*—hasn't changed that much.

What a photograph is *of* rarely carries the image; this is what I mean by being seduced by subjects, or more specifically, subject matter.

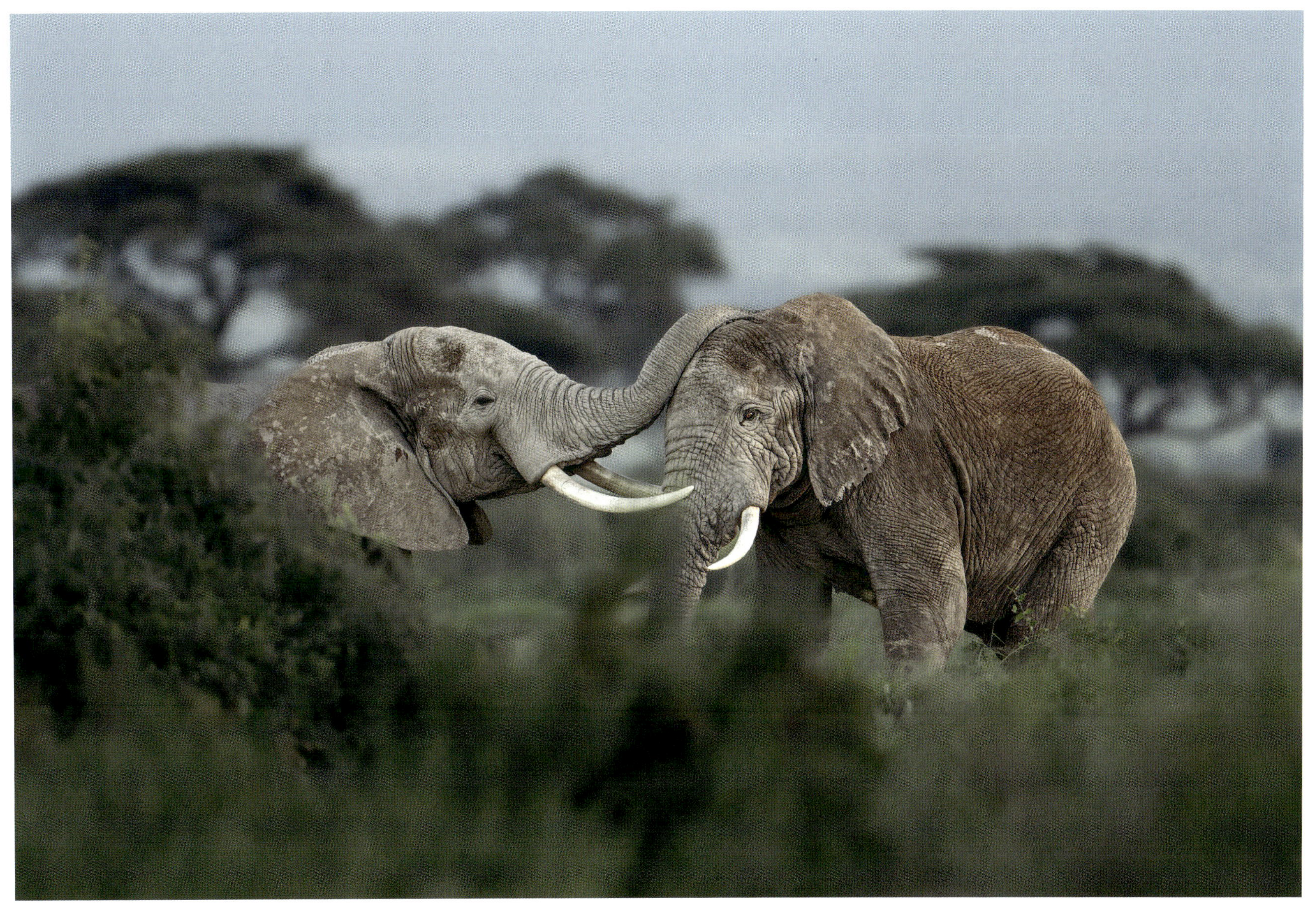

I've found it helpful to think less about what I put in front of my lens and more about the ideas I'm exploring—to think less in terms of what my photographs are *of* and more in terms of what they are *about*. The biggest benefit has been a change of thinking: I'm less likely to get seduced by the subject matter in front of me.

I have guided safaris in Kenya for over a dozen years and have observed with amusement, after doing this myself, how clients react to their first elephant. "Wow! An elephant!" they say excitedly as the motor drives whir on their cameras and memory cards begin to fill. Within days, however, that reaction turns to something closer to, "Oh, it's just an elephant," and they're less likely to raise their cameras. They don't lose their wonder at seeing an elephant; they're seeing more, not less. They're now seeing an elephant in light that doesn't interest them or suggest a possible photograph. They're seeing an elephant against a background that doesn't appeal. They're taking in the entire scene and all the possibilities we see when we stop being seduced by what the photograph might be *of* and begin to ask what it might truly be *about*. And

that's what drives them to pick up the camera. Not because of a reaction to "Elephants!" but rather, "Look at the intimacy between that mother elephant and her baby." The elephants are the subject matter, but the true subject is the intimacy.

What a photograph is *of* rarely carries the image; this is what I mean by being seduced by subjects, or more specifically, subject matter. A beautiful sunset does not always make a beautiful photograph. A handsome face alone does not make a handsome photograph. I've seen some unappealing photographs of some otherwise very appealing faces. But give me a face a photographer finds interesting and can translate into a photograph that conveys what they see in that face, and you'll see an image that's not only *of* that face but *about* something more. It could be something as simple as an emotion: the weariness of a comedian just off the stage, the lines of age on a face we're so used to being presented as young, or the complexity of a person we've always believed to be simple.

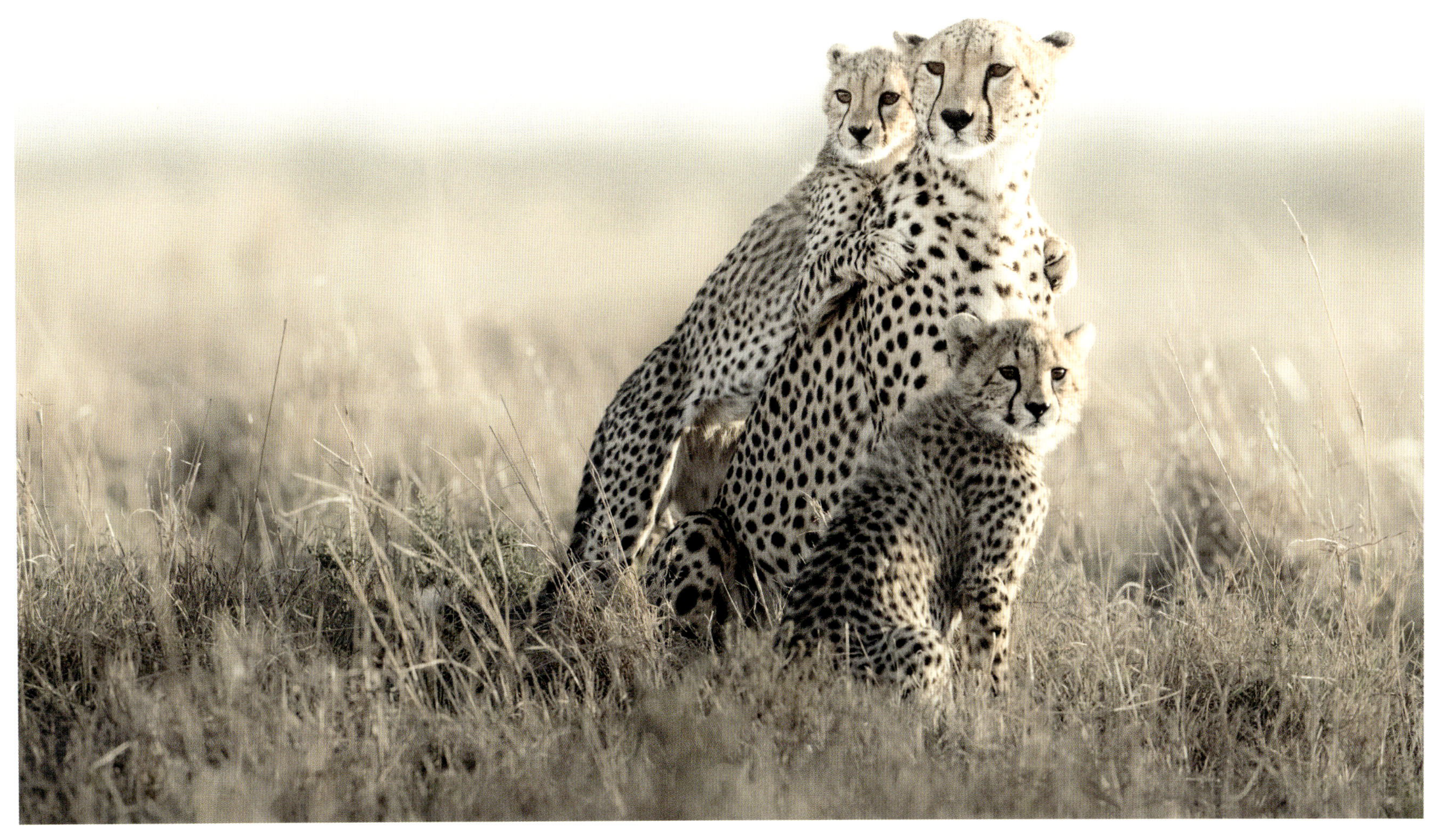

To define yourself by (or let your thinking be defined by) the objects you photograph only reinforces the idea that those things are also what your photographs are all about.

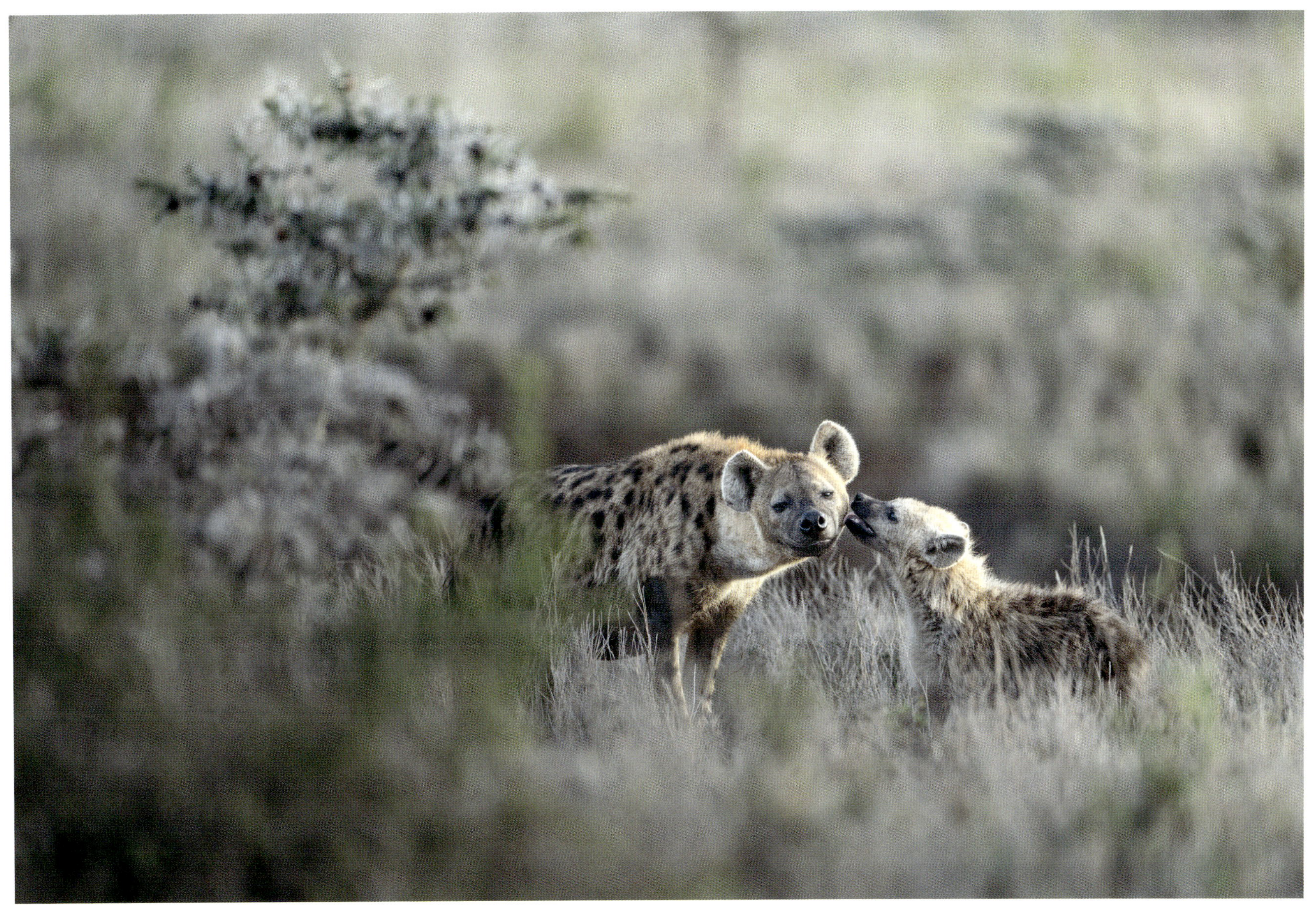

We talk about the things in our photographs as "subjects," and that's not going to change. But wouldn't it be clearer if we spoke of them as "subject matter" or "objects"? They are the *matter*, the *substance* in the frame. They are what the photograph is *of*, but how we see them and what we think or feel about them are the true subjects of an image. To define yourself by (or let your thinking be defined by) the objects you photograph only reinforces the idea that those things are also what your photographs are all about. Yet the street photographer's real interest is rarely the street itself. It might be life and the human drama, but not roadways. The so-called travel photographer doesn't usually photograph travel itself but rather culture or faith or how the differences in those cultures only point to the commonalities. The most compelling landscape photographers don't photograph only trees and water but beauty and wildness or the encroaching hand of man. To put it another way, they don't photograph the matter; they photograph *what* matters.

Maybe this is what Edward Weston was suggesting when he said his task was to "photograph a rock, have it look like a rock, but be more than a rock." What did he mean by "more than a rock"? There is a sense in which a rock stops being a rock the moment we make a photograph of it. The original rock remains what it is, but the one in the photograph is something else. It *looks* like a rock, but in the two-dimensional world of

the photograph, it isn't a rock: it is line and shape and colour resembling a rock, but not.

How much it resembles a specific rock falls to us in our choices, but it could be more. From the right angle and using forced perspective and an absence of scale, it could be a mountain. From another, it could resemble something more symbolic. From yet another, it could be personified, an implied character in a story. At the very least, it becomes a graphic element in the frame that will contribute to the composition of the image. It might add to the balance of the frame, but it might also be a distraction. Much like Weston's rock, yours might become more than a rock—a picture *of* a rock, but *about* something more, but it could also become *less* than a rock if you choose an angle from which it doesn't look rock-like at all. Either way, there's no benefit in thinking of it as only a rock and not a possibility.

Perhaps this change of thinking is one path beyond the banal. If cliché is to be found not so much in *what* you photograph but rather in what you *say* through what you photograph, then perhaps this is the answer for you if you're frustrated that your work rings hollow or lacks depth. It is certainly the more challenging path, but it's where you can find hope that your photographs can be something more meaningful and more uniquely yours.

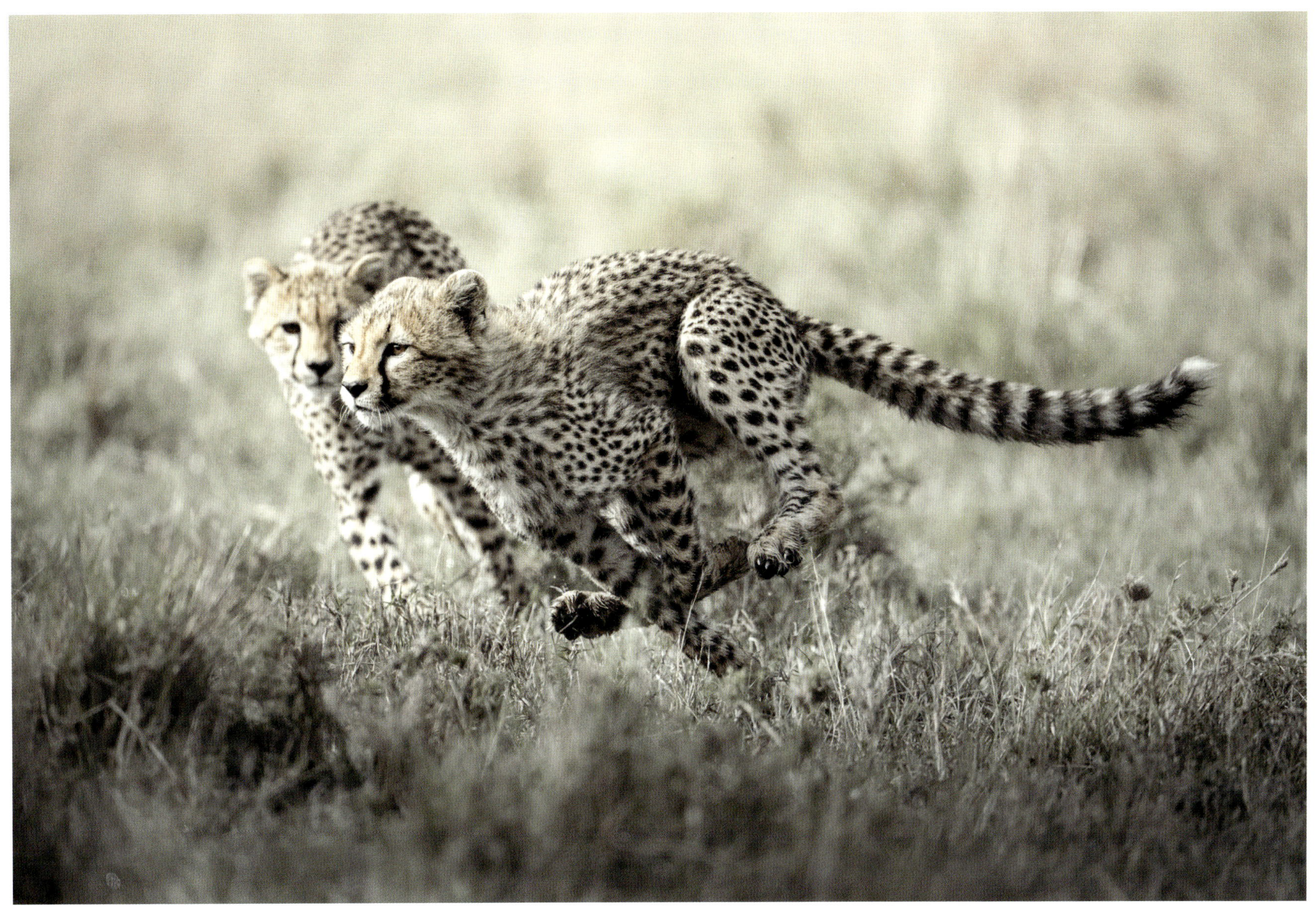

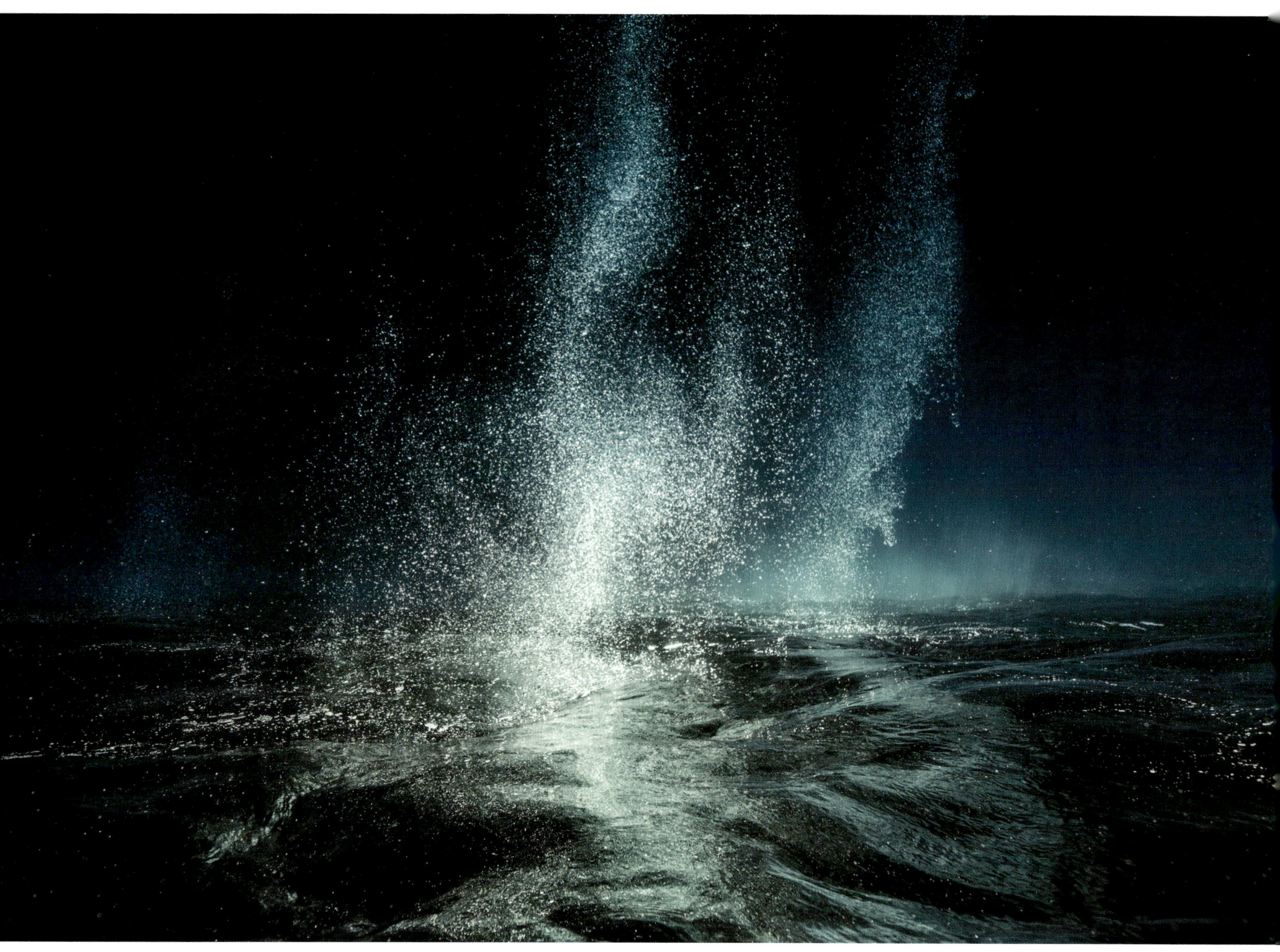

The Freedom of Flow

Photography is hard. Changing our thinking is hard. Seeing the world in new ways and finding ways to express that changing vision through the capabilities of the camera is hard. That's evolution. That's growth. And growth, too, is hard.

Hard things beg for shortcuts and detours, enticing us back to what has worked before, to call on familiar tricks rather than venture into new territory or embrace the forward call of creative growth. There is nothing wrong with this; we naturally return to the techniques and tools that, after so long, finally feel comfortable in our hands. Abandoning the subjects you've been exploring through the subject matter you enjoy makes no sense at all, even in pursuit of something as worthwhile as new directions or those moments of creative grace we call flow. We just can't *stay* there.

In my experience, evolution as a photographer (or any creative artist) does not come in dramatic changes of vision or U-turns in our way of working. It comes not in abandoning old or familiar approaches but in *combining* them either together or with new influences. Reaching a plateau in your creative work (often the point at which you get bored or begin the self-recriminations so common to all artists) is not a sign you've peaked, but that the challenges that have brought you to this point have leveled off and it's time to find something that reintroduces new challenges: an idea to explore, learning to use a piece of unfamiliar gear, or a change in subject matter you find interesting. It might also be something as simple as *combining* different techniques with which you're already adept. The techniques are comfortable, but the combination might not be. What matters isn't so much what that combination is, but that it introduces *challenge*.

The challenge of photography is not something that needs fixing, which is why shortcuts and rules (or, worst of all, anything touted as a "secret") are more likely to sabotage the creative process than help it; they attempt to remove the challenge, and challenge is *necessary* for creative flow. We all yearn for that way of working that feels intuitive, when time slips away as you work and the best decisions seem to come out of nowhere. That's flow, and shortcuts do not get you there. Making things easy doesn't get you there. Counterintuitively, it's challenge that gets you there.

Challenge pushes growth; it is the friction that causes creative sparks. When you look at your work and find it missing something that matters to you, or it no longer resonates with you, or you're bored in the making of it, it is challenge that pulls you forward and back into flow. We need something to push against. Creativity needs a problem to solve. And as you become increasingly comfortable with your craft, as you work with familiar subjects and your growing skill solves the earlier problems you once wrestled with, it's up to you to introduce that element of challenge anew.

Sometimes, life itself pushes you beyond that plateau on which you've been resting, but more often, the decision to move forward needs to be your own, and what got you to where you are now is usually insufficient to take you farther. That's why it's challenging. Whether through circumstance or choice, you need a new, more challenging problem to solve. And the more *interesting* that problem is to you, the better. In choosing your creative problems, more interesting is better than more difficult. Interesting problems keep our attention by forcing us into experimentation, healthy risk, and pushing the limits of our craft, driving us to expand our skill and knowledge.

Interesting problems lead to flow; they pull you forward in ways that racking your brain for that next great idea can't. Have you ever *tried* to think of a great idea? Our minds don't work that way. Not only do our brains seem to object to the pressure to perform, but they also need raw materials to work with—specifically, raw materials we find interesting. Because it's only those problems that interest us—the ones that distract us, occupying our thoughts when we should be thinking about something else—that our brains subconsciously work through. And only those problems excite us enough to pick up the camera and work through them, sketch image by sketch image.

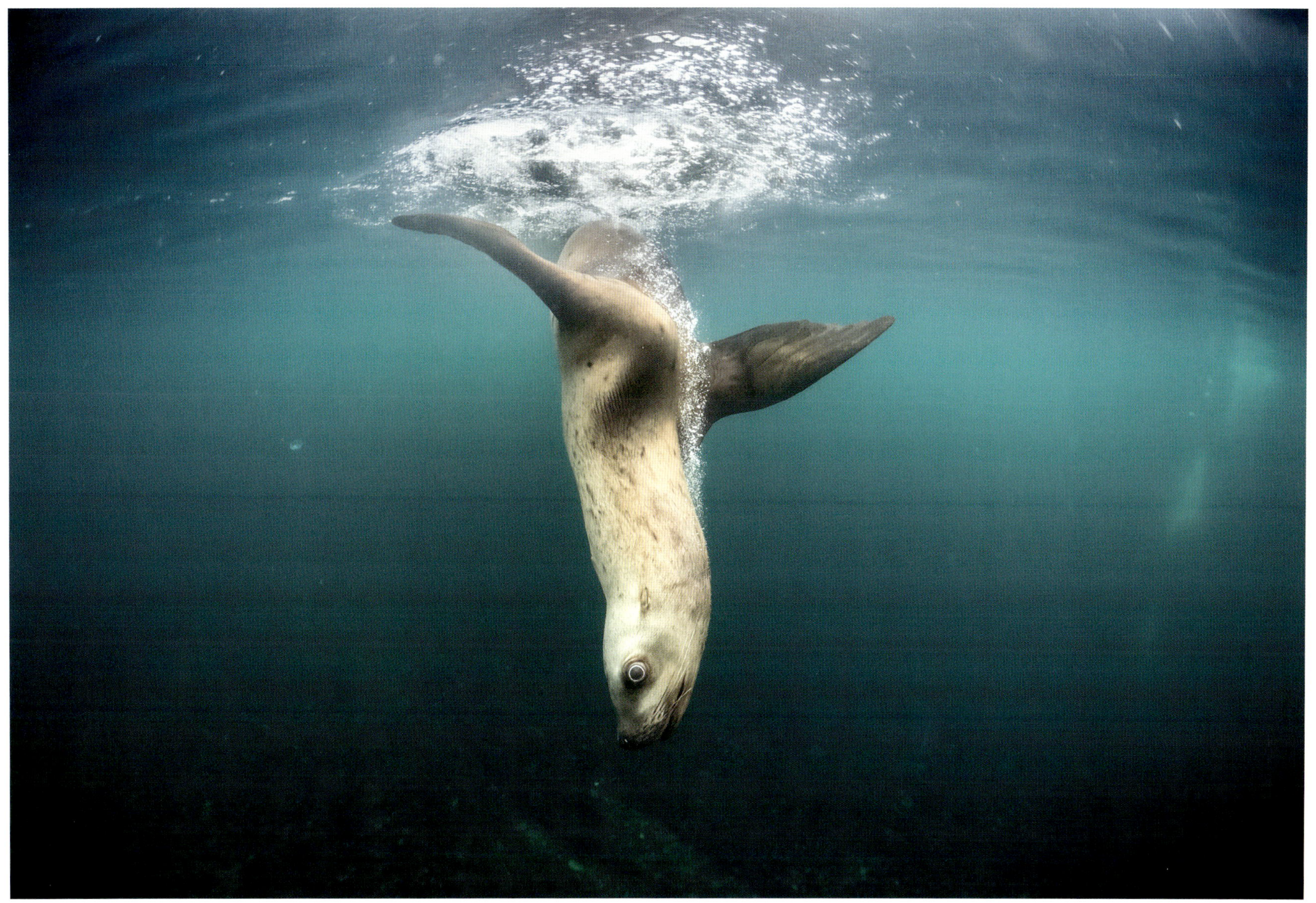

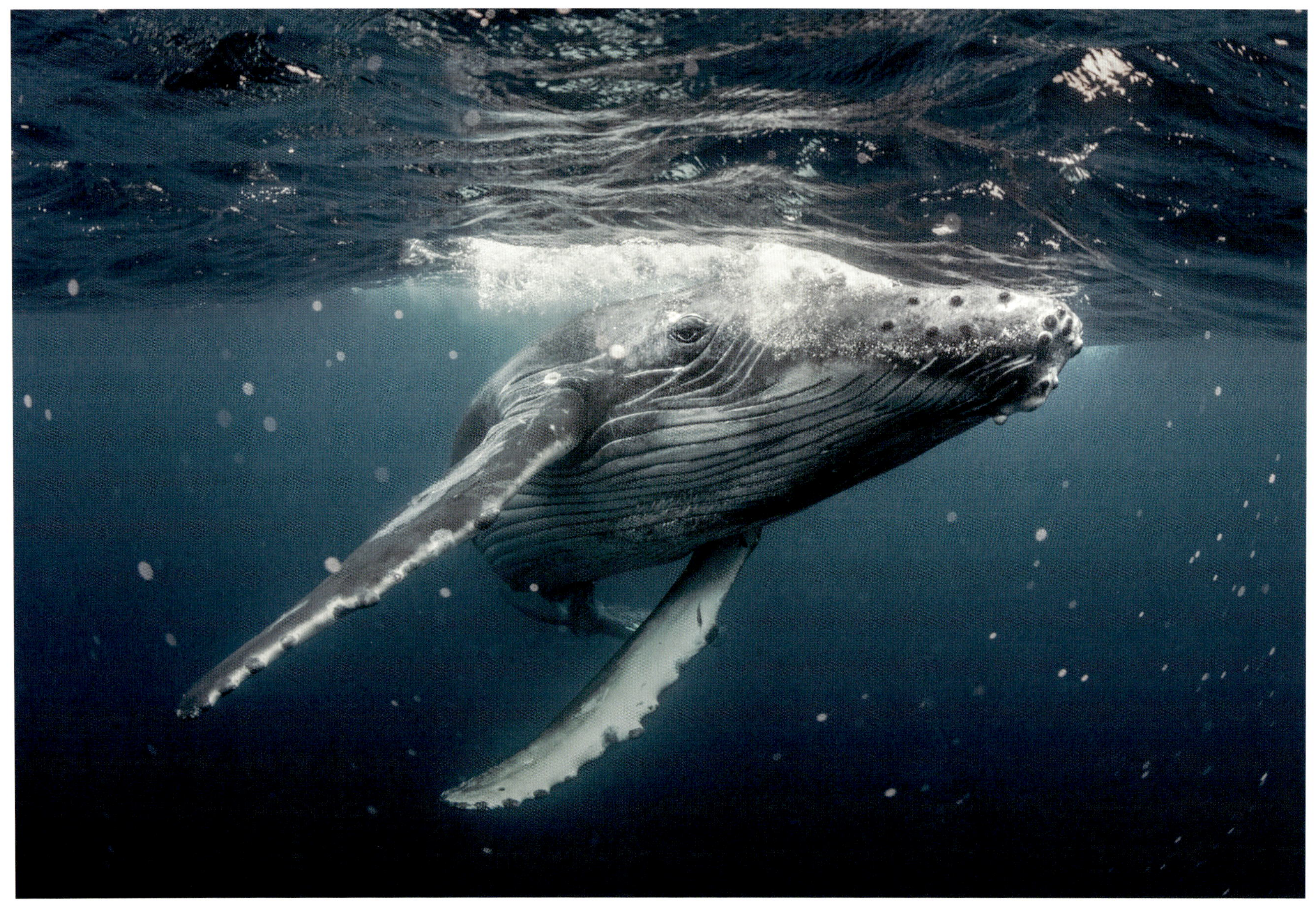

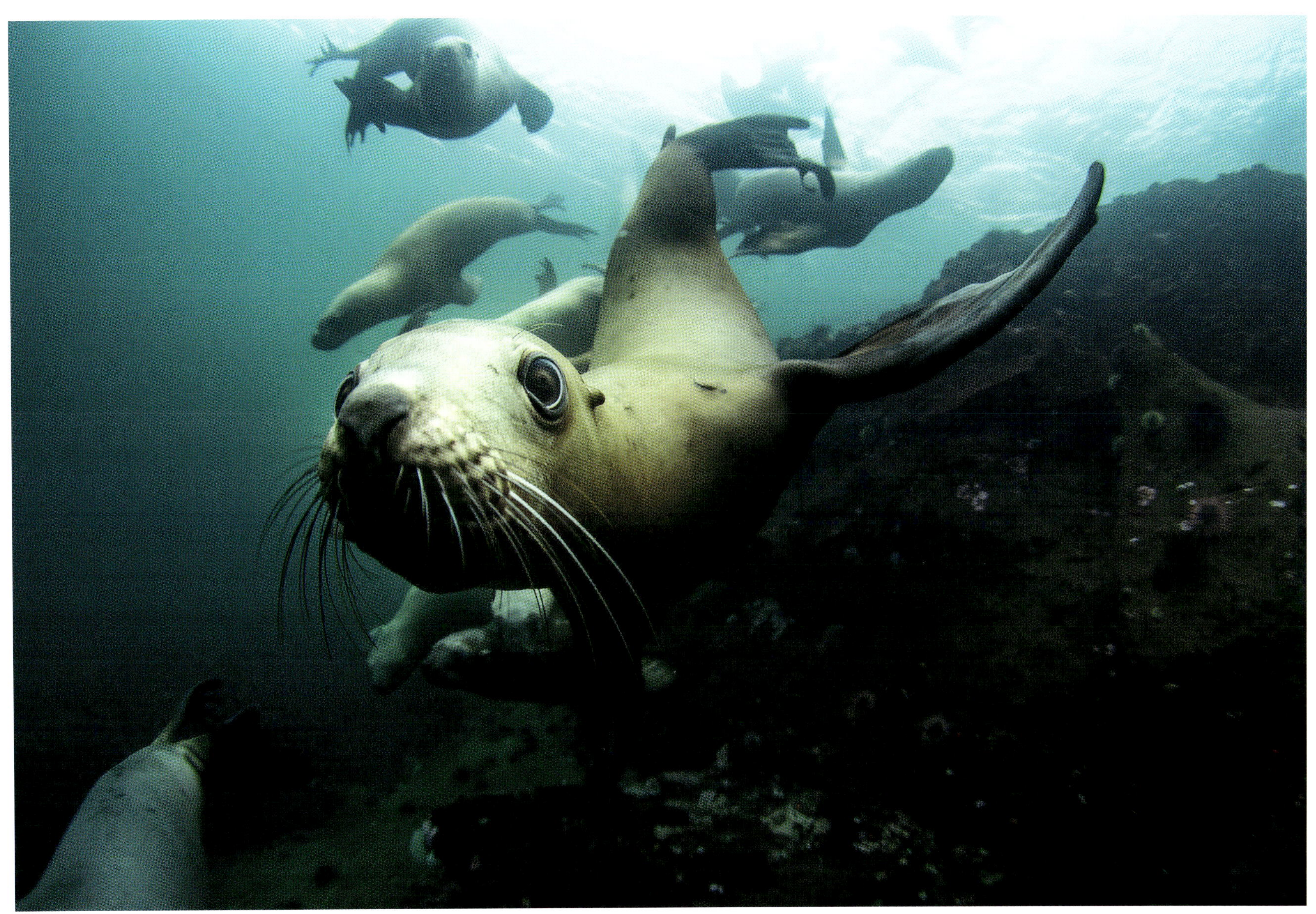

The wisdom to "shoot what you love" is good advice, although I think it's probably more accurate to say "shoot what interests you." Go in the direction your brain is already running. Follow the direction of your own interests, no matter how far they take you from the mainstream. *Especially* if they take you far from what others are doing and how they're doing it. That's where you'll not only find flow, but flow that takes you to places that are uniquely you. And that's where you'll find your voice.

Maybe this is just a more complicated way of recognizing the danger of your comfort zone, the calm center of which offers many potential directions where you could step out, not all of them helpful. Going against the grain of your interests or attempting to leap too many steps ahead of your skill level is more likely to result in fear, frustration, and paralysis. There is nothing especially redeeming in suffering for your art or making things more difficult than they have to be. The muse finds us when we're working and not cowering in the corner, which is where we're more likely to land when we follow a sense of obligation and the *oughts* and the *shoulds* rather than curiosity and fascination.

Flow is the word adults give to play to make it sound less frivolous and more legitimate. Yes, photography is hard, but that's what makes it flow (or play) if you approach it the right way. Play requires challenge. Play results in discovery, and from it, we learn about both the thing we're playing and about ourselves. Play is never forced; it always flows with the grain of who we are and toward our interests. If it doesn't, it's not play. And it's not flow.

It is necessary that creating work you are proud of is difficult and feels a couple of steps out of reach. This difficulty and discomfort are not problems to be fixed but challenges to be embraced. There are many paths to more interesting photographs; finding more interesting challenges is one of them. Finding an *easier* path, one that circumvents the challenge, is not. This is how creativity works, not because there is magic in challenge but because that's where you are more likely to learn and be forced to look deeper into what you already know to find solutions through combinations you've never tried. Taking the next steps in your craft and finding those steps difficult doesn't represent a deficiency on your part. It's just an area to explore as you continue moving forward. You'll know those next steps are right not because they're easy but because you are interested in where they can take you.

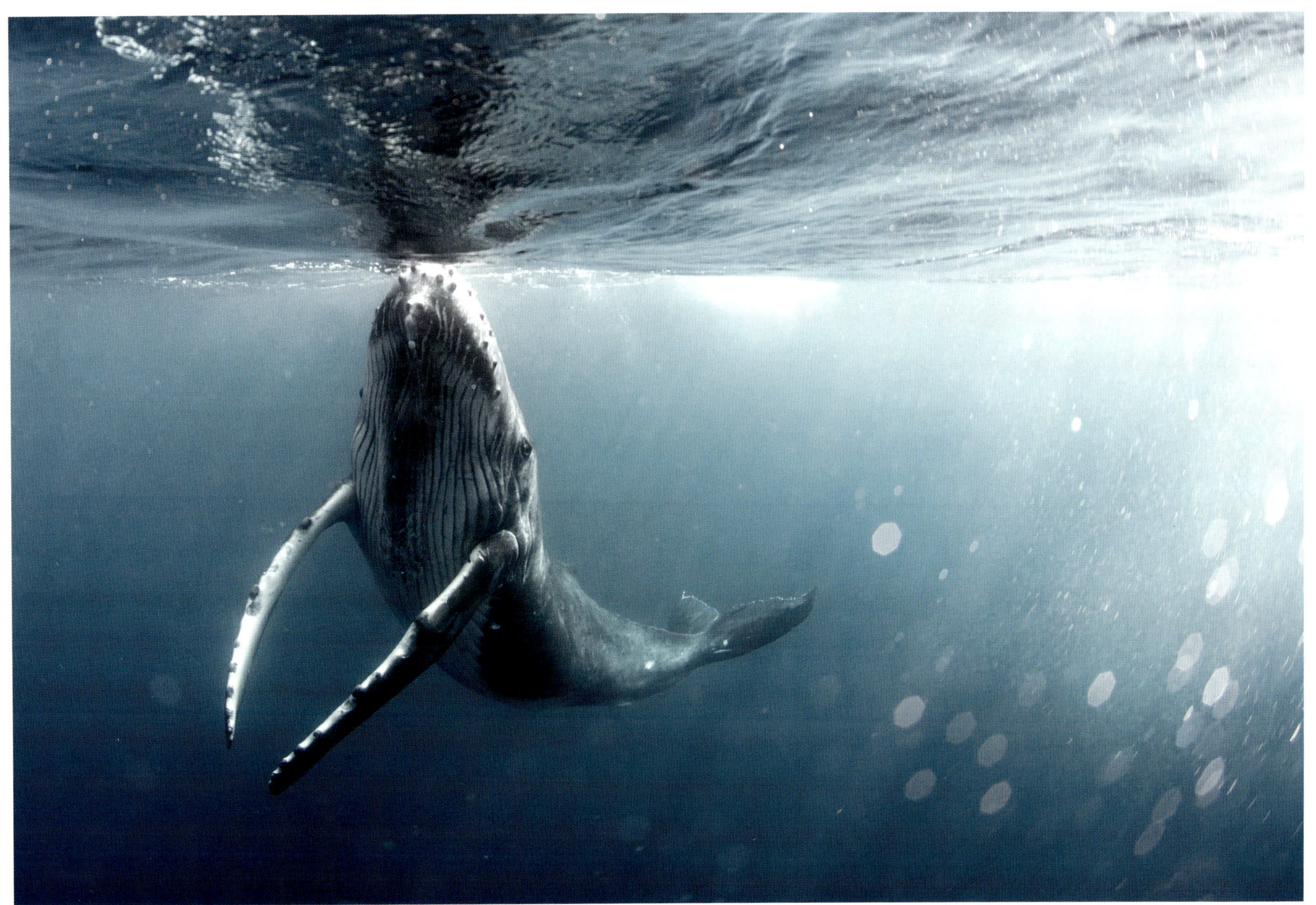

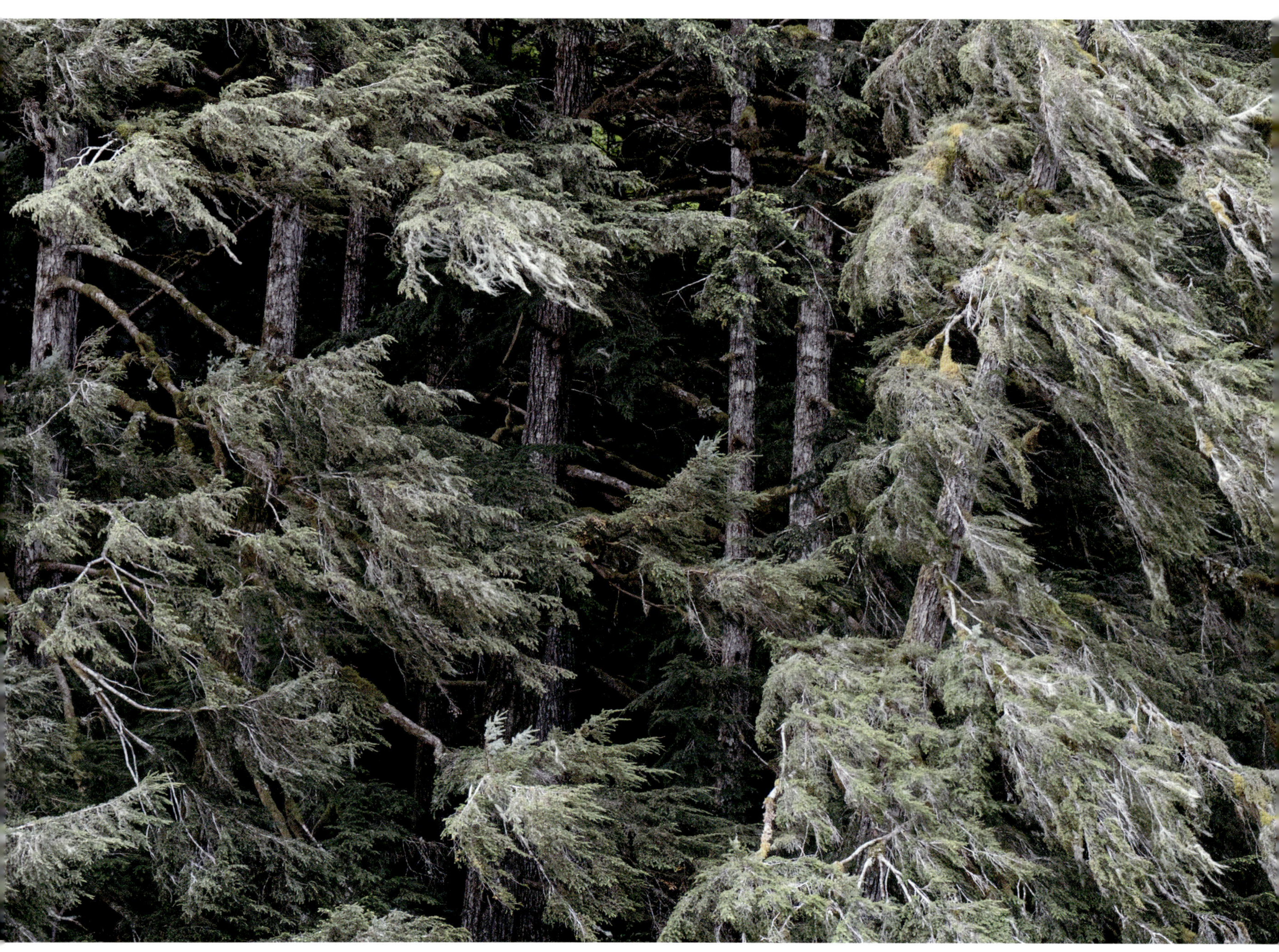

10

We're All Missing Something

Any creative effort is vulnerable to the thought that the process would be so much easier if only we had . . . and then our minds fill in the blanks. A different lens. A better camera. A 10-stop ND filter rather than a polarizer. A tripod. And while we're at it, a little more talent. God, I wish I were more creative.

In the bigger picture of the context in which we live our creative lives, we're all missing something. We are all a Gordian Knot of what we are, what we have and do not have, and what we've both gained and lost. The blessing of some of that is easily understood, while some of it is hard not to see as a curse or a deficiency. All of it comprises the constraints that shape our lives. As a photographer and a teacher on matters of creativity, the word *constraint* is important to me. Easily misunderstood as a *barrier* to creativity, constraints do not *prevent* creativity; they drive it. Accepting (and working with) this is the key not only to a challenging and fruitful creative life but to life. Full stop.

When I say "creative," does your mind immediately jump to painters, musicians, filmmakers, or that neighbour who wears too much purple and makes macramé owls? It's true; creativity thrives in the arts (though the arts are also sometimes where true creativity goes to die). But creativity also thrives in engineering and the sciences. It's the realm of inventors and great teachers and struggling parents and baseball coaches. Creativity is an imprecise idea, but it implies *making* something. Creating—whether making a family, a meal, a photograph, or a presentation. It might be making time for what's important or making a difference in your community. All of these come with their own constraints and challenges. They contain within them a problem to be solved—often several problems.

In this craft, it's the creative photographer who thinks differently about those problems and looks at them from a different angle, conjuring the courage to take the risk on possible solutions and the perseverance to work through the failed first solutions. The truly creative photographer isn't confined by what they have or do not have but sees them all as possibilities or challenges to drive them forward.

When people want to "get creative," there is much talk about thinking outside the box, but true creative thinking is about what we do within the box. For you, that might be the very specific circumstances in which you are photographing: the light, the weather, what background you have to work with, where you can or can't place the camera, and which gear you do (or don't) have with you. That's your box, and the photographer who spends their time trying to get out of it is not trying to solve their challenges but escape them. Creative thinking with a camera in your hand is not so much about thinking outside the box as figuring out how to work best within it in a way that results in images that feel right to you, delight you, or teach you something new. The box is the challenge, and challenge is underrated.

Too often bemoaned as distractions that keep us from our busy lives—lives in which we otherwise might be more creative if only we had the time and fewer of these challenges—it is challenge itself that primes us to be at our creative best, and gets us into flow.

Challenge is the gift given to us by our constraints, filling the void opened by what we lack: time, natural talent, insight, resources, or—as is so often bemoaned—gear. Challenge is not the reason our creative efforts fail but is why we need those efforts in the first place; no one needs to "get creative" about problems they do not have. Human ingenuity has always been driven by what we lack. Without lack (or the challenge of filling it), there is no flow, no creativity, only boredom, which has been described as "the lack of a lack." We *need* the challenges that arise when our constraints bump up against our desires.

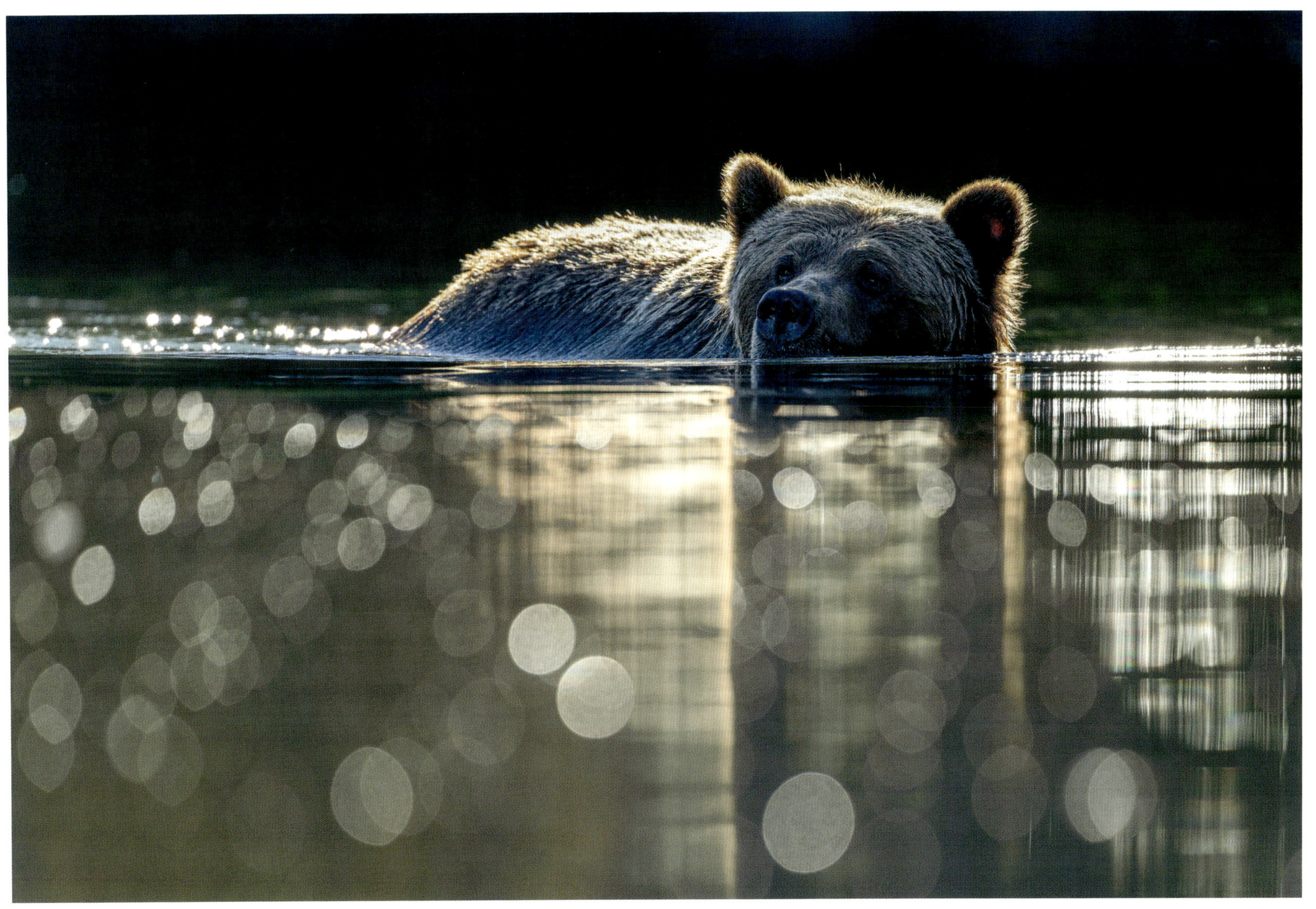

When people want to "get creative," there is much talk about thinking outside the box, but true creative thinking is about what we do within the box.

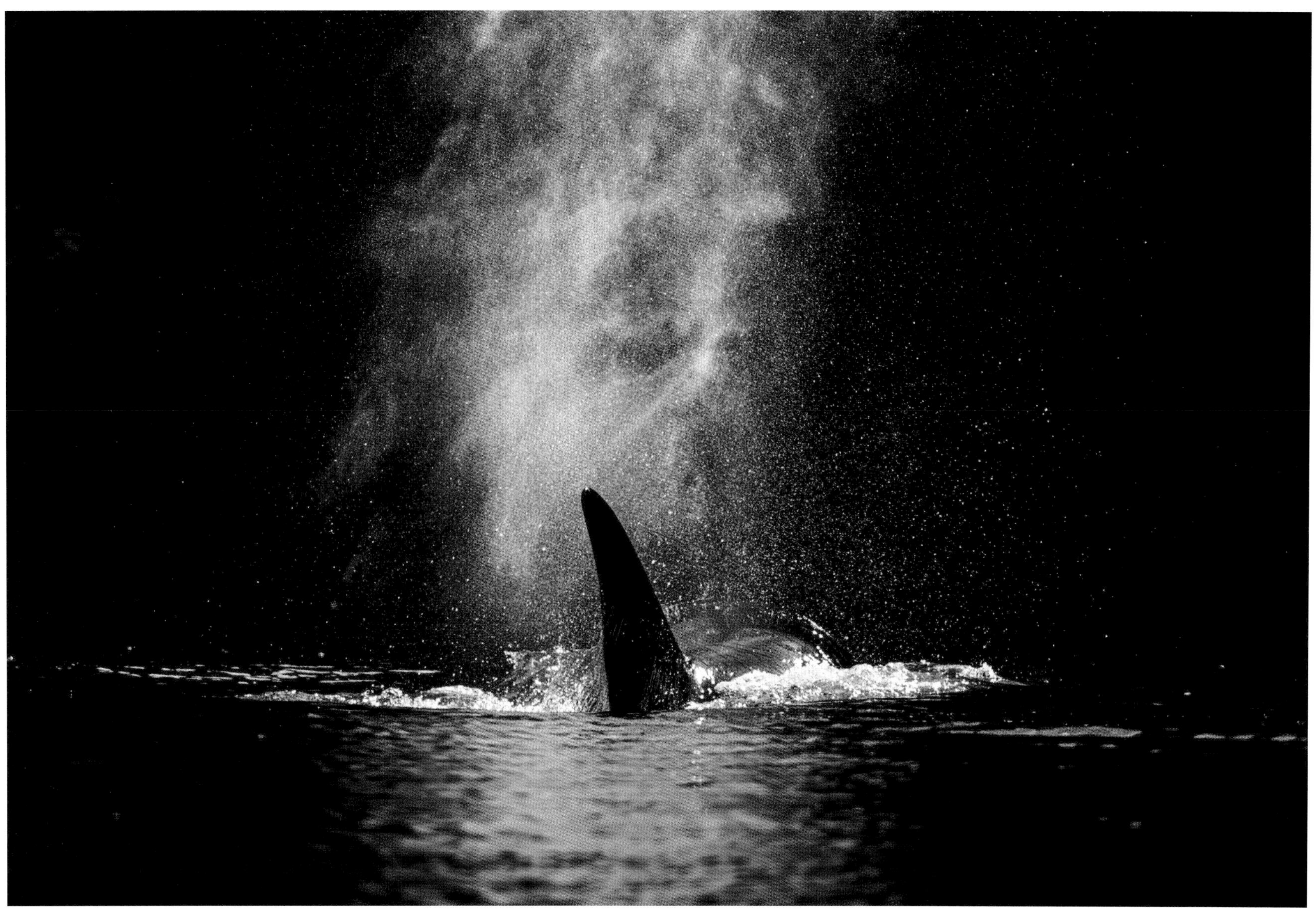

Creative people—photographers or otherwise—rise to the challenge of fulfilling those desires in the face of their constraints. They do not necessarily get it right the first time, but they do try from different angles. They are not the most flamboyant, nor necessarily even the most outwardly innovative. You can be creative without glitter and glue; you cannot be creative without a problem to solve. These problems, particularly those that are new to us, require a different approach or solution, one that doesn't come from our usual way of thinking. Exploring these problems usually has us returning to that long-muttered mantra of "What if . . . ?"

This is all made so much harder by how uncertain it always is. Creativity isn't necessary to apply a known solution to a familiar problem but to fresh challenges with possible outcomes that are hidden or shrouded. We ask "What if . . . ?" because we truly don't know. But we have a hunch. A curiosity. A suspicion that we're on the right track. It might not be the track that leads directly to the solution and our Pulitzer Prize, but it might lead us to the detour that leads us to the rabbit trail that leads us to the path. Life is labyrinthical, and creativity happens in the unknown. That's one of the lacks, one of the constraints.

Creativity isn't one thing; it's not one characteristic of the human soul or mind, but many traits found in aggregate. Among other things, it is a combination of curiosity, resilience, and courage, all of which are responses to an obstacle or constraint. Curiosity is a response to a lack of knowledge, resilience is a response to failure, and courage is a response to fear. Without those counterparts, they have no reason to exist.

Creativity is not only the stuff of pink pipe cleaners and rainbow sparkles; rather, it's an imaginative response to lives that often prove increasingly difficult as we get older and find ourselves missing more and more, keenly aware of what we've been missing all along and that our time to act is drawing short. Being creative doesn't happen when conditions are perfect but rather in response to conditions that are far from perfect. Being creative is leaning into that.

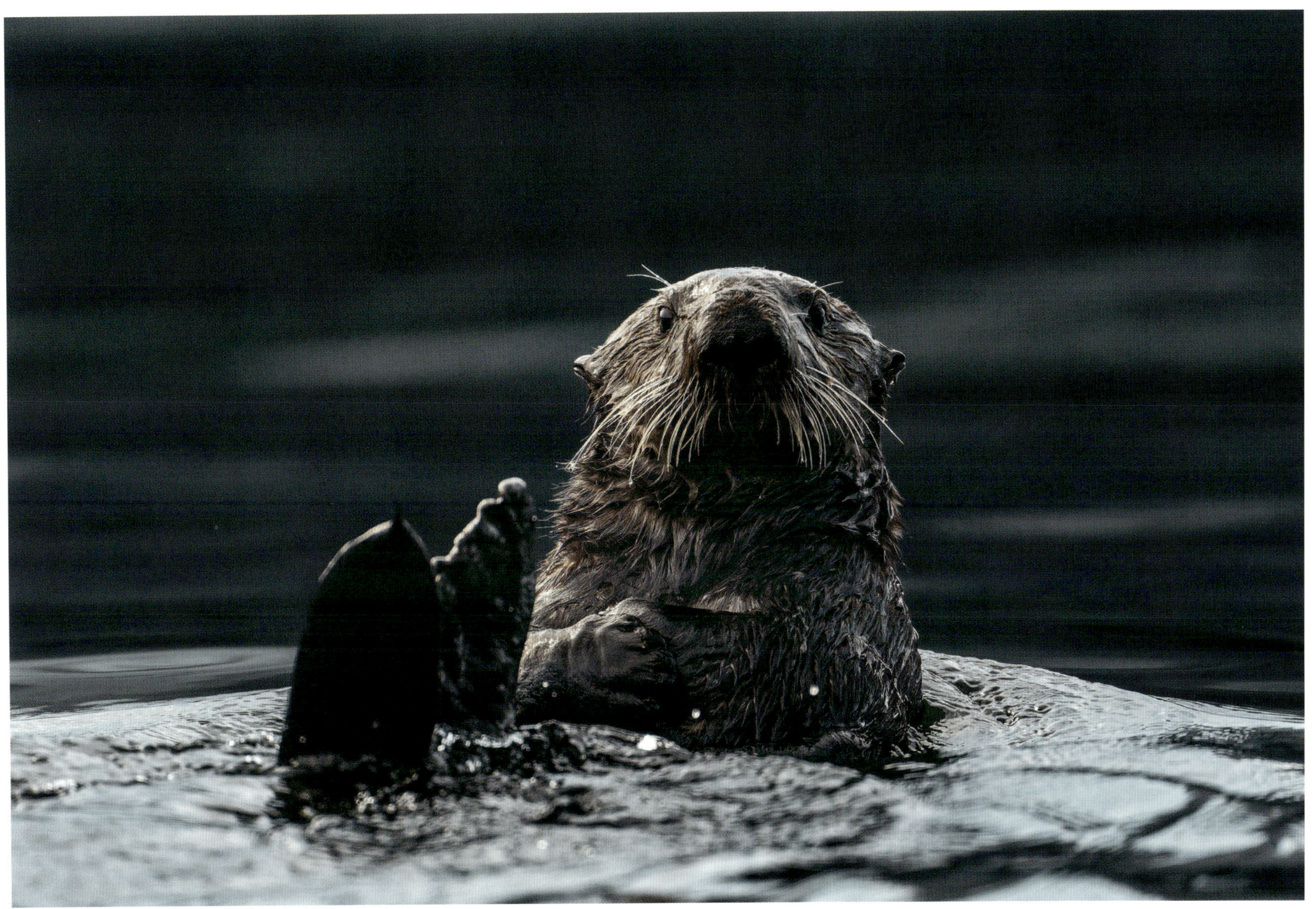

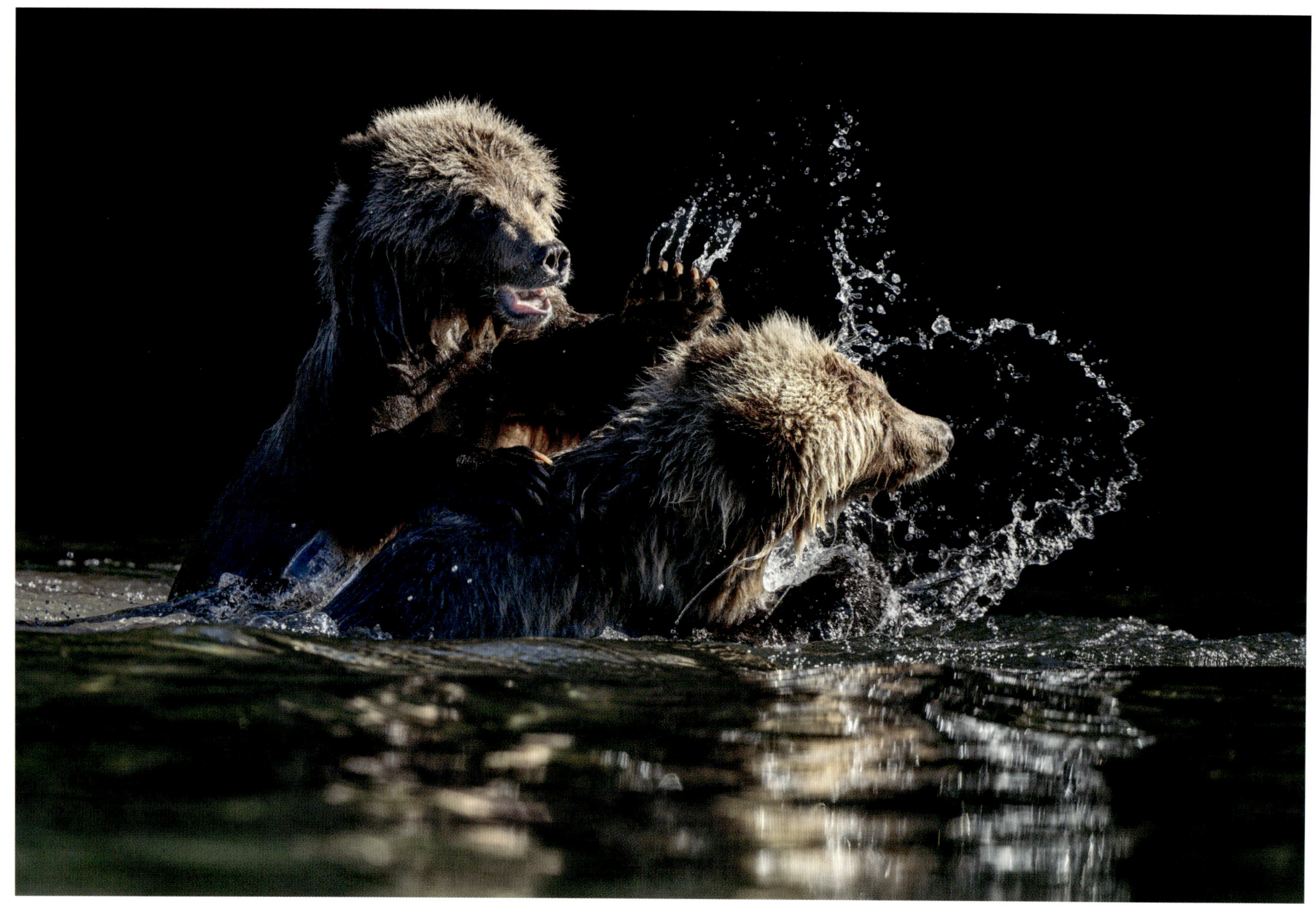

What is missing in our lives becomes, in part, the core of the songs we sing and the art we make. We write about the hunger for the things we do not have (often, love). We photograph and paint to find the beauty we long for, and in all forms of art, we ask questions to look for answers we do not have. And although scientists, engineers, and teachers don't usually call themselves artists, they do this as well and are no less creative. We respond to the lack; it's where the challenge of our days comes from. How we face those challenges becomes our chance to shine.

Our lack—and how we respond to it—becomes our chance to put our unique fingerprint on our lives and those we touch. Our challenges give us the chance not only to shine but to do so in ways unique to us. Leonard Cohen famously sang, "There is a crack in everything; that's how the light gets in." I believe it's also how the light gets out. It's why some people shine more intensely than others. More cracks, more light.

Marcus Aurelius said, "What stands in the way becomes the way." He might have added the word *maybe*. Sometimes it does not. Constraints do *not* always become possibilities; they often become excuses. They turn us around in the fear that we don't have the resources, don't know where the path leads, and have no guarantee of success. In short, it might get hard. And who can blame anyone for wanting an easier path? For wishing they had what they do not, or looking over their shoulder and wishing for what others seem to have in abundance? Creativity is not found in wishing.

Art doesn't imitate life; it *responds* to life. In the same way, courage is a response to fear, or faith is to doubt. Art doesn't happen only when the struggles fade and the traumas are forgotten, but as a reaction to them. A creative life is not something we succeed at only when we've got all the right pieces. Everyone is missing something, which isn't a deficiency; it's a path. A challenging path, to be sure, but stepping into that gap and finding ways to fill it brings us meaning and purpose, and if that's not artful living, I don't know what is. That's what creativity is to me.

Want to be more creative? Find the gap. Find the constraints and embrace them. It turns out that where creativity is concerned, if you're not missing something, you're missing everything.

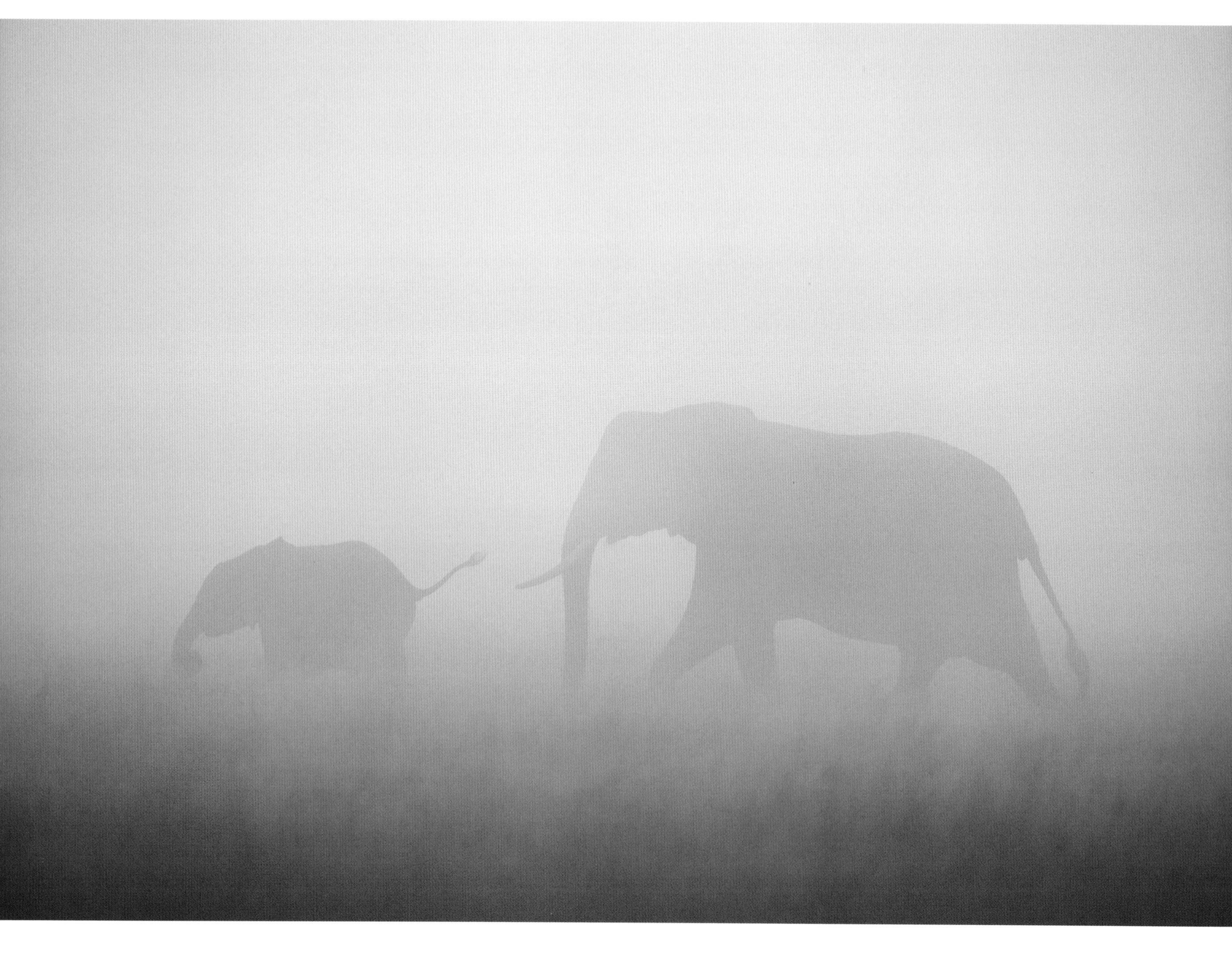

11

The Power
and Possibility
of Constraint

The idea of working within constraints is so important that it's worth exploring more pragmatically. We all face limitations, and the more gracefully and creatively we respond to the challenges those limitations place on us, the better. If you don't have the lens you want, you work with what you've got, right? But there is much to be said for intentionally choosing the constraints within which you practice your craft. If constraints lubricate the wheels of creative thought, why not be more proactive in choosing them?

The benefits are many, and one of them is mastery. There is no better expression of this idea than Edward Weston's observation that "relatively few photographers ever master their medium. Instead, they allow the medium to master them and go on an endless squirrel cage chase from new lens to new paper to new developer to new gadget, never staying with one piece of equipment long enough to learn its full capacities, becoming lost in a maze of technical information that is of little or no use since they don't know what to do with it."

The reality is that the photographer who works with a carefully chosen bag of tools will have greater proficiency, and the photographer who limits their subjects and focuses the direction of their work will be more articulate in speaking about them through their photographs. They will have a stronger and more recognizable voice, a more intimate knowledge of their subject, and a better understanding of the creative possibilities those subjects represent.

Mastery comes with focus. By definition, focus is constrained—it's a tighter beam. So is creativity. And in the times I have found myself floundering, either for a starting place or for direction once I've begun, being intentional about the limits I work within has only made that work better. Increased constraints lead to increased creativity rather than the paralysis of too many choices.

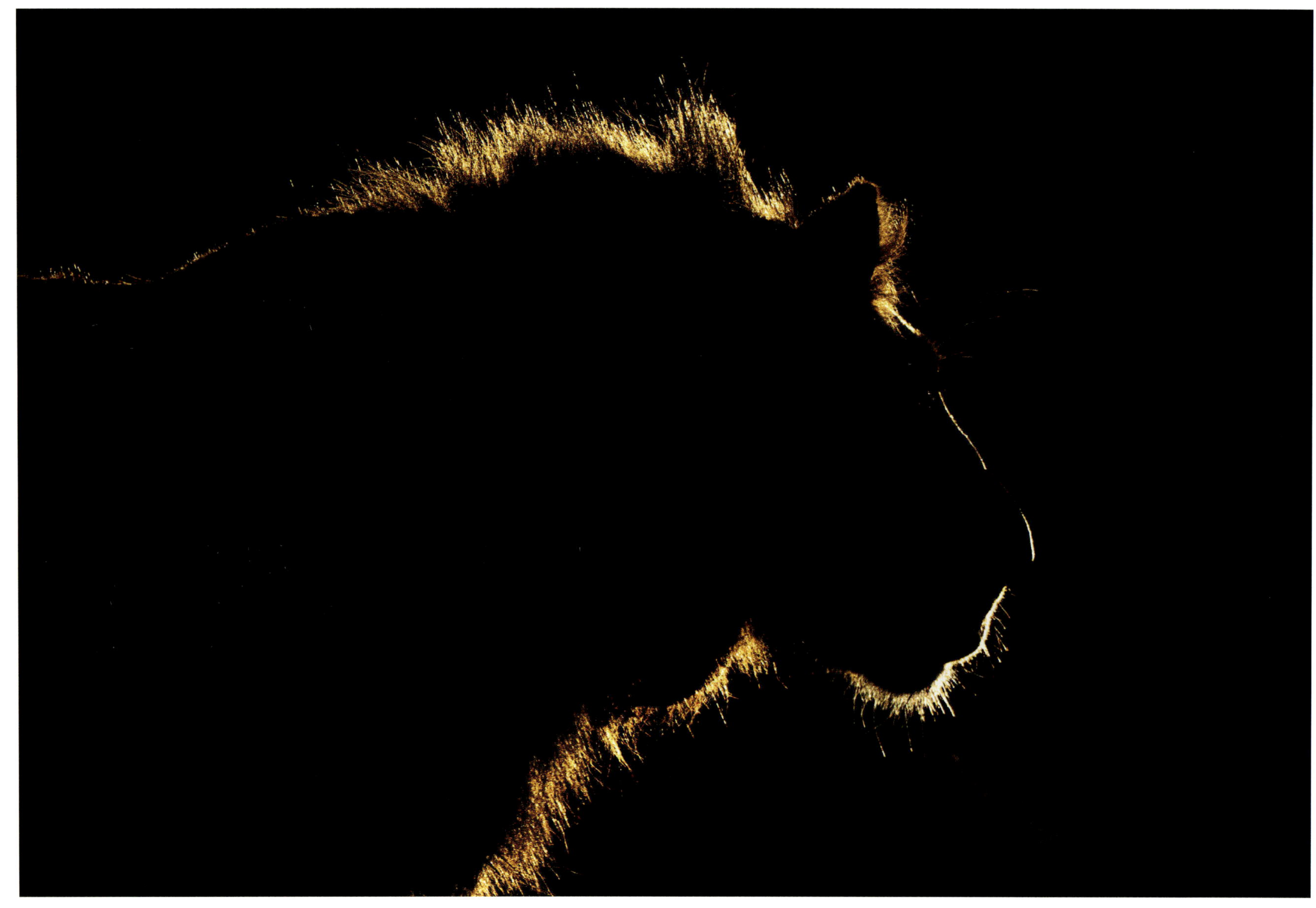

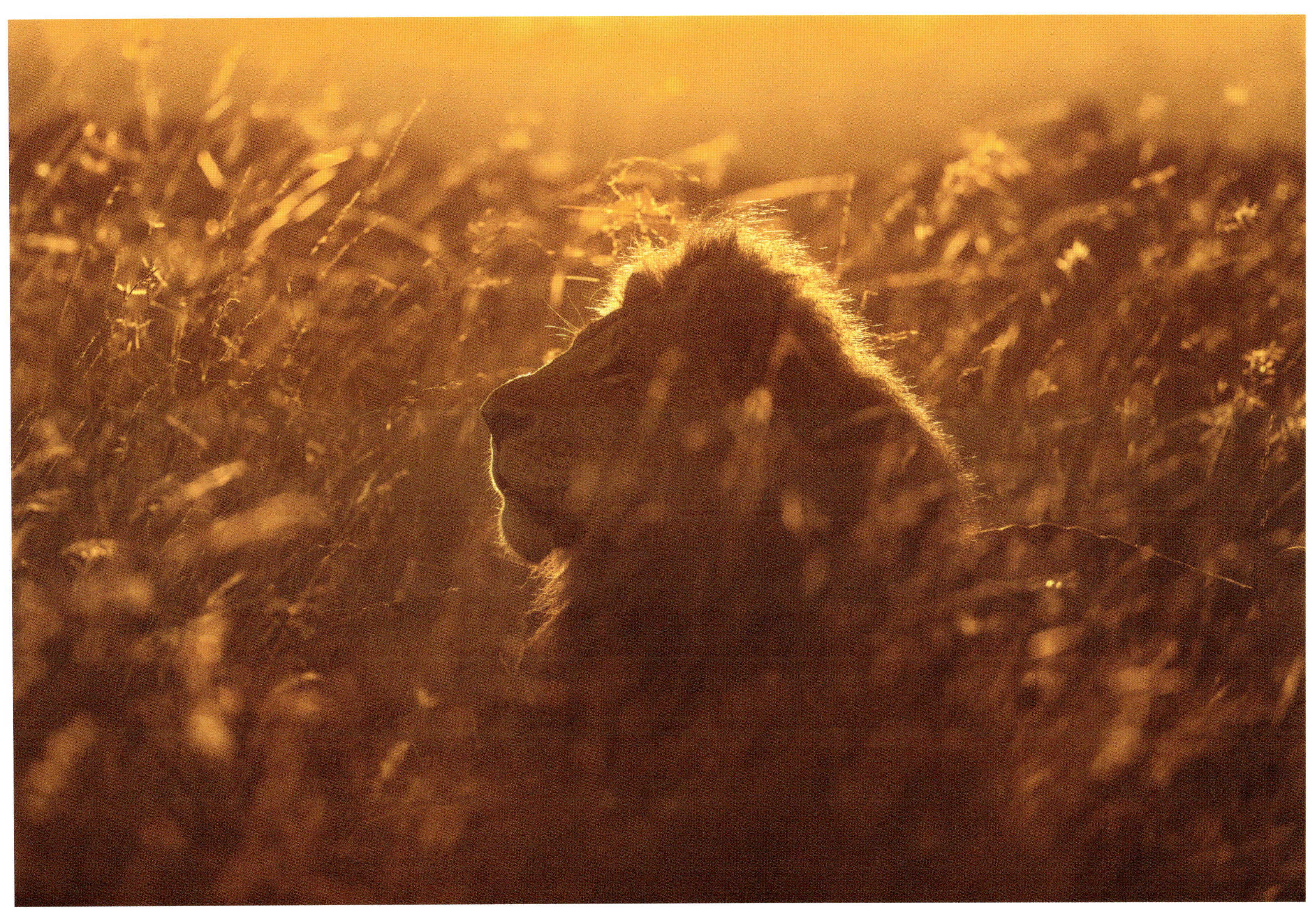

The photographer with only one camera and a single focal length isn't caught in the trap of asking which lens or focal length to work with. They have other challenges, but not that one.

The photographer choosing to work without strobes is never stuck trying to figure out where to put them or how many to use (and at which ratios). For that matter, the photographer who constrains themself to work mostly with artificial light avoids the challenges and unpredictability of working with natural light.

The photographer choosing to work only in monochrome is spared the questions and choices that colour photographers face.

Constraints drive creativity and allow us to be more specific about the challenges we choose to tackle. They don't help us think outside the box (or boxes) but allow us to be more specific about *which* boxes we most enjoy working within—the boxes that are more "us."

The international workshops I teach in places like India or Italy revolve entirely around constraints. My students choose to work within the confines of a particular theme that captures their interest, but they are limited to that one idea. It might be faith, juxtaposition, or street life, but they stick to whatever the constraint is while also being encouraged to consider other creative limitations. For example, some choose to work only in monochrome or one focal length, but because of the focus their chosen limitations impose and the way this challenge ignites their creativity, they all create work they might not have otherwise.

When you make the choice to work almost entirely within the constraint of a horizontal frame or to limit your aspect ratio to the classic 3:2 frame, your creative problem when you raise the camera becomes "How do I make this scene work within my preference for horizontal compositions?" rather than "Which frame orientation do I use?" The photographer whose constraint of working with lower shutter speeds to elicit a sense of movement in their photographs is presumably interested in that specific constraint, or they'd have opted for different limitations. Choosing to limit your work to a particular theme, technique, or tool narrows your focus; you're still working inside the box, but this box is a constraint of your own choosing that presses you closer to your own preferences and, ultimately, your own voice.

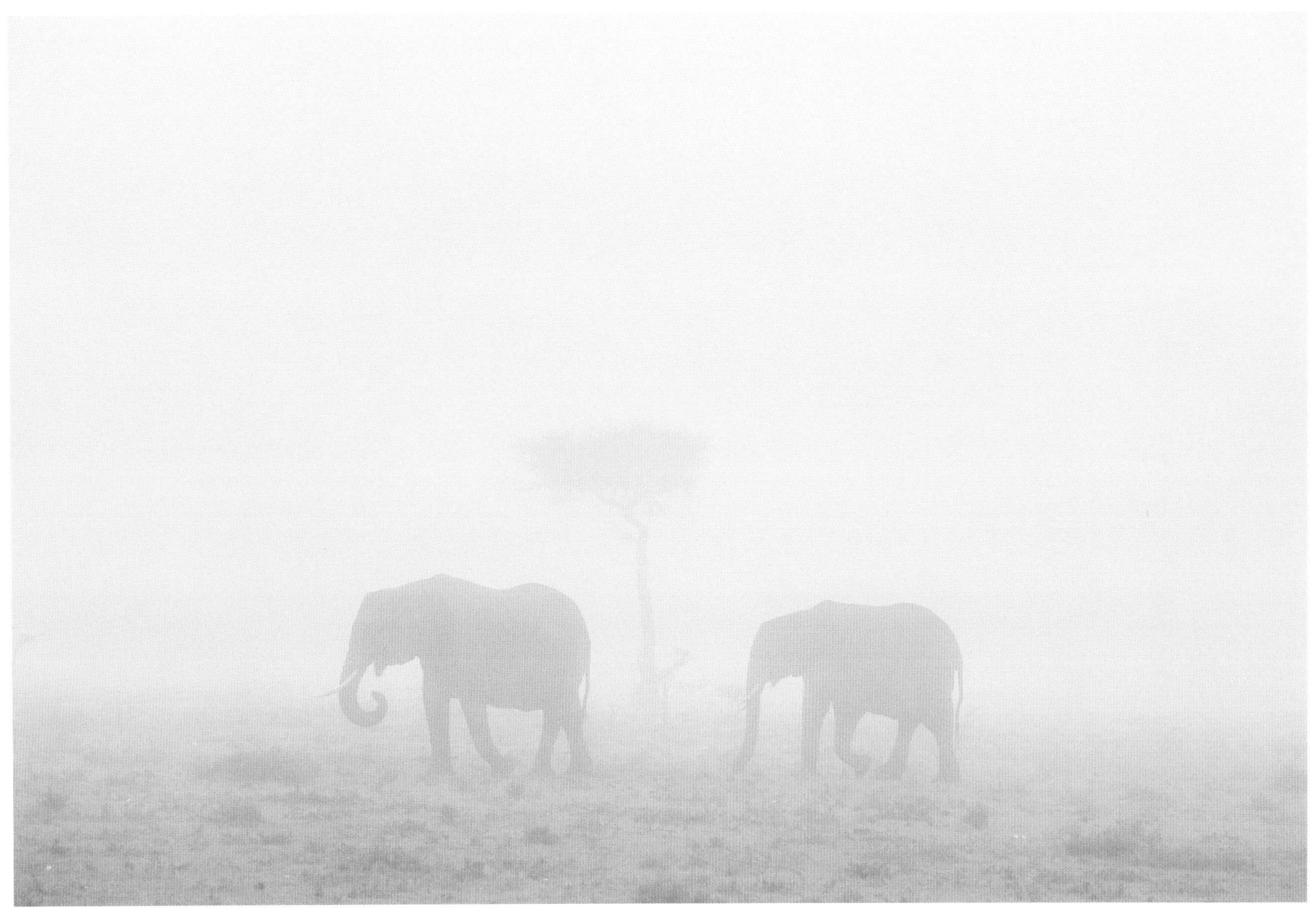

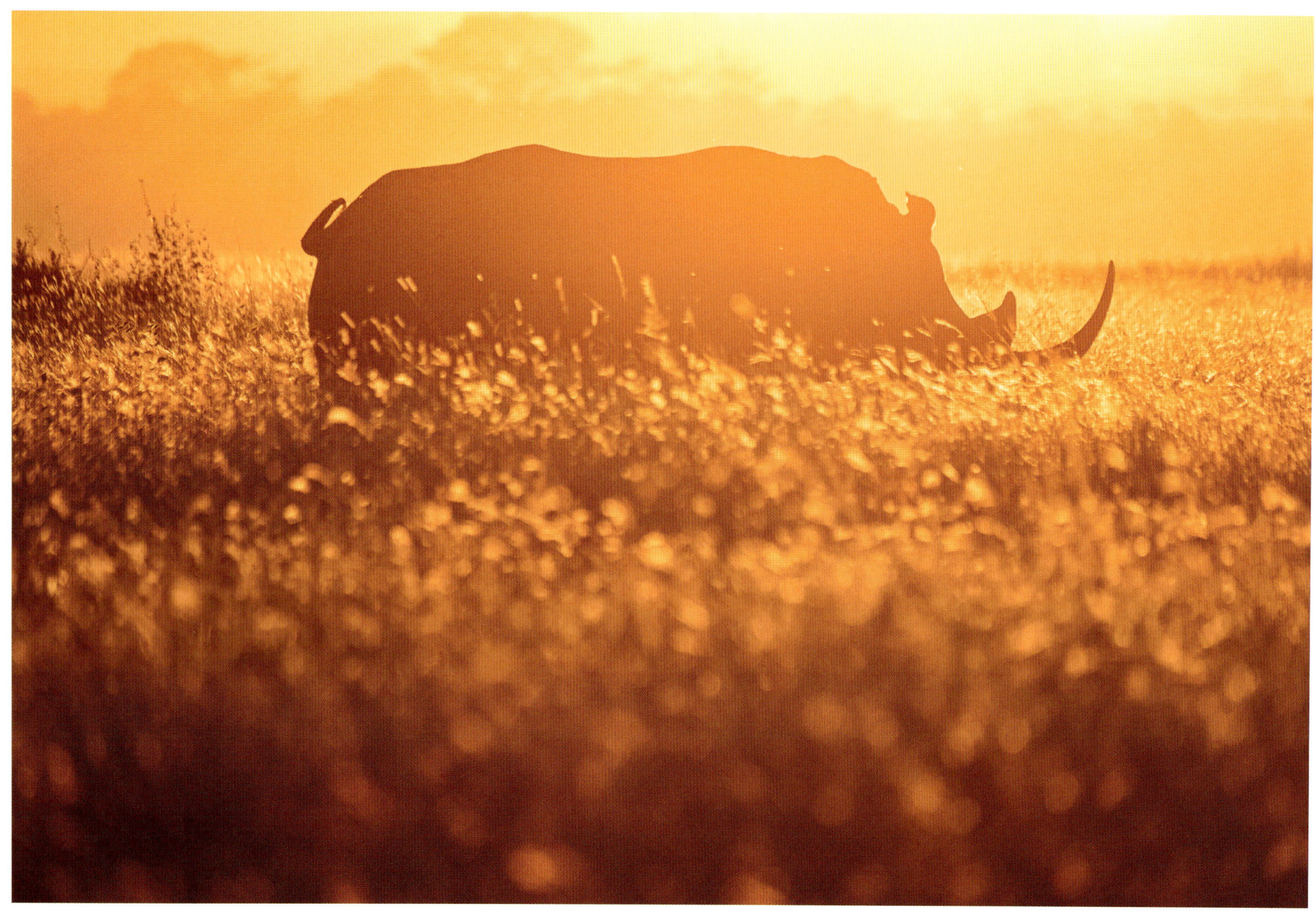

Aside from what life hands me (and the inevitable challenges of circumstance), intentionally choosing to work within constraints allows me to select the challenges I most enjoy. I photograph here and not there because I prefer here. I work in one format and not others because that format pleases me. I work with wider lenses and more inclusive points of view because those are my preferences. And so the more I choose my constraints, the more my work truly becomes mine. Constraints don't only guide creativity and provide its spark; they help you find and express your voice.

As my tastes and preferences have changed over the years, I've chosen different constraints that have made my work easier and created well-defined channels for creativity and flow. This approach has also made my work more unified and less all over the map. There have certainly been phases. The work in this book differs in several ways from my last large project, *Pilgrims & Nomads*: one body of work is colour and focused on encounters with wildlife and the natural world, particularly megafauna, and the other is monochrome and explores human subjects, specifically the Christmas pilgrimage in Ethiopia and the lives of semi-nomadic pastoralists in northern Kenya. Different choices about the constraints I was working within came from my preferences about the subjects I was exploring and how I thought they might be best expressed.

Too little is said about personal tastes and preferences in photography. There are trends and rules (and opinions aplenty), but what freedom we would all find in our work if we did it just because it pleased us. You find your voice in the unique combination of all the many things you *like*, the challenges you *enjoy*, and delving into these aspects to discover where they ultimately lead you.

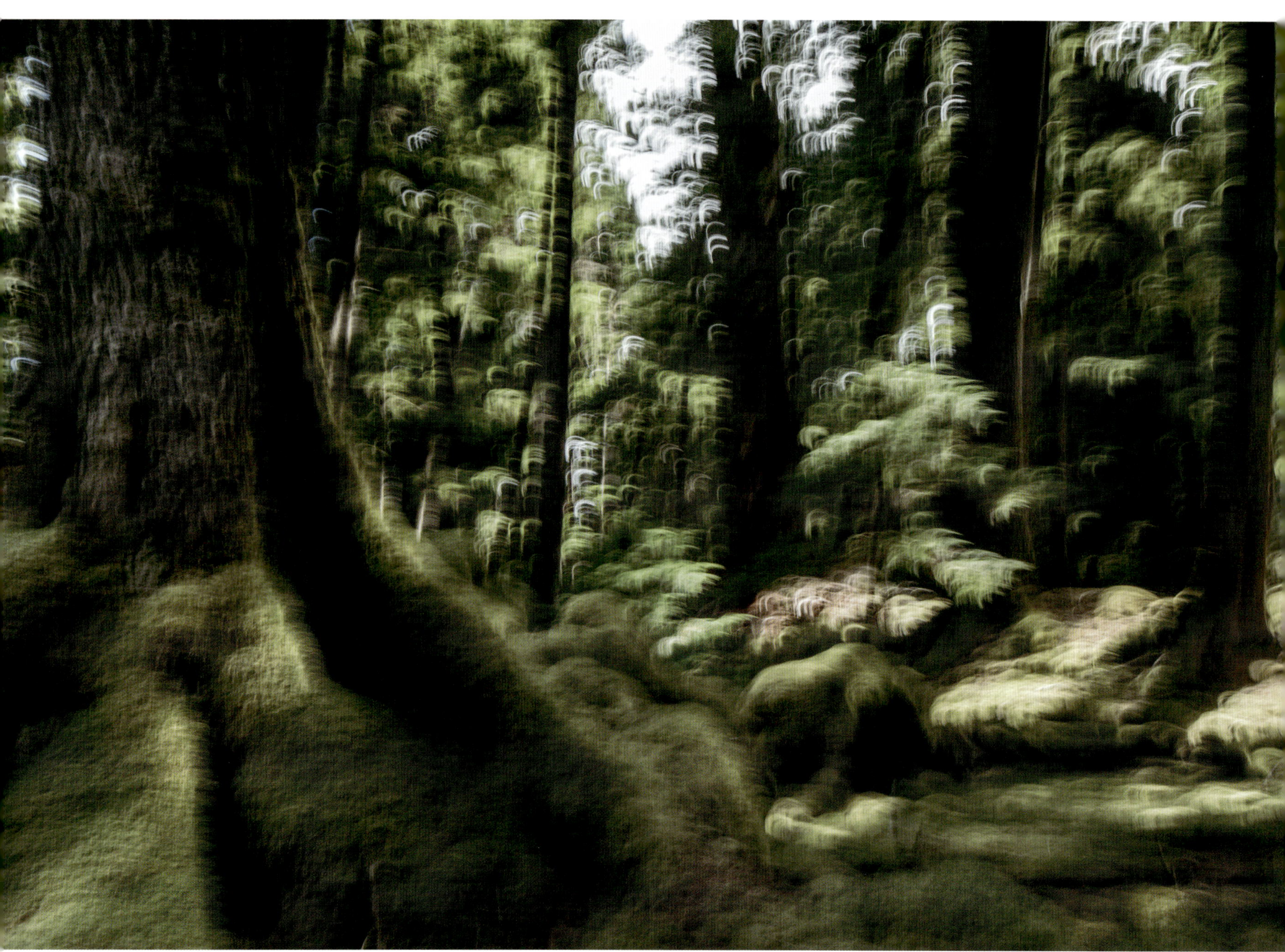

12

Comparison and Creativity

I have never once compared my work to that of Pablo Picasso or Vincent van Gogh; it's just too different. Not only is my chosen medium as different from theirs as the themes I explore, but our work exists so many miles apart that it invites no comparison whatsoever. On the other hand, the work of a peer creating photographs with vision and creativity, or worse (for me, not them), creating work that is getting attention where mine is not makes for very easy comparison. I wish I could say I no longer felt the pangs of envy when looking at the magic others are creating, but I suspect it's a very human thing to do.

I've heard it said that comparison is the death of creativity (and for the most part, I agree), but quick sound bites and pithy quotes tend to lack the nuance of longer conversations. Focusing on the differences between your photographs and those of your contemporaries can indeed sabotage a healthy creative life, but it can also be a learning experience. Identifying an area of technical weakness in your work because it's so conspicuously absent in someone else's photographs can give you the encouragement to embrace a little more rigour in your photography. It can help make you more aware of blind spots. Recognizing stronger storytelling elements in the photographs of a contemporary (or a more nuanced understanding of colour, for example) can be the nudge you need to understand yourself and embrace new ways of thinking about and practicing your craft. There is a sense in which comparing your work to others' can be exactly what you need to look at your work from a different angle. Asking, "Why are my photographs so unlike these others?" can hint at the interesting problems your creativity thrives on exploring if you're receptive to it.

Voice is found exactly in the differences between what makes you and other artists *unlike* one another; it is not found in the pursuit of similarities.

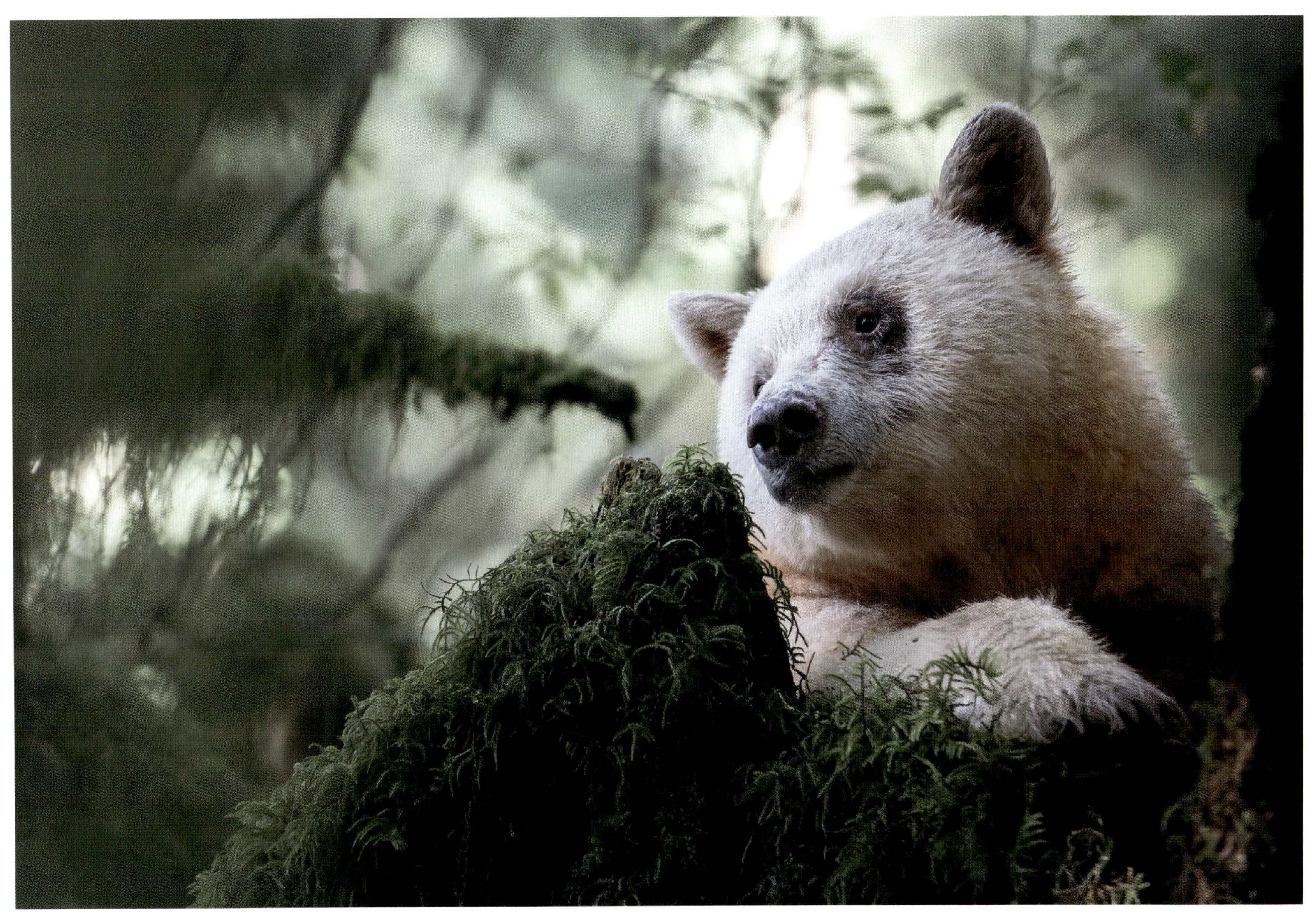

Keep your eyes open long enough, and you'll see photographs so compelling that they put a knot in your stomach or make you dizzy; some photographers create work so strong it occasionally makes me want to quit altogether. Aside from the temporary despair this may induce, I usually come around to the happy recognition that, in a craft I have become so familiar with, there is still something to discover—that there is room for me to grow and move forward. It's good to stir the paint once in a while. But discovering what is yet missing in how you think about or practice your art is not the same as believing that you yourself are deficient.

Comparing my work to that of others can be a learning experience, but comparing *myself* to other artists has only ever sent me into a tailspin that not only steals my joy in the process but also takes my work farther away from what is really me.

Voice, that intangible thing that makes you distinct as an artist, is found in the many differences between us. Voice is found exactly in the differences between what makes you and other artists *unlike* one another; it is not found in the pursuit of similarities. Voice is not found as we seek to be more and more like the others to which we compare ourselves, but as we discover the cracks between us and go all in to widen them. Voice (and what others might one day call authenticity or originality in your art) comes from a willingness to be different, not the effort to be the same.

The differences you discover as you make those comparisons and the photographs you make are not to be criticized or lamented; rather, they are to be celebrated. There's more life and creativity to be found in leaning hard into what makes you different than in leaning toward sameness, and instead of worrying about whether you're doing it "right," focusing on doing what works for *you*.

Doing it your way beats doing it the right way every time. If people like Jim Henson, Jimi Hendrix, or Pablo Picasso had made puppets, played guitar, or painted like everyone else, we would never have heard of them or experienced the magic of their very individual genius. Their voices were so distinct you could point at any of them and say, "That's not how it's done." Exactly. Jimi didn't play guitar the "right" way. He played it *his* way.

Photography is limited to some degree by physics, but it is gloriously free from rules. We are constrained by the optics and the mechanics that result in images that are focused or blurry or dark or light, but not by what we are permitted to do within those constraints. There is no right and there is no wrong in photography; there is only what works, and specifically, what works *for you*. This is not easy to discover, making it all too tempting to look to photographers who are doing what obviously works for *them* and hoping it

There is no right and there is no wrong in photography; there is only what works, and specifically, what works *for you*.

might also work for you as a kind of shortcut to making something that resembles your own. It usually doesn't, though it can often contain hints.

What *does* work is found at the unique intersection of your perception of the world (let's call it vision) and the many ways the camera can render that world (let's call this craft) in the form of a photograph. Unless you see and think about the world in exactly the same way as others, the craft they appear to so effortlessly and effectively use to express *their* vision won't work for you. It's tempting to believe that others have figured out how to be a "real" photographer and want to emulate them in an effort to be the same, but what they have discovered is nothing more than how to be themselves. They don't know the *right* way to make photographs any more than you do, but if they've found a trail that seems to lead to making photographs in a way that is uniquely *right for them*, then blindly following that same trail will only take you farther from what is right for you.

I've often looked at someone else's photographs and wondered why I don't see the world the way they do. I know that if I had been in the same place at the same time, I'd have been looking at completely different things or even at the same things but *seeing* them completely differently. I can learn from this if I stop beating myself up about it. We all can. This is one way our vision grows. The more exposed we are to new per-spectives or ways of seeing the world, either through the eyes of others or the unique "eyes" of the camera, the more we are able to open our eyes to the possibil-ities and think differently about what we see when we look at the world.

You might not see the world like an impressionist photographer, in brush strokes created with slower shutter speeds and motion, but if you try your hand at it to see whether those techniques might become part of your craft, you might *see* the world very differently in a year or so. The answer to "Why didn't I notice that?" is often as simple as having never tried long enough to discover a new way of seeing. Another photographer might see more (or differently) than you, but they don't see *better*. There is no "better" when talking about individuality.

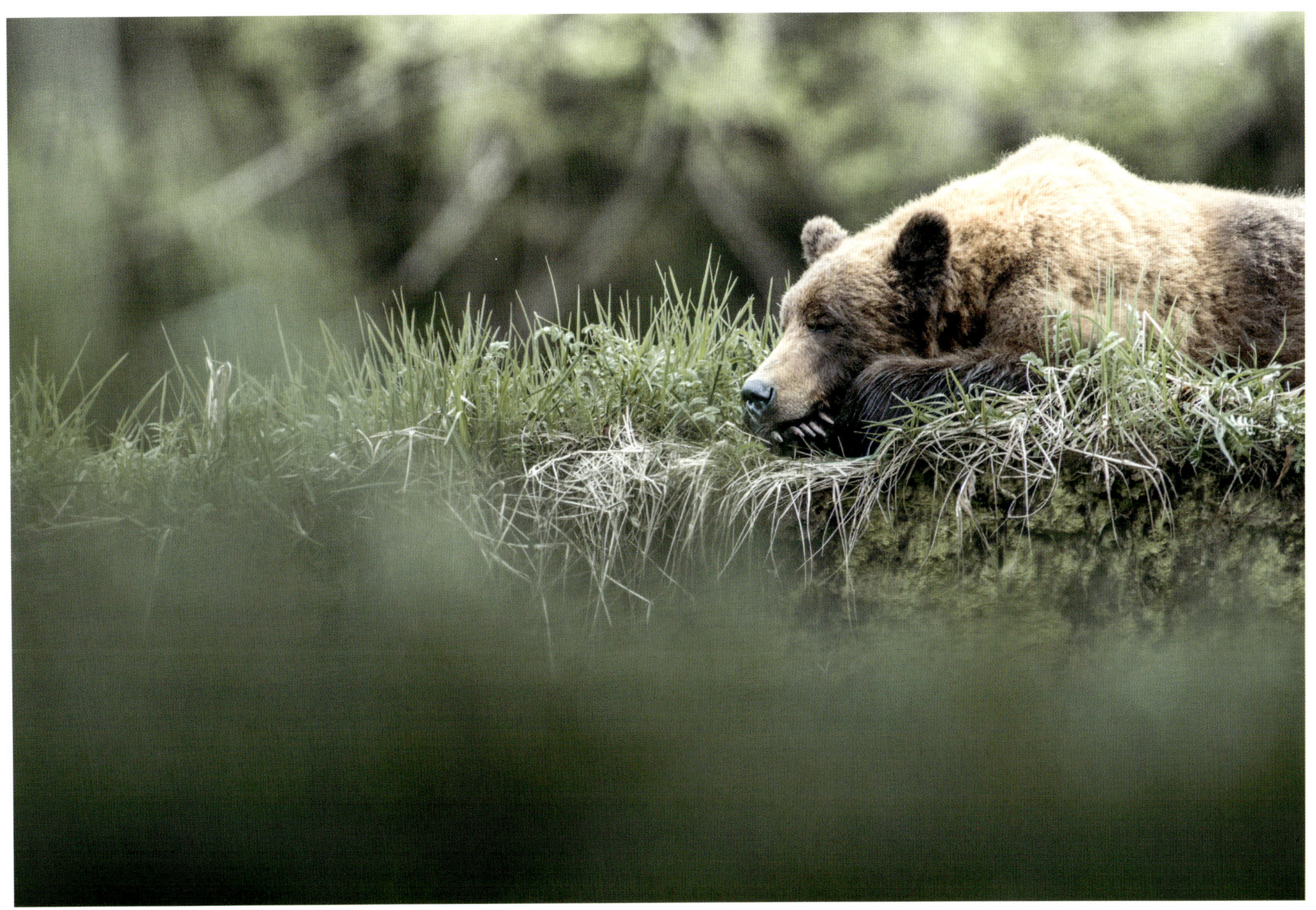

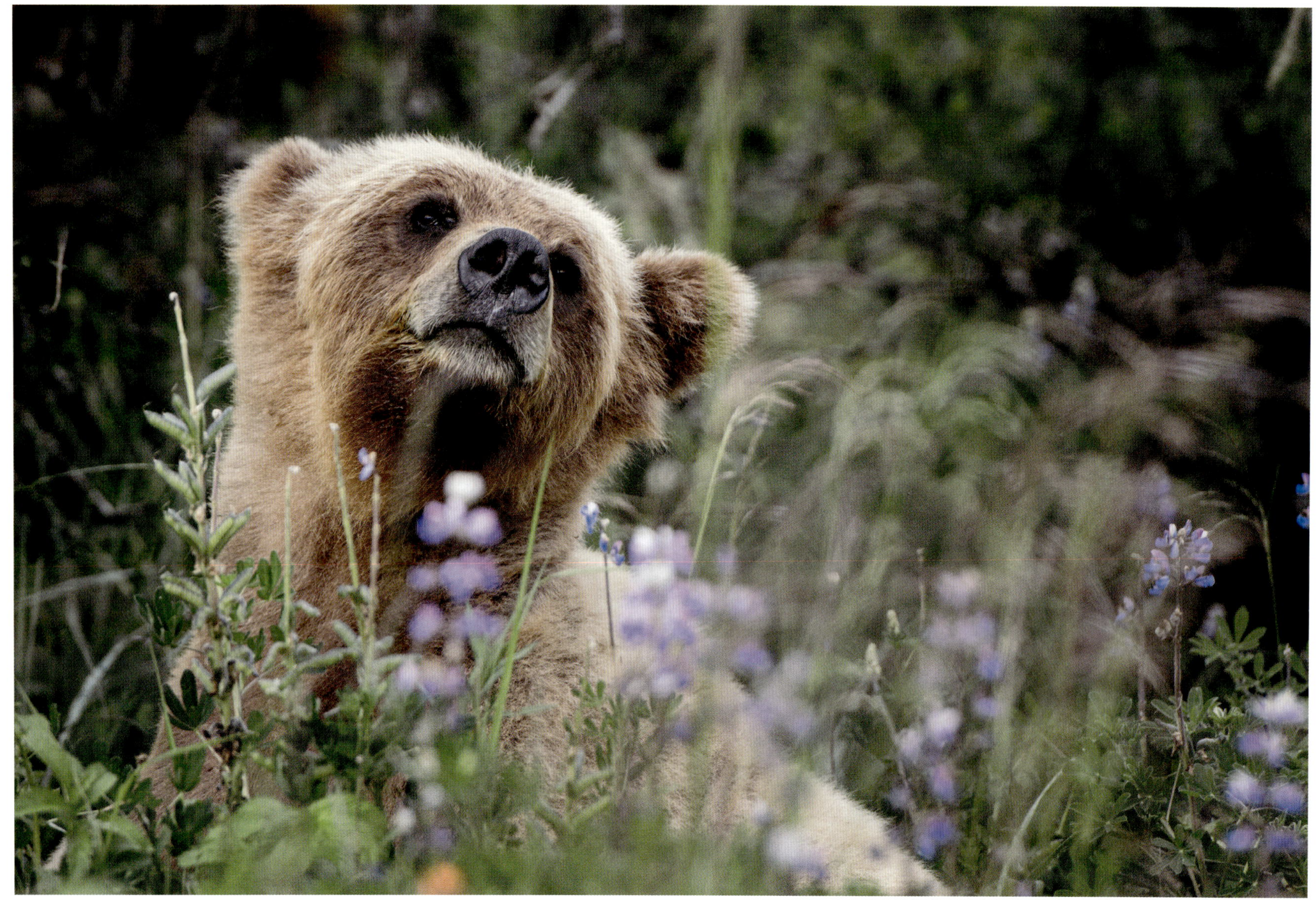

There is something else: we react to what is unusual. Could it be that when we look momentarily through someone else's eyes and wonder why we don't see as they do, we're merely comparing what is novel to us to what is familiar and obvious to them? It's easy to be seduced by what is new or different and to forget that someone else's way of seeing is as obvious to them as yours is to you. The knife cuts both ways: you don't see the way they do, but they don't see the way you do, either. Different, but not better.

Just as the unique way you see the world comes from the combination of a lifetime of interests, tastes, preferences, and the thousands of influences that are yours and yours alone, so are the ways you learn and use your craft. In 2009, I wrote *Within the Frame: The Journey of Photographic Vision*, which deeply explores the role vision plays in our craft. But photographic craft is also a journey that's neither shorter nor easier than finding your vision, nor can craft and vision really be disconnected from each other.

What you see and how you photograph will grow and change, but that change is an internal journey that is mostly invisible and can't be compared with what you see in other photographers.

Comparison works against you when it averts your eyes and attention from your work; you'll discover your voice and refine your craft as you do the work, not as you look over your shoulder. There will always be someone in your periphery making photographs that feel more successful than yours, and the more you expose yourself to the work of others, the harder it is to keep your eyes facing forward. This is already a challenging task, but in a world so saturated with images, it's even harder. How many times have I gone looking for "inspiration" in others' work (or so I had convinced myself) and instead found only discouragement? Comparing my work to yours, I might learn something helpful. Comparing my work to the hundreds or thousands of others I might see in 30 minutes online, I'm more likely to become paralyzed, pulled in every direction but my own.

Every artist or creative I've spoken with has expressed some version of this struggle. I can only tell you what works for me: studying (not scrolling) and creating more than I consume. I learn better when I look more deeply at the work of one artist at a time and consider their life, find the markers that make their voice recognizable, see how they create what they do, and ponder why. The more I get to know them, the more I'm pulled to celebrate their work rather than only comparing it to mine. They become mentors to me as I thoughtfully study their work and methods before asking, "What can I learn from this?"

The experience of scrolling through online media, on the other hand, offers no such benefits. On the days I let my guard down long enough to fall into those rabbit holes, I emerge not inspired or having learned something but distracted and discouraged, overwhelmed by all the directions my work is *not* going. Being mindful of what I expose myself to visually (and how) has made my inner life a quieter, less confusing place from which to do my work. Creating more than I consume flows from that and probably needs no more explanation than this: your voice is found, polished, and evolves only when you do your work.

When your eyes are on your work, they aren't looking around at what others are doing. When you're in flow, the only thing that matters is the here and now, you and your work, and the thrill of discovery when the pieces finally come together and the photograph you just made feels like the one in your imagination. Doing your work and finding enough challenge to spark your creativity to get into flow as often as possible is what gets you to that moment of reward or grace—when you make something so uniquely yours that what others are making just doesn't matter. Doing your work and getting to creative flow more often is the antidote to the negative effects of comparison.

When I was learning to drive, I was told that I would steer toward wherever I was looking: "Don't look at the wheel; look where you want to go. Focus on the ditch, and that's where you'll end up." How you create—and find your voice as you do—can't help but be affected by what you look at. There is much to learn from the work of others (and much to celebrate in the diversity of that work), but if you want to move in the direction of creating work that is truly yours, then *that* is where you need to be looking. Attention is a limited resource, and the more you spend it on other things, the less you'll have to give to your work.

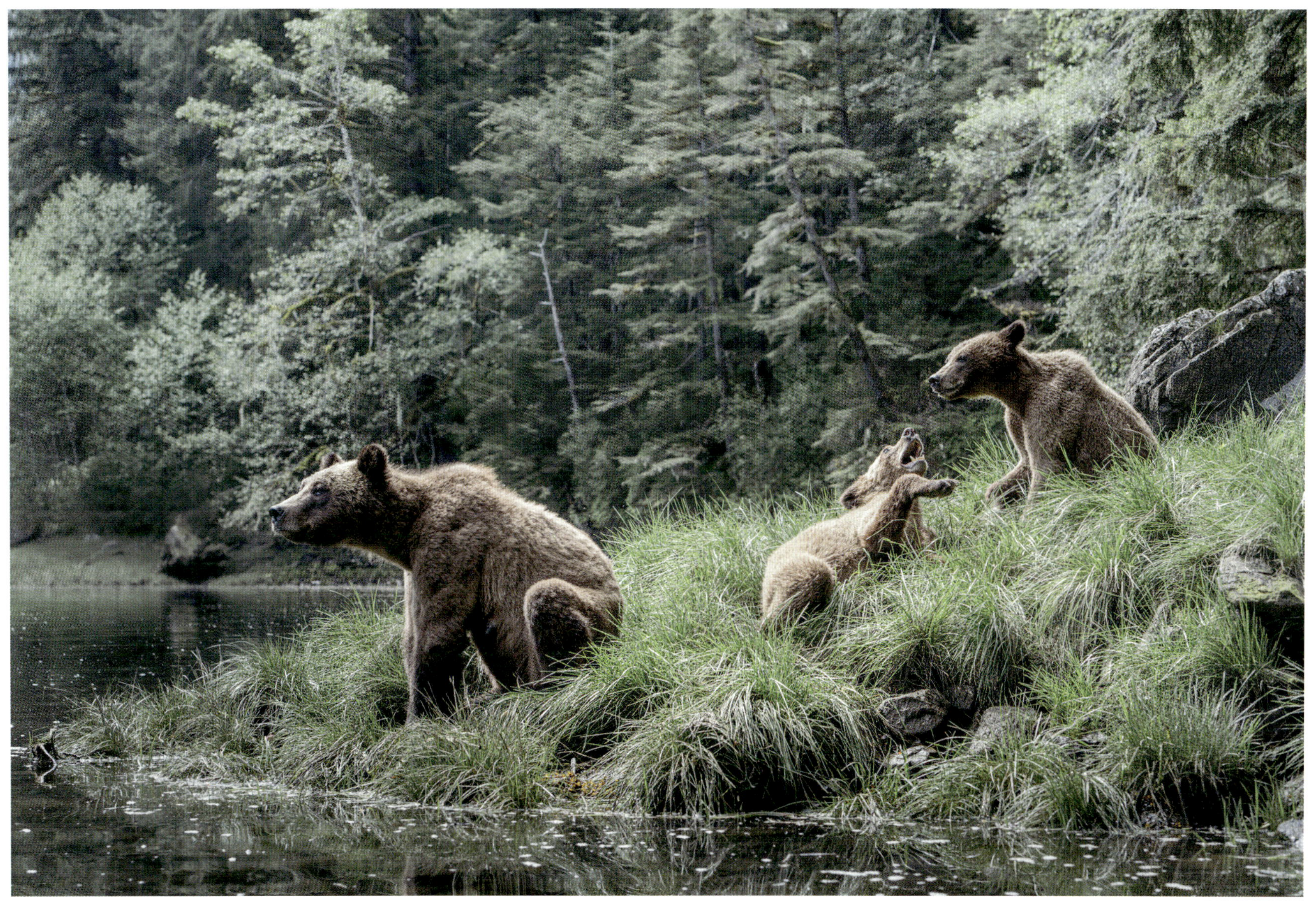

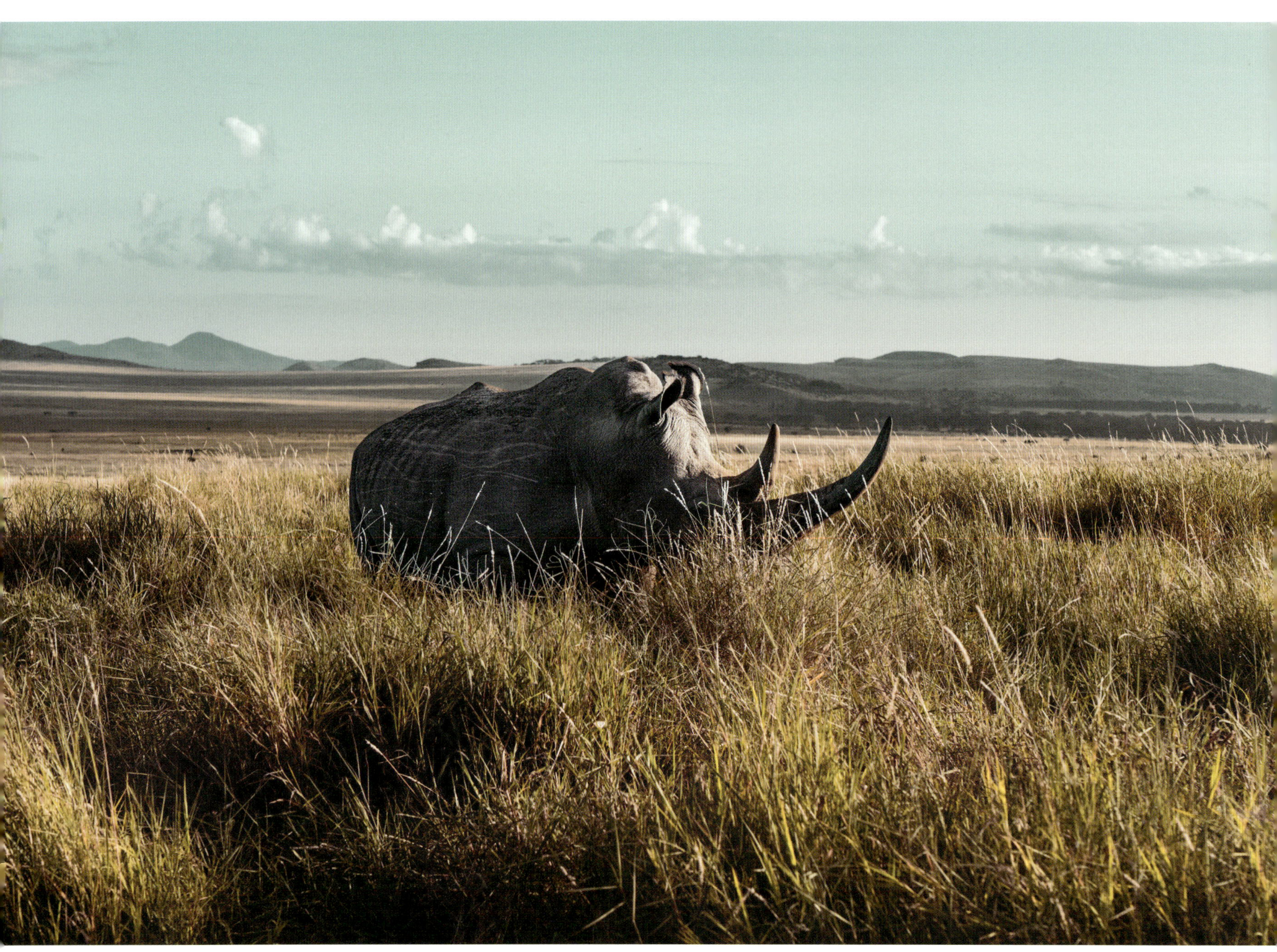

13

Beyond
the Settings

I received the gift of my first well-used SLR camera at the age of 16, complete with a crappy tripod that pinched my fingers when I closed it and collapsed at the worst possible moments. It also came with a stack of magazines and a much-treasured book by Freeman Patterson, and what I found on those respective pages turned out to be my main source of inspiration and instruction; the photographs in those publications knocked me sideways with how beautiful they were. When I looked for an explanation of how they were made and what accounted for their beauty, it was always right there, in small print under the image: a code I learned was what we now call EXIF data, which read something like "Nikon F3, 105mm, 1/250, f/11, ISO 800."

Those numbers felt like an incantation to me, a little like math but more like magic. I would look at them and take mental notes about the cameras, lenses, and various settings recorded under the pictures as if to explain the magic trick and think, "So *that's* how it's done." I wasn't wrong; it was a lot like magic, just not in the way I'd hoped.

In my 20s and early 30s, I was a professional comedian and magician. To learn a new trick, I would spend hours in front of a mirror practicing the moves—most of which came down to some form of misdirection. For example, a quick movement of the left hand would draw your attention while the right hand did the actual work unseen.

In hindsight, there was much misdirection in my early years in photography: I pored over the pictures that so inspired me and hoped to find an explanation in the small print underneath, wishing those settings would get me a little closer to understanding, only to realize with time that the real explanation lay elsewhere.

The settings published with your favourite photographs tell only half-truths, which matters if you hope to learn from them. They tell you which camera, but not whether that *particular* camera made a lick of difference in making the photograph or whether another camera might have done the same (or a better) job. They tell you which focal length, but not how close the photographer stood from the elements in the scene or whether that photograph was cropped after the fact, making it next to impossible to reliably use that information for much more than fueling your next gear purchase.

If you were looking at one of my photographs, the settings might tell you which ISO I used but never hint at *why* I chose it. In some cases, I want my camera to select the ISO, so I set it to Auto ISO with a maximum of 6400, allowing me to think about the more visually significant choices of aperture and shutter. In other cases, it might be left ridiculously (and unnecessarily) high after emerging from a dark scene where I wanted the highest shutter speed possible and, distracted by some new scene unfolding in brighter light, I didn't so much choose my settings because I *wanted* f/32, but that's where I ended up in the spontaneous rush not to lose the passing moment or overexpose my scene. But you wouldn't know that just by looking at the settings. If you could see behind the veil, you would learn that sometimes you do what you have to—that your settings (so long as they get the job done) are as often a matter of expedience as they are an explanation for why the photograph looks the way it does.

Sure, 1/8000 might be overkill, and dropping it to 1/1000 would have given me an ISO of 100 instead of ISO 800, but at some point, you have to say "good enough" and make the damn photograph. If this reads like a confession, that's probably a good thing. None of us gets it right all the time, yet some of our photographs miraculously turn out beautifully despite ourselves—but the settings will never tell you that.

There is so much more that goes into the making of a photograph than what can be discovered by looking at even the most robust EXIF data. Imagine looking at a painting that blows your mind. You ask the artist how they painted it, and they reply, "I used some colours, two of which were red and blue, and some brushes, one of which was a No. 8." This information isn't helpful because it's only half the story; it can't possibly speak to the real work of making the painting. Even if the artist gave you a complete list of all the colours, the exact brushes, and the brand of easel they used, how much closer would you be to understanding how they made the painting? Are colour choice and brush selection the real work of painting? Is that what you're responding to when you feel awe standing in front of it? It's undoubtedly more than that.

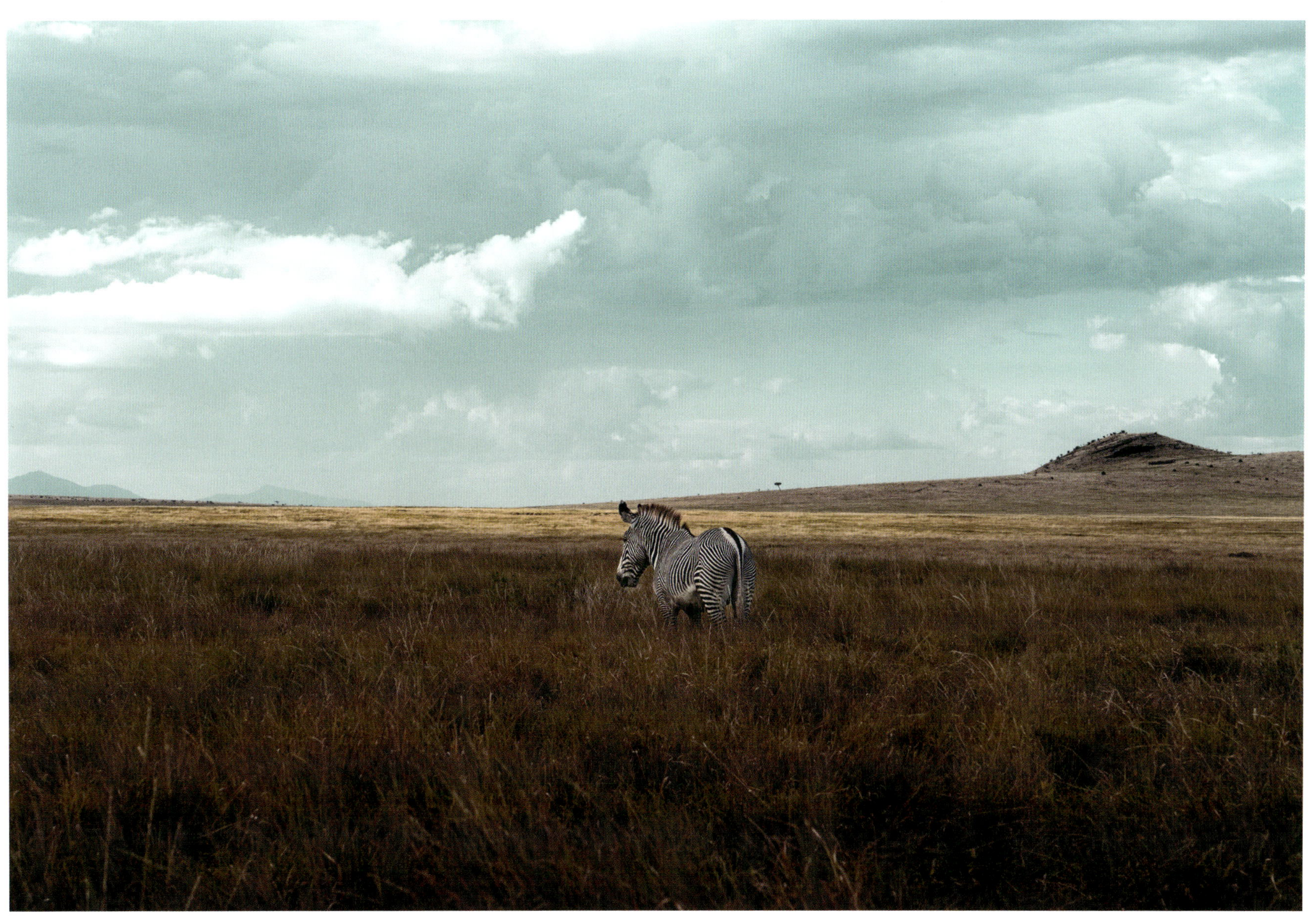

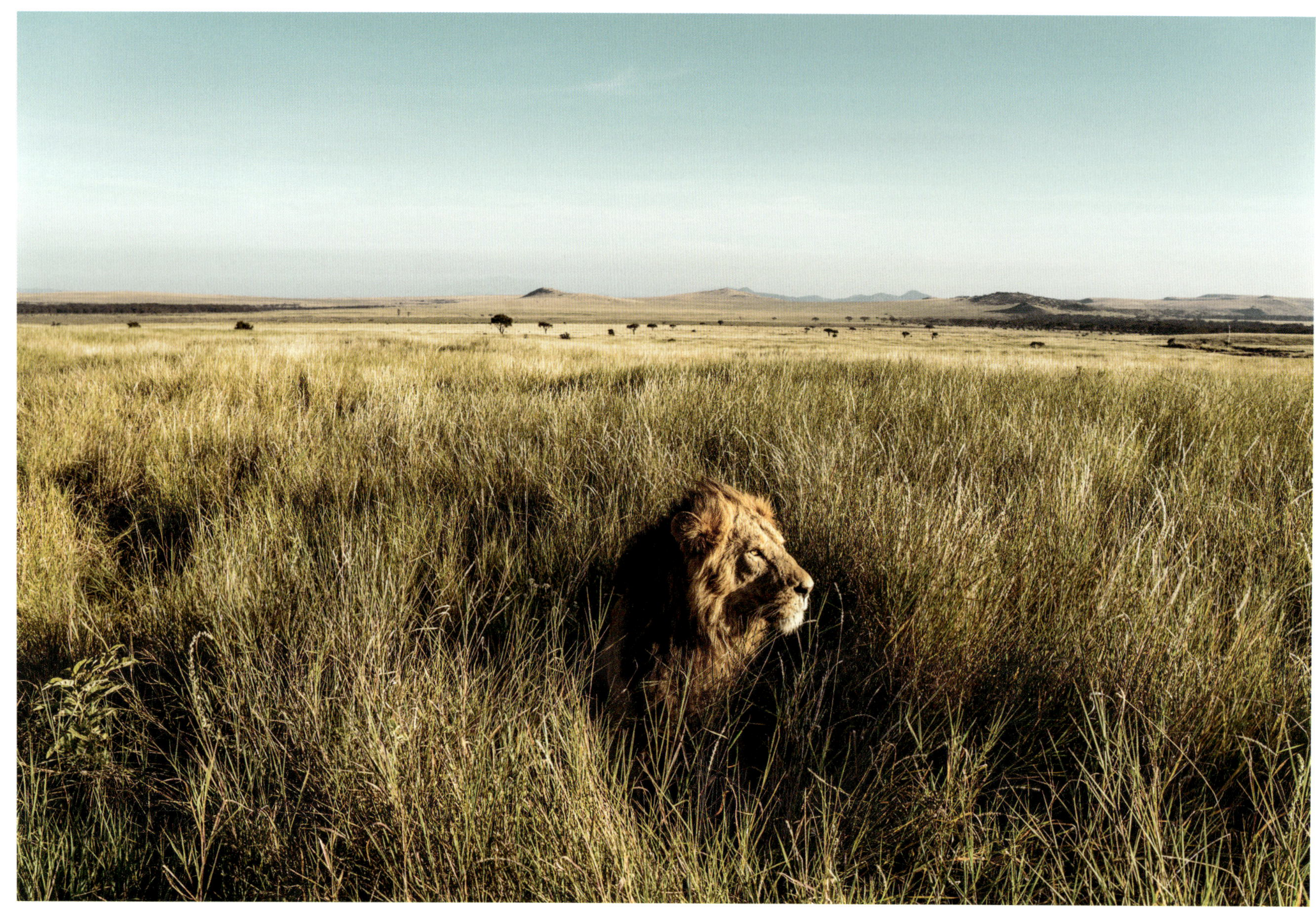

At best, EXIF data represents a puzzle and a half-told story. For the photographer trying to learn from it, this misdirection can throw you off the scent entirely. You can see that the aperture was f/8, but was that intentional? Is the resulting depth of field, combined with the focal length and the proximity of the camera to the nearest elements, even an *important* part of the photograph? Is *that* what makes it sing? Would it be similar if the photographer had used f/4, or would there be more impact if they'd used f/11 instead? Perhaps. But maybe not. The shutter speed was only 1/30, but does it *matter* in this image? Could it be that 1/30 represents a truly *terrible* choice of shutter speed—that every other frame of the 100 shots you're *not* seeing was a messy blur, and this one just happened to work out? Where is the notation in the EXIF data for sheer dumb luck, to which I give at least partial credit for so many of my photographs for so many reasons?

Settings can tell you *something* about exposure decisions, but not that the photographer intentionally underexposed the scene relative to what the camera was screaming for. I don't think I've ever seen settings reflect choices made with exposure compensation to intentionally darken or lighten a scene when the camera's meter indicated different choices. Seeing that a photograph was made at 1/1000, f/5.6, and ISO 200 isn't remotely helpful if you have no way of knowing that the decision to underexpose the image by three stops makes the photograph feel the way it does. Mood is often amplified in an image by making it darker or lighter than the meter suggests is correct, but you won't learn that by obsessing over EXIF data.

Settings give no credit to point of view, choice of moment, or quality of light. They do not speak to mood or mystery, balance or tension. They don't give the slightest nod to composition or story, to colour harmonies, or whichever choices might have been made in development after tripping the shutter. They give no hints as to *why* those technical choices were made and only partial glimpses into the simplest of those technical decisions.

The settings you choose matter; they are one part of the bigger process of making a photograph. Looking at your settings in context (and remembering *why* you chose them) and which effects they have on your images, learning from those, and allowing those choices to be guided by what you want your pictures to *look and feel like* is how you discover *your* way of making photographs. Observing the settings of other photographers without the ability to ask *why* they selected those settings and which priorities informed those choices only results in an adventure in missing the point.

Observing the settings of other photographers without the ability to ask *why* they selected those settings and which priorities informed those choices only results in an adventure in missing the point.

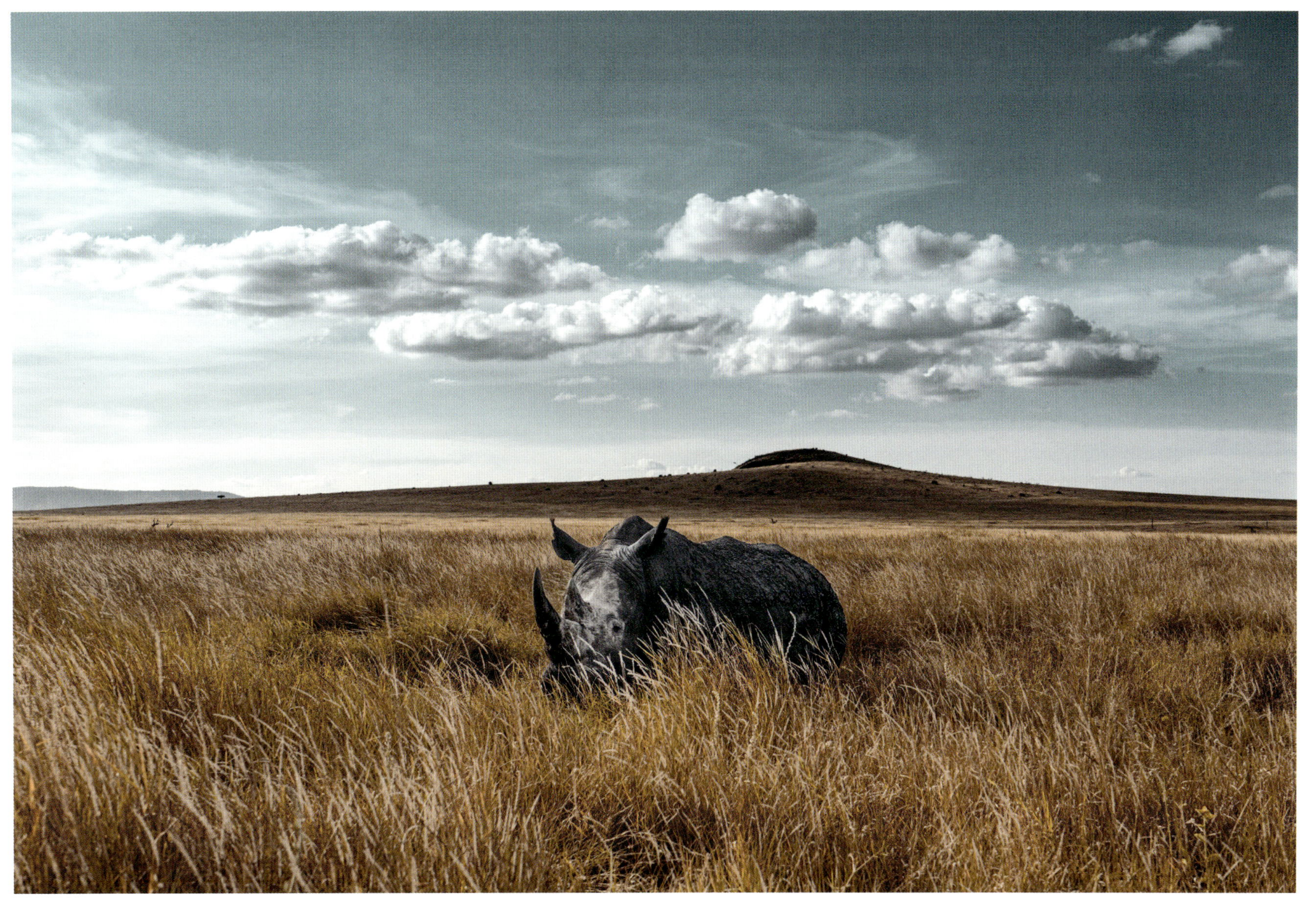

A good photograph remains a technical marvel. That we can turn light into the kind of wonder we experience when we finally make the picture that matches or exceeds what we imagined will never stop being amazing to me. Without the technical, foundational choices of our craft, we would spend our time looking at blurry images that are either too light or too dark. But remember, you can get to an exposure value that you can work with in many ways.

Imagine you're working old-school-style with a roll of ISO 400 film in your 35mm camera. Putting the camera to your eye, the meter tells you that 1/500 and f/5.6 should do it. That's one choice. But so is 1/1000 and f/4. One stop faster shutter, one stop wider aperture. And 1/250 and f/8 works, too. Or 1/15 and f/32. Or if you own some fast glass, 1/8000 and f/1.4. Using full stops, there are at least ten possible combinations or equivalent exposures that will get you to the same place in terms of how bright or dark your photograph is. Which one you choose is not only a technical choice but also a *creative* one. Add ISO into the mix and we're talking about (counting on my fingers and mumbling math sounds to myself) a *lot* of possible combinations, all of them "correct." Now it's time to ask what you actually want the photograph to *look* and *feel* like. 1/15 and f/32 together can make a photograph that looks and feels much different than 1/8000 and f/1.4, even though both exposure values are the same. The former could have a beautiful sense of motion and almost infinite depth of focus. The latter would freeze any motion but have an incredibly shallow, almost dreamy depth of field. Same exposure value. Totally different aesthetics. Which do you prefer in that moment?

Now engage this same thinking when choosing focal length and how close you stand to the elements in your scenes, then add the nearly limitless options for where you place the camera and which moment you choose. For each of these (and so many more), you'll quickly reach the limits of technical dos and don'ts and enter into the domain of the creative and the poetic. As your thinking changes, so will your photographs— because your desire for how those photographs look and feel also changes. A brief look at the settings of another photographer can't give you a glimpse into that kind of thinking, and it probably can't help you with your own.

Technical choices are important, but they are insufficient. If you want to learn from the types of images you hope to one day create for yourself (and after 40 years, this is still true for me), there are better questions. *Why* does the photograph look like that? What choices did the photographer make, and why? What other options were possible? If you had been the photographer, what might you have chosen to do with light, space, and time? Might there have been other ways to make a photograph that were not only correct but also creative and, most importantly, uniquely yours?

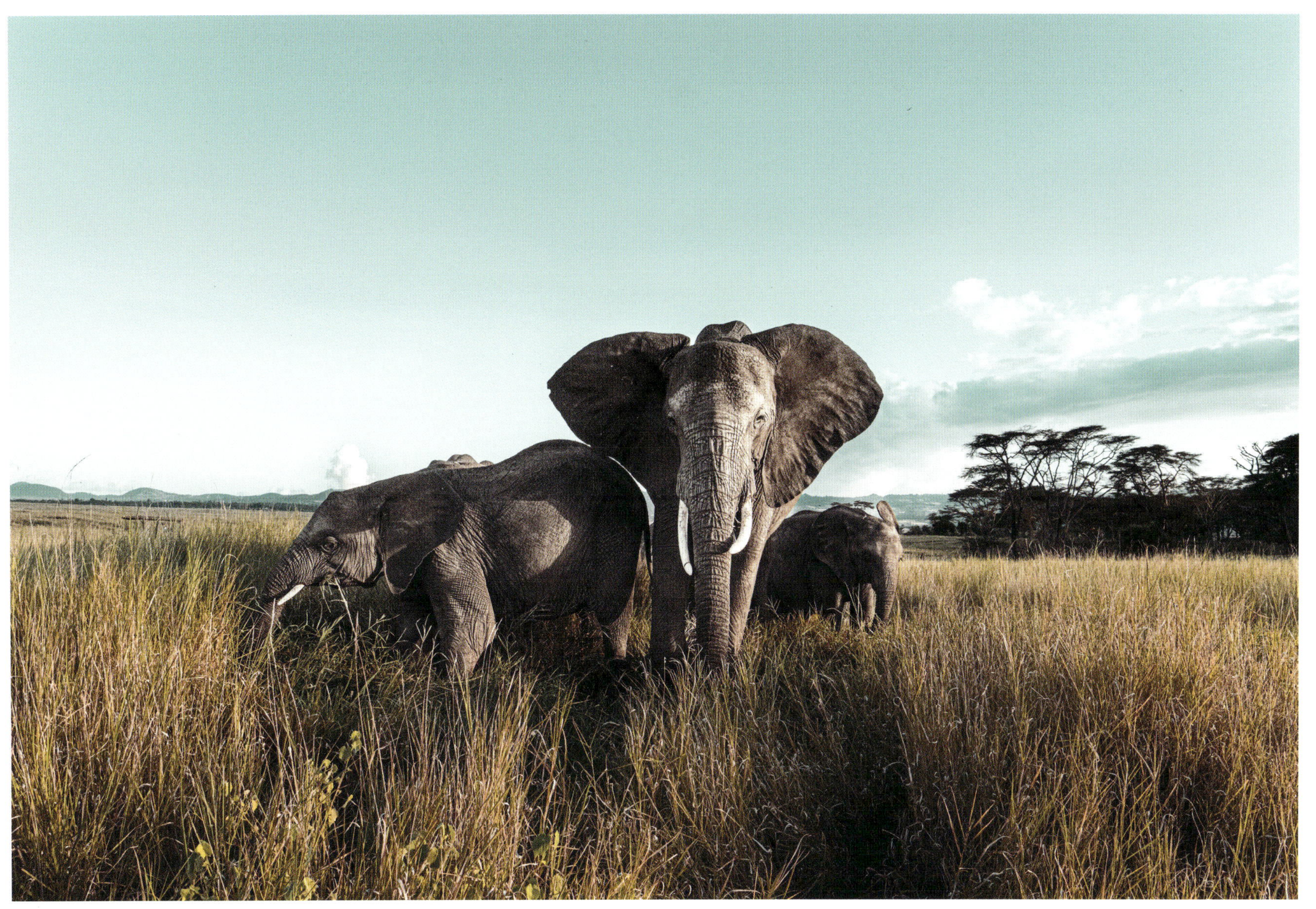

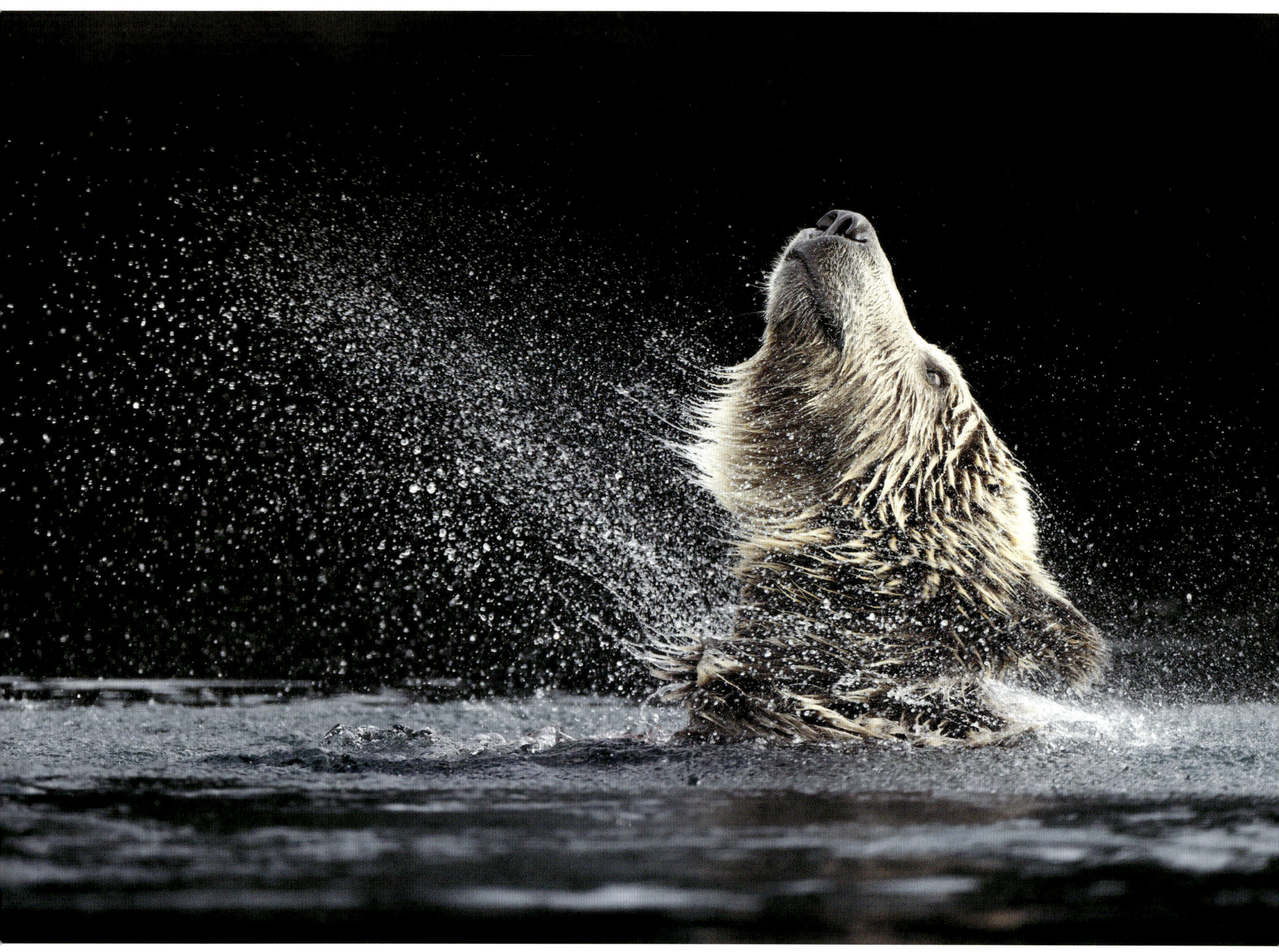

14

In Praise of Luck

Every photograph I've ever made has been a lucky shot. The light was just right; without it, there'd be no mood in the image. The weather cooperated, or it didn't, but in the end, the resulting rain or fog made for a much more visceral photograph. The elephants lined up just so, and I was lucky. That I even get to be in the extraordinary places I make my photographs is so, so lucky. Of course, I'm referring to the final images that get edited out from the sketches, developed, and printed. Many among the sketches are very unlucky, and still far more fail for reasons for which I have only myself to blame.

Luck is underappreciated in conversations about creativity. As a younger man, admitting that luck played a role in what I had made felt like giving away the credit; I had worked hard to get where I was, I had learned to use my gear, and I had anticipated the shot, so if someone implied that it was a "lucky shot" I was both offended and defensive. It has taken me some years to change that response to gratitude and to think

differently about luck. It's not a question of whether we credit our best work to either luck or skill but whether we're open to taking advantage of it being *both* luck and skill. Creative work is a dance between you and the circumstances in which you do your work.

As a photographer, artist, or human being, being creative is about responding to circumstance or luck. You've probably heard some version of "the more I practice, the luckier I get." As aphorisms go, it certainly has a ring of truth to it, but it still feels a little disingenuous—like it's not so much acknowledging the role of luck but claiming the credit. "I wasn't lucky," we say, "I was prepared." Perhaps, but it wouldn't be the worst thing in the world if we let happenstance have a moment in the spotlight.

It's not a question of whether we credit our best work to either luck or skill but whether we're open to taking advantage of it being *both* luck and skill.

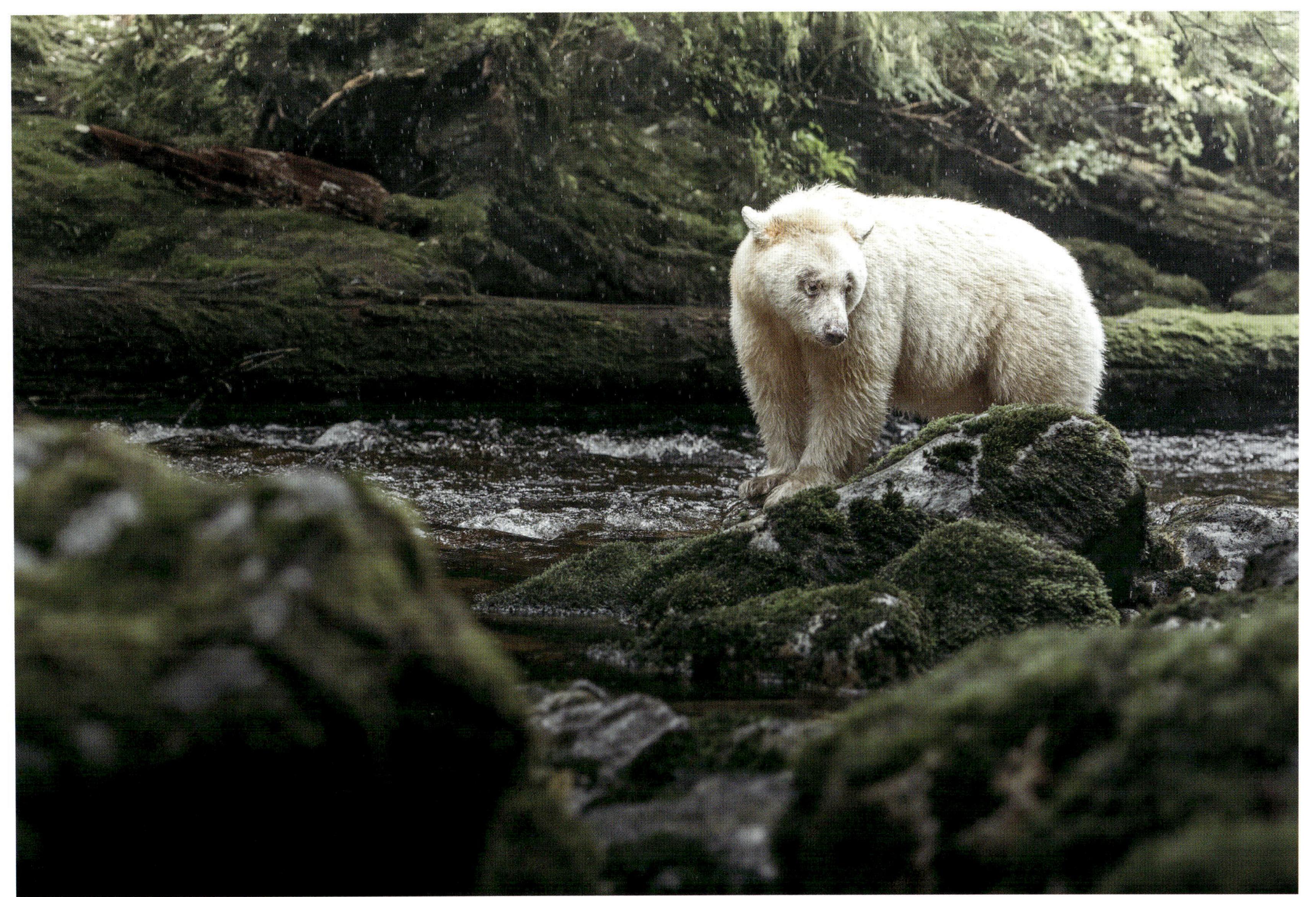

I've long been a proponent of being intentional in art-making and in life. In my early writing, I talked a lot about vision, which, depending on how you use the word, could probably be swapped out for "intent." There's great value in planning and forethought. Still, especially after making an unexpected shift into photographing wildlife, it's been harder to kid myself about the serendipity on which I've been relying. It turns out being intentional in my work isn't exclusive of sheer dumb luck.

So, luck being what it is, why talk about it at all if we have no control over it? Acknowledging luck probably keeps us humble, and there's value in that where being perceptive is concerned. But there's more value in being truly *awake* to luck—even looking and waiting for it.

The more you practice, the less likely it is that when luck does come, it will find you fiddling with your gear. The more practiced you are, the more intuitive your craft will be for you, and the easier you'll settle on a pleasing composition, dial in an exposure that's not merely correct but truly expressive, and anticipate the strongest moments. Making a photograph might be a dance with luck, but it's still up to you to follow that lead and be responsive to it. The more comfortable and practiced you are, the smoother that dance will be, and the better you'll be able to improvise when your dance partner changes things up and your luck and circumstances go in a direction you didn't expect, as things tend to do.

But there's something else—the blind spot that occurs when you get too self-assured and stop being aware of luck and the magic you can find if you're awake and looking for it. Almost every photograph in this book has a backstory that begins with my expectations and hopes—and ends somewhere else entirely, usually somewhere better and completely unexpected. I owe the credit to an openness to luck—and those crazy random happenstances. In most cases, I was looking or hoping for something else. Perhaps not something wildly different (though in some cases, that is certainly true), but very seldom does what I see in my mind's eye match what I eventually see in my final picture, for which I am grateful. The best of my work has *always* been unexpected and is a creative response to that.

If this is true for you, it pays to be careful what you look for and to be mindful of your expectations. Expectations focus us; they narrow our gaze and give us the patience to wait for the moments we anticipate. But they can also make us unobservant of everything *else* that is going on, stopping us from seeing what would be very lucky indeed if only we were open to it.

Making a photograph might be a dance with luck, but it's still up to you to follow that lead and be responsive to it.

The challenge of thinking or perceiving creatively as a photographer is being able to look for specifics without becoming oblivious to the unexpected. I have found it helpful to breathe. To loosen up a little. To put the camera down and look around. To sit back and watch what's going on. To be aware of my thoughts and be present. How many times have I invested time and attention in one scene, waiting for the moment, waiting for things to pop, only to realize the real opportunity was in an entirely different direction? That the stronger photograph was begging me to pivot and reimagine things? It happens so often that I've become suspicious of my first instincts; second-guessing my expectations has become my (rather counterintuitive) *modus operandi*. You've got to trust your gut, but that doesn't mean you can't ask it to consider *all* of its options.

You can't photograph what you're not open to seeing in the first place. I never thought I'd say this, but our very specific vision as photographers can be our greatest liability as much as it can be our greatest asset, and sometimes more so if what we're looking for (or expecting to see) blinds us to the unexpected.

Years ago, in the Great Bear Rainforest in British Columbia, we had been photographing a Kermode (or "spirit") bear, an American black bear with a recessive gene that makes it white. We had waited for hours to photograph this bear, so we were thrilled when it briefly appeared. But then it was gone just as quickly as it had arrived, and with it went my hopes for the kind of photograph I'd worked so hard to make: a spirit bear fishing in the creek. Dejected, I sat on a rock and waited for the bear to return, feeling the muscles in my shoulders and neck tightening, fearful I had missed my chance and was wasting my time. The rain was only making things worse. And then I heard my guide, Tom, whispering my name. I was annoyed; he knew I was looking for a bear and didn't want to divert my gaze. As I reluctantly turned to look at him, he made a gesture—a subtle upward glance with his eyes and a tilt of his head. And there, just a few feet above him, was our bear, sitting with its head on a log, watching me from high on the river bank (page 131). The resulting photograph pleases me immensely, never mind the magic of that unforgettable moment.

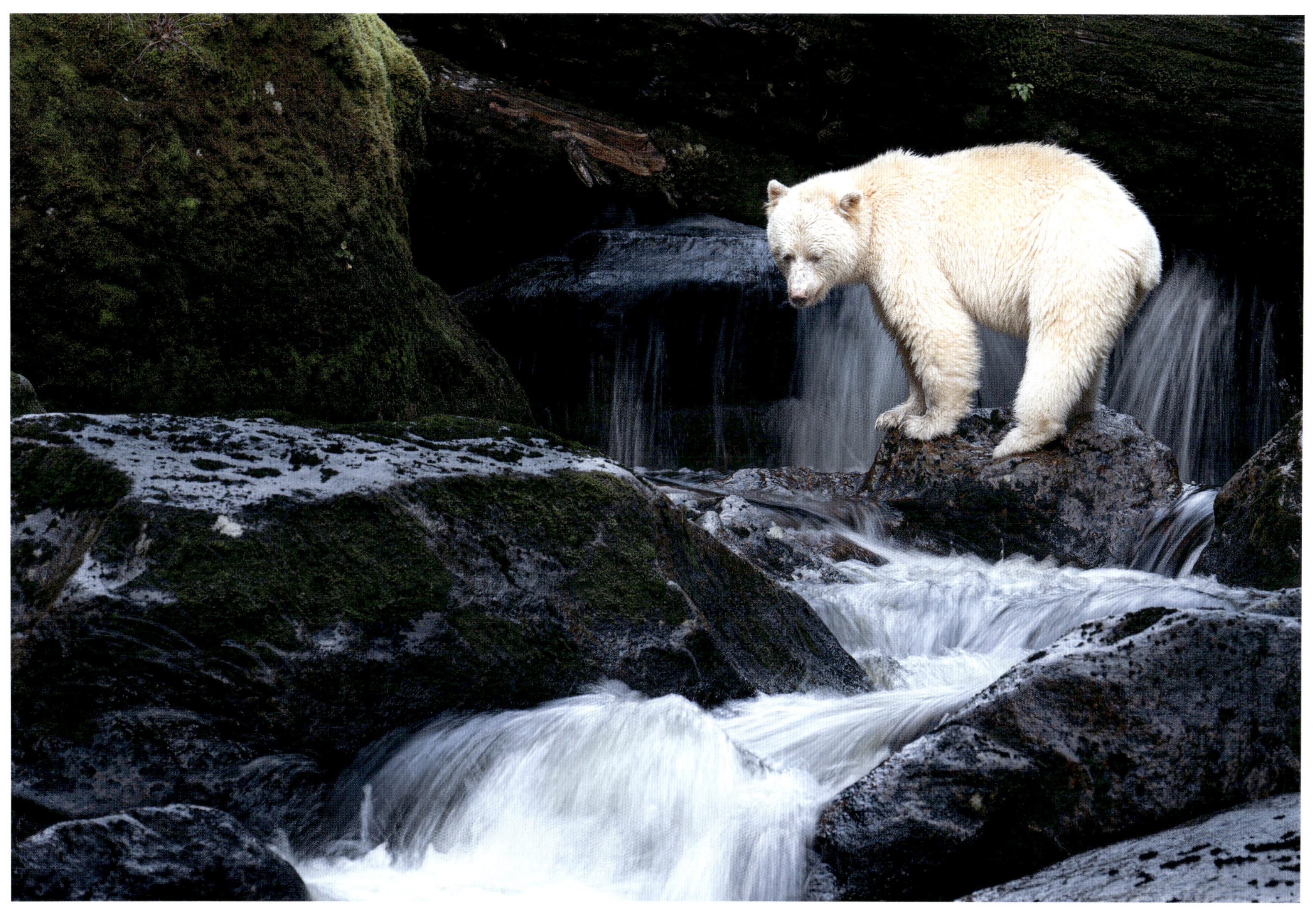

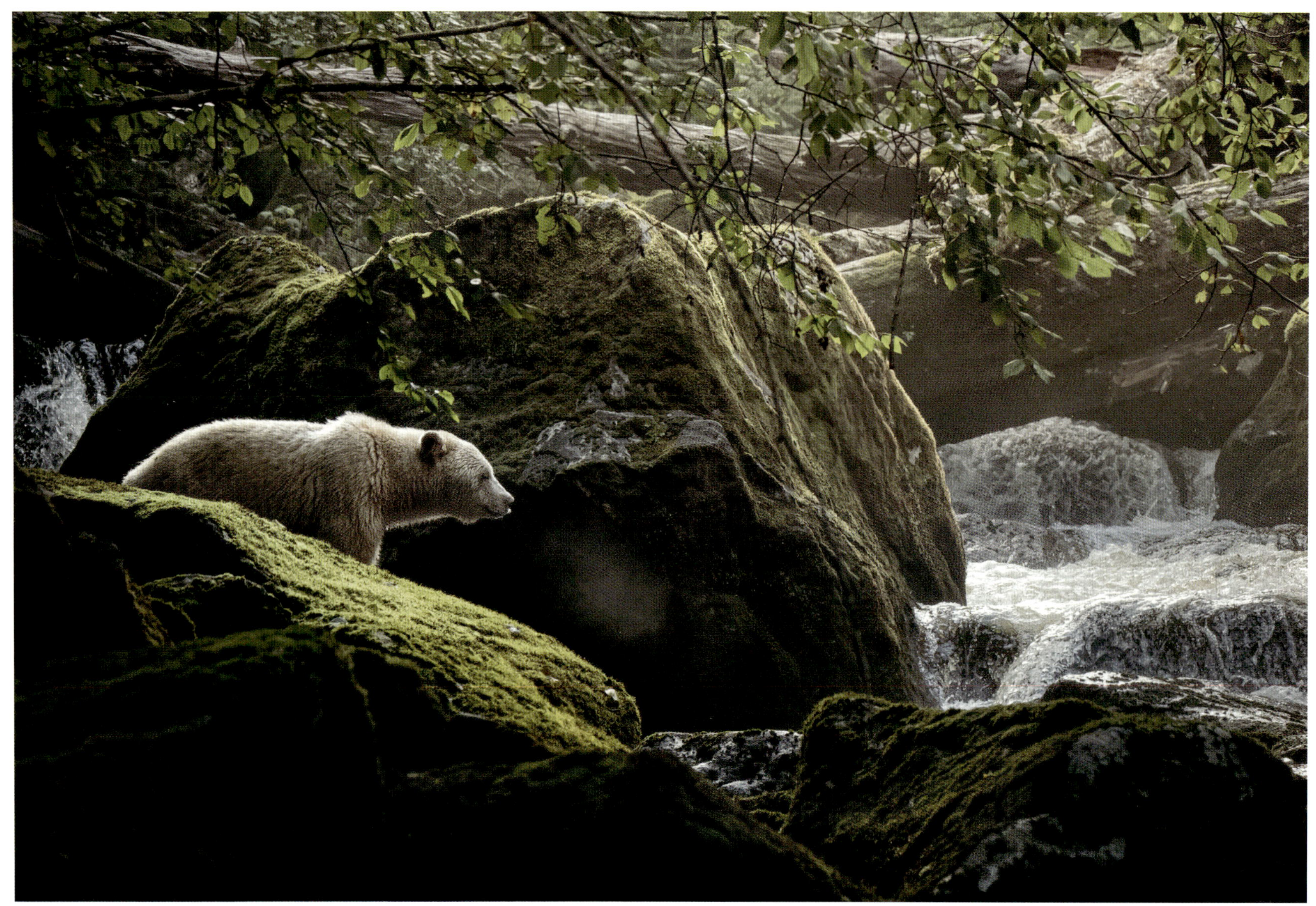

If the strongest photographs happen at the most unexpected intersections of light, space, and time, then the longer you spend awaiting (and remaining open to seeing) those intersections, the better the chance you'll be there when it happens.

I was looking so damn hard I wasn't seeing. Being awake to luck isn't the only thing; you've got to be there. If the strongest photographs happen at the most unexpected intersections of light, space, and time, then the longer you spend awaiting (and remaining open to seeing) those intersections, the better the chance you'll be there when it happens. Yes, chance favours the prepared, but it also favours the *present*. Sit in one place long enough, revisit a subject often enough, and you will be luckier. You must be there long enough for things to happen, for the light to change, for you yourself to become more aware of these changes, and to develop interesting ideas about what you see. The more time you give it, the luckier you will be, but that time will also give you more chances to do something unexpected and to think differently about how you turn that luck into a photograph. At the risk of abusing the metaphor, it's more time on the dance floor.

I don't pretend to have the creative process figured out; it remains mysterious, and I like the wonder that that instills in me. Yet, with each passing year, it's a little less unpredictable, a little less scary. What I do know is that any creative effort, like making a meaningful photograph, happens in the liminal space between what we can and cannot control. There is such freedom in this. The more willingly I relinquish the desire to control what I can't and relax my grip on things, the more grateful I am for luck and the more likely I am to be both prepared and present when I turn and find it sitting there, head resting on a log, waiting for me.

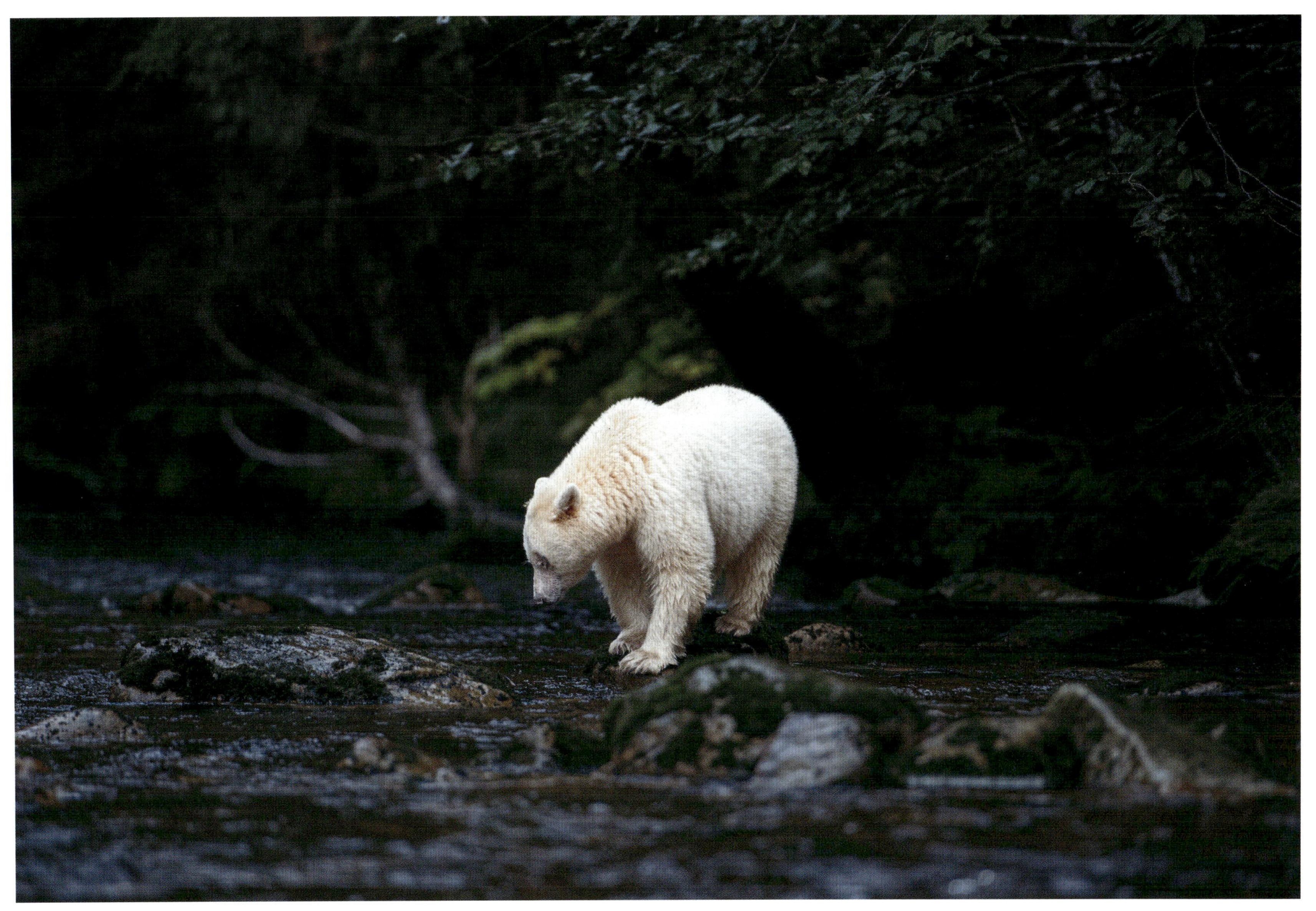

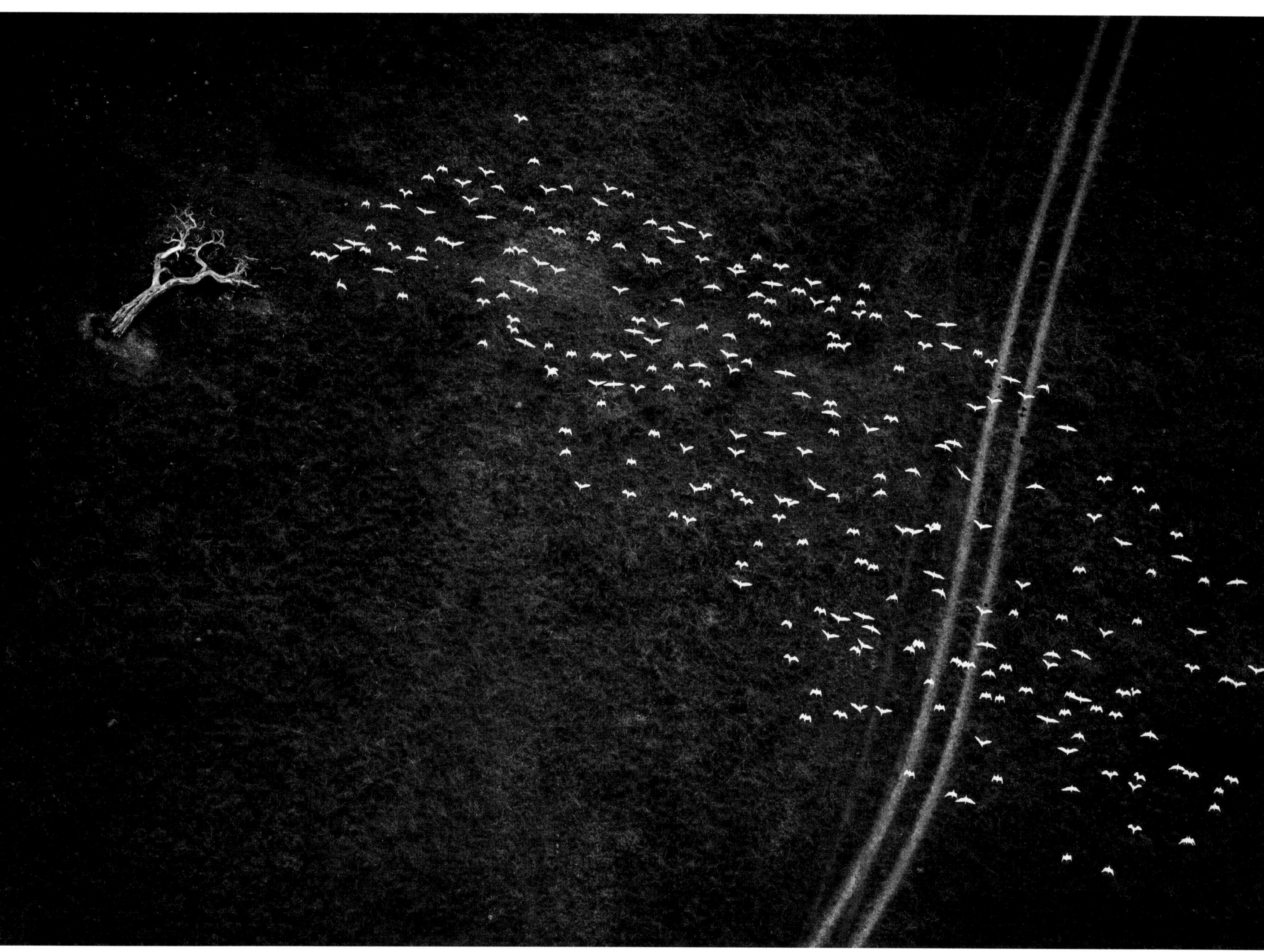

15
Talent
or Time?

I am suspicious of the notion of natural-born talent. I've been told it's out there, that some people seem to come into this world leaning so much more powerfully in one direction than others that you can't help but notice. We call them *prodigies.* I've never met one. I have, however, met many people who are *astonishingly* creative. Far from being prodigies, they're as ordinary as you and me—just plain folk, as they say. If there is something about them that makes them more than ordinary in their creative lives, it's an uncommon drive to keep chasing the thing for which they are now celebrated.

Happily, if there is a secret to creativity, it is not in winning the genetic lottery but in being highly prolific, which comes from perseverance. In short, you've got to make a lot of photographs over a long period of time. You've got to make photographs when other people are doing other things and misunderstanding your work ethic as obsession. If you do this over a span of years and don't give up, you will be mistaken at some point for being talented.

Perhaps "mistaken" isn't the right word. "Recognized" is better because you can *become* talented. As far as I can tell, talent can develop. It can form and evolve, and while it might not be there at the outset, it can most certainly be there later in life. The big question is, how do you get good at something? How do you get *so* good at what you do that it appears effortless? The answer is simple, if not easy: you do it over and over again.

This gives such hope to the many of us who weren't born as prodigies! All it takes is focused work, applied over time. All it takes is the humility to fall, get back up, and eventually learn how to find your balance and not fall.

How do you get *so* good at what you do that it appears effortless? The answer is simple, if not easy: you do it over and over again.

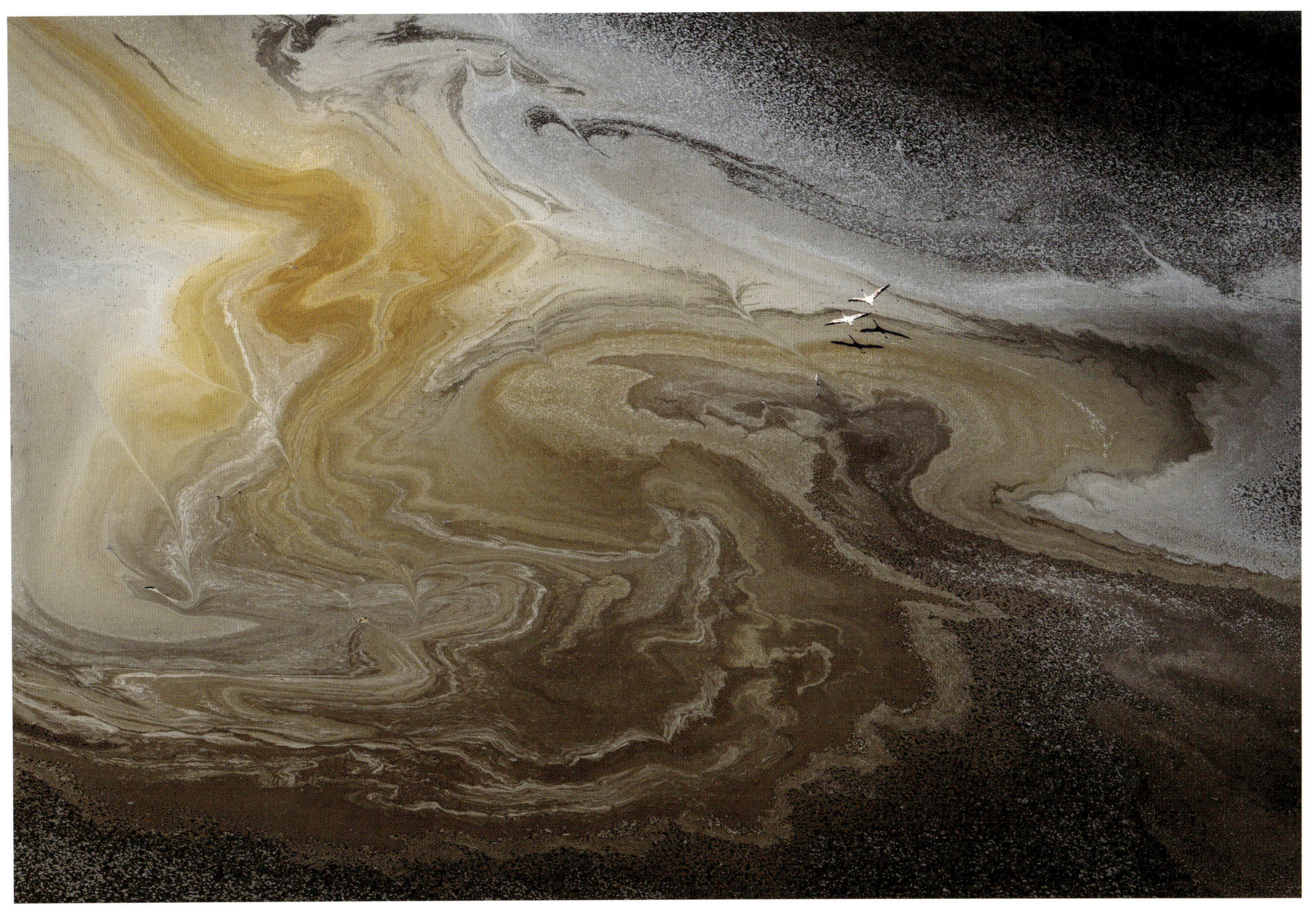

All it takes is holding that camera in your hands so often that you know the buttons by touch, by instinct.

All it takes is looking at so many photographs that you begin to sense what does and doesn't work and, ultimately, what works for *you*.

All it takes is focusing on your chosen subjects so many times that you can predict their behaviour so well that others believe you must have a sixth sense about them.

All it takes is looking through that lens so many times you can see through it with your imagination while it's still in the bag, knowing exactly what the camera will see when you mount the lens to the body.

All it takes is knowing the light well enough to dial in your exposure value before the camera gets to your eye, and to do that, it's merely a matter of repeating the process over and over, for a very long time.

All it takes is doing all of this (and more) well past the point where any sane person would be distracted by some other pursuit. But not you; you're still at it after all these years. Or you will be.

It's often suggested that creative people need only follow their passions. But passion isn't a direction; it's a fuel. And you'll need it to put in the kind of time that gets you to the point where people mistake the results of your hard-earned perseverance for God-given talent. Passion fuels perseverance, and over time, this becomes the winding road toward mastery. However, some people are uncomfortable with the term *mastery*, so perhaps it's easier to call it *control*. After showing up and putting in the work for so long, it's possible to gain the kind of control that looks like instinct, like something innate.

Passion matters because something powerful has to fuel that lifelong effort to make it feel like more than just putting in the time. It's passion that gets you through the challenges that get you to creative flow and make you feel like there's nothing else you'd rather be doing at that moment. Even when it's tough, even when you can't figure it out or you feel like a fraud, as so many of us do. Passion gets you through that and makes it all meaningful—a scenic route on that long road to mastery (or control).

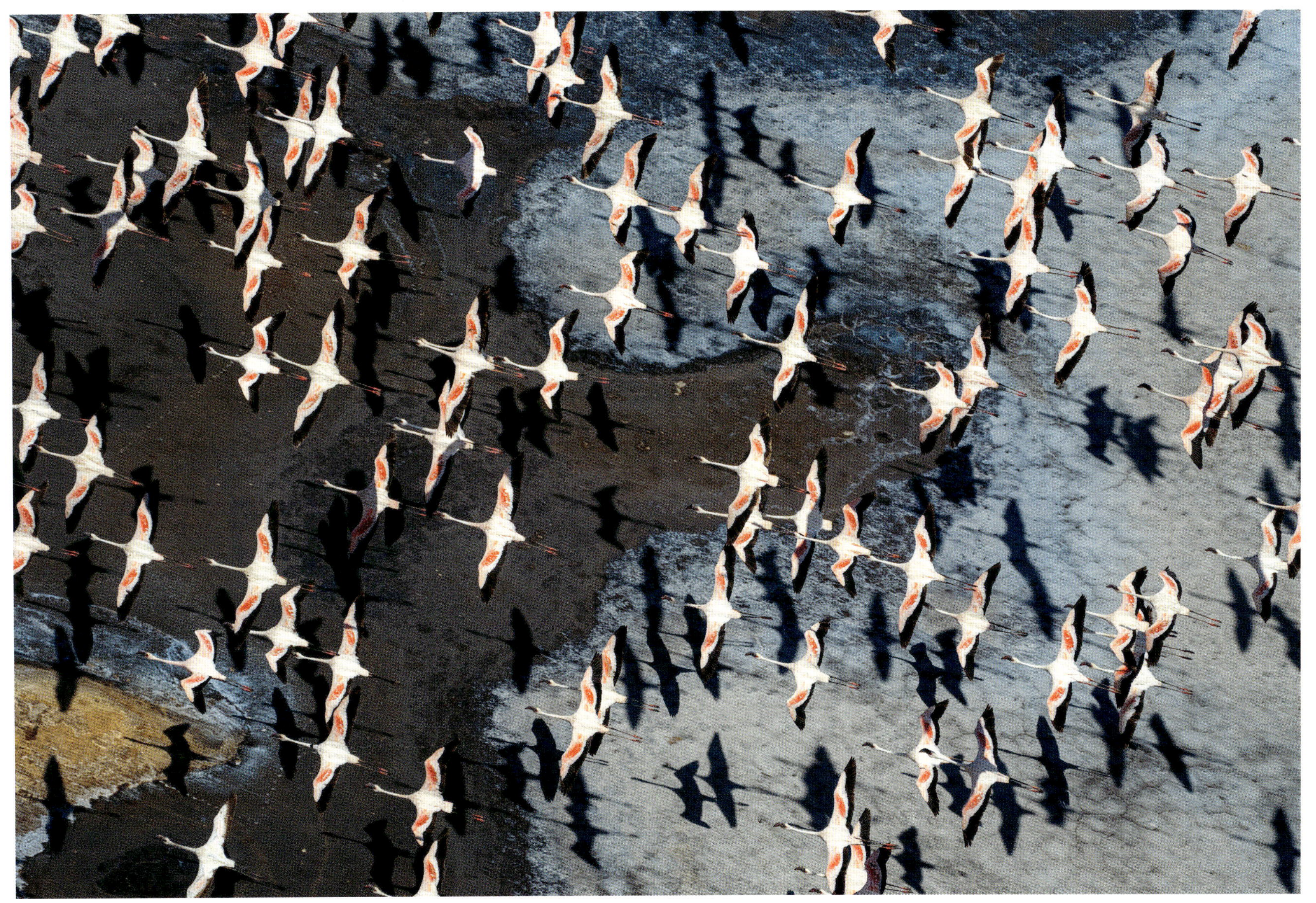

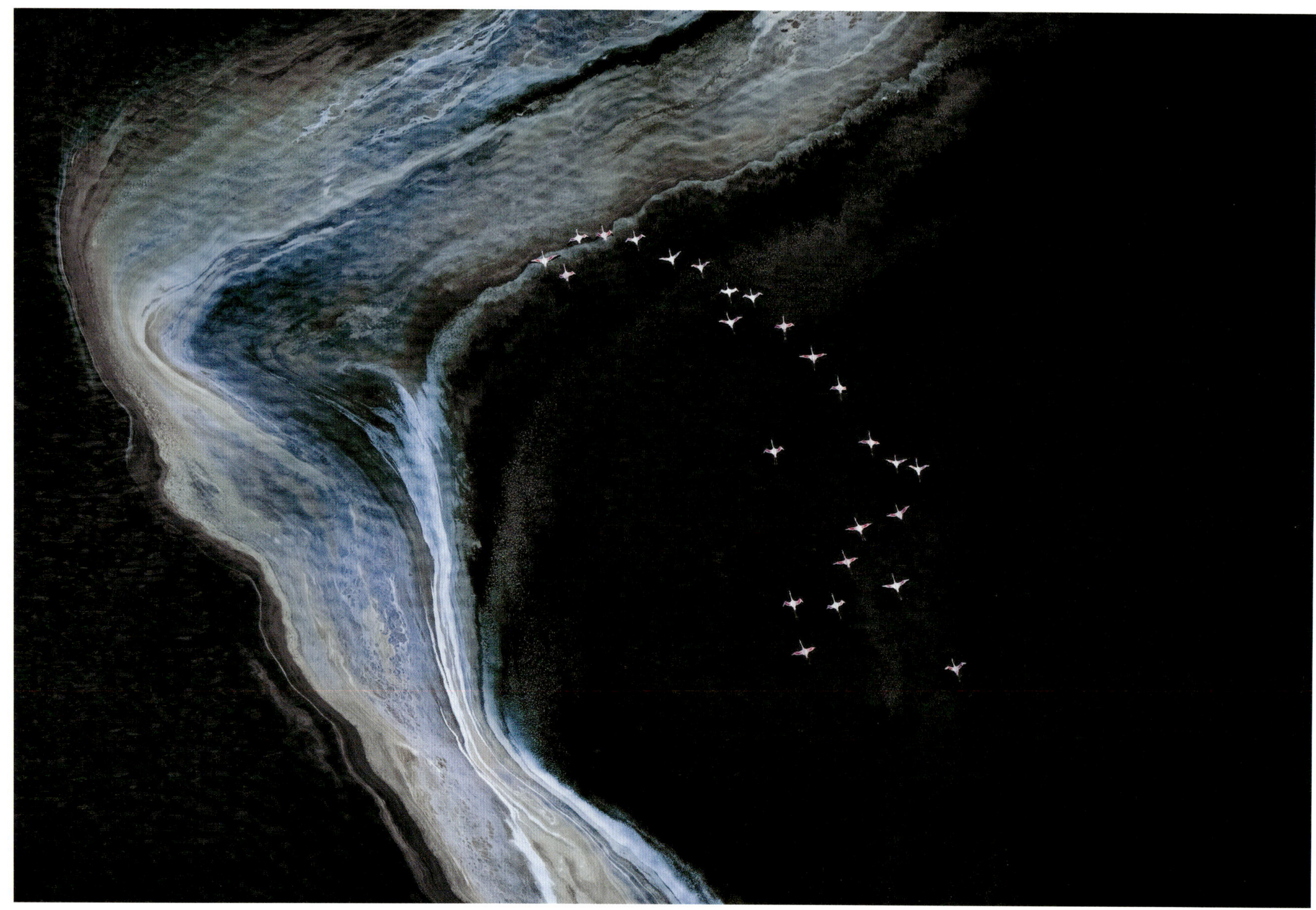

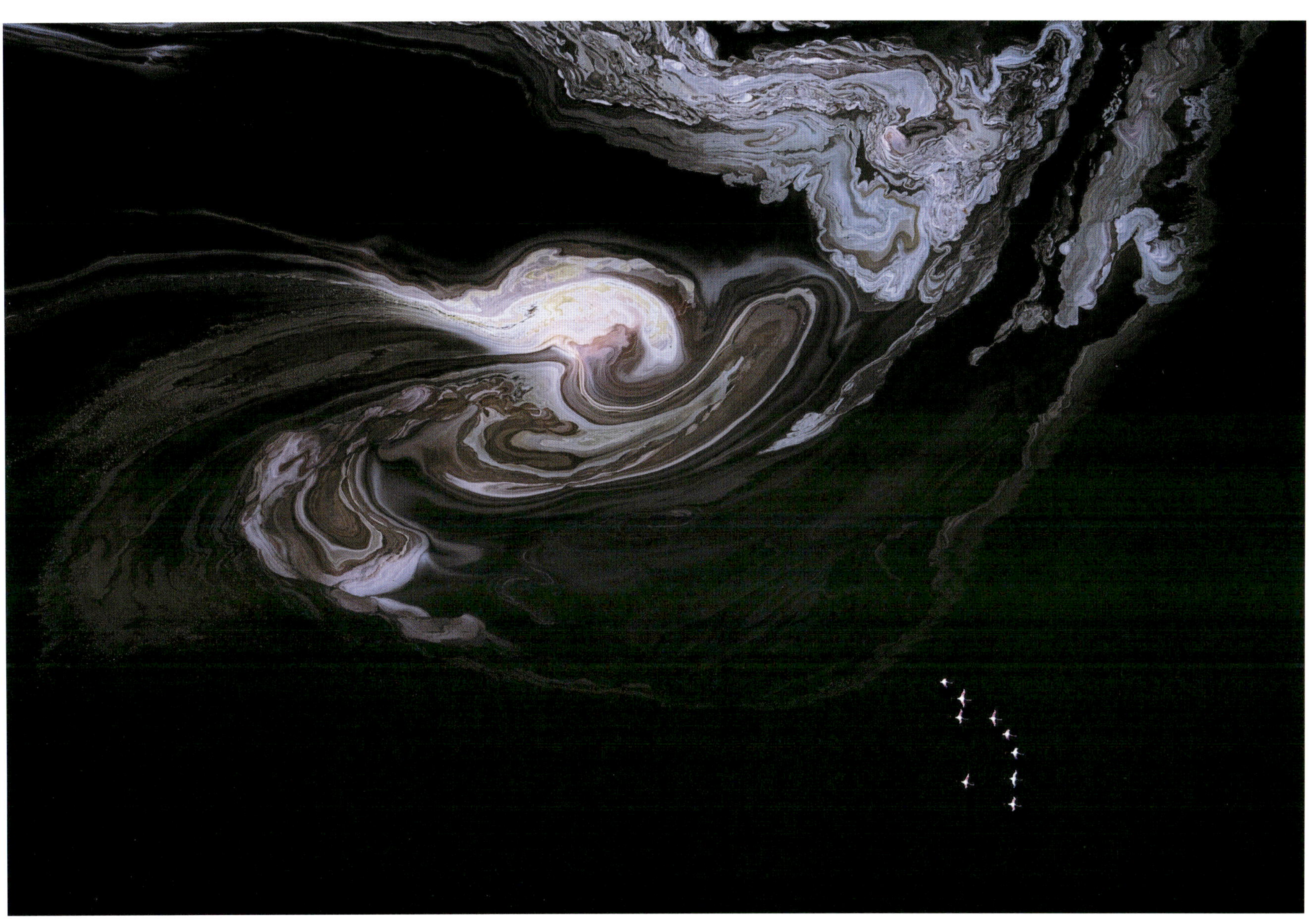

Would it be easier to use the word *skilled* instead of talented? Perhaps. Talent seems to imply some kind of gift from the gods; it feels like hubris on our part to lay claim to it. But skill? Skill is a little more down to earth. Skill is the stuff of hard work, and it's not a stretch to believe you can learn it. If you don't believe talent is within reach, surely skill is.

The question isn't whether you were born skilled or not. Most of us weren't. It's whether you are *becoming* skilled or not. You can do nothing about the former but you can do everything about the latter. That should give you hope.

But it might be worth digging deeper and making sure that what you're truly asking isn't whether you are *more* talented or skilled than others—a terrifying question because you will never answer it and because of what it will do to your creativity. Using your art to measure yourself against others will turn it against you; it'll kill your impulse to try new things, to follow your curiosity, and to find joy wherever it is you once found it in abundance.

I don't know if skill can genuinely be compared or measured; it exists in such infinite combinations that it feels futile to try. But I am certain it can be nurtured

and honed. If you never make another photograph, your skill will most likely decline as your learned instincts get dull from lack of use and your interests fade over time. But if you continue to pick up the camera, allow yourself to experience the world through its lens because you love it and find joy or meaning in this practice, then your skill (or talent, if you prefer) will grow and your photographs will become more specifically your own.

Thinking about my camera craft and creativity in terms of skills to be gained over time makes me take responsibility for them. It puts the ball in my court. And it makes it easier to credit others with the hard work it has taken them to get where they are and applaud them for it. Most of all, it gives me hope and lights a fire under me to get back to work, to keep at it and be grateful for the passion that has fueled my journey to this point. I don't know to which degree I might consider myself to be skilled or to have mastered this craft, but does it matter? I can do what I love and am growing in my capacity for it. So will you.

It is unlikely that the artists you look to in wonder have succeeded because of a surplus of natural-born talent, and even more unlikely that you will fail for want of it. Put the time in. Do the work. The talent will follow.

It's passion that gets you through the challenges that get you to creative flow and make you feel like there's nothing else you'd rather be doing at that moment.

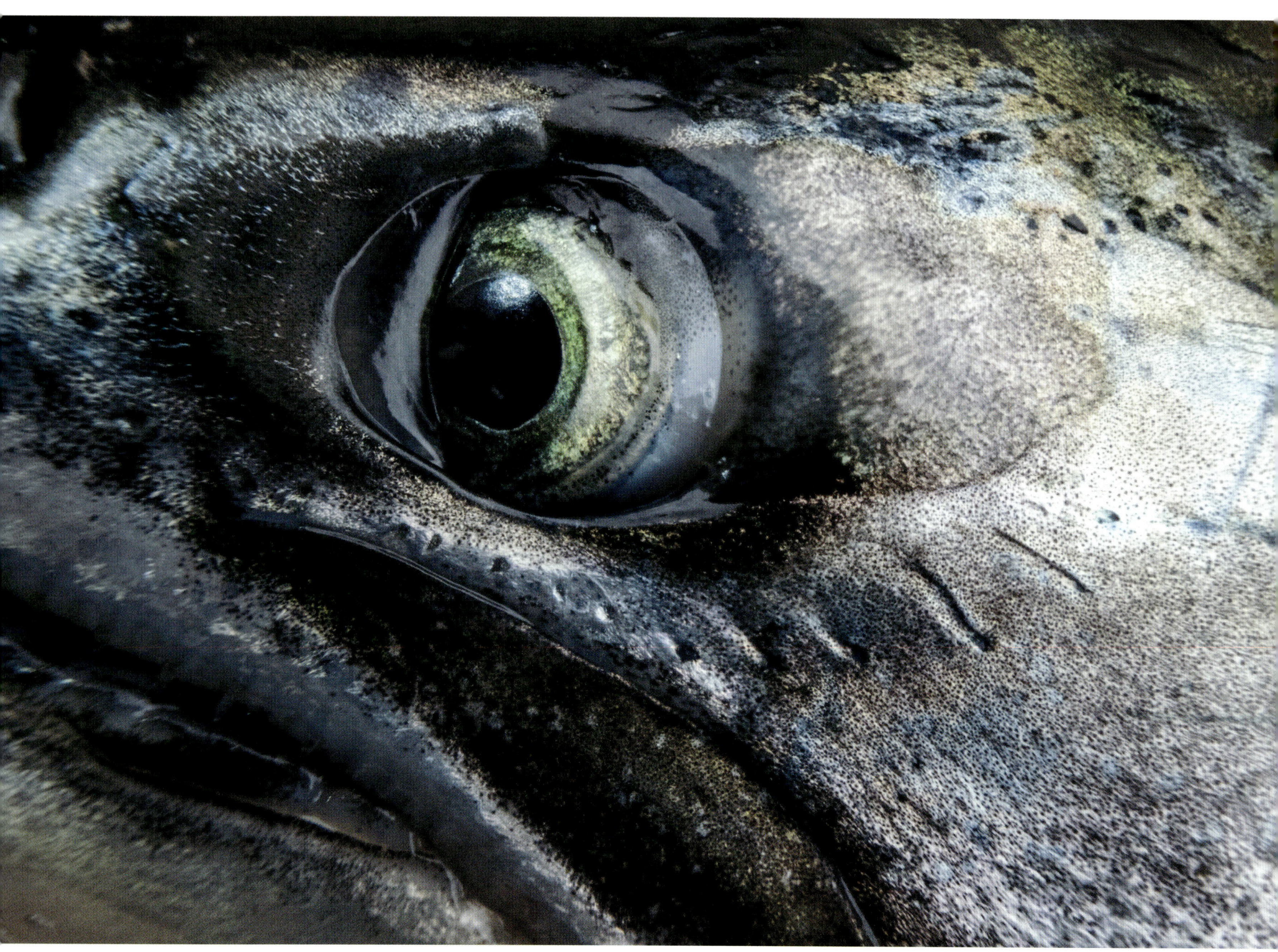

16
Ever Forward

Shortly after my return to photography, having taken a break to pursue comedy in my younger years, I self-published a book of my work and had the audacity to offer it to the world for far more than it was worth. To my shock, many people purchased it, including my best friend, Jon. Now, years later, he still brings it out occasionally, presumably to keep me humble and remind me from whence I come. I cringe at the mere thought of it.

I have that same cringe response when I look back at much of my past creative endeavours, specifically, my writing and photography. I like to view it as a representation of my past self: the writing of a younger me and the photographs that younger man made. It's not necessarily regret, but rather a visceral reaction to work I would now do much differently. I can't be the only one who feels a sense of embarrassment when reflecting on early efforts.

Not all our work, or our once enthusiastic reaction to it, endures. I believe this is precisely because it was made by the younger photographer you were—one you've grown beyond in your vision, your craft, and your taste—so your current reaction can be more detached and critical than it once was. Far from being something to be embarrassed by, the fact that there is work in your past that now fails to make the grade is a sign that you've evolved creatively.

The passage of time makes it easy to plateau; looking at your past work and cringing is a positive sign that you're still moving forward. The work that no longer resonates with you is a mile marker in your journey. What is most beautiful and freeing about this is that the work you make today might also one day elicit the same response: the truly magical photograph you labour over today might, in the not-so-distant future, arouse little more than indifference (if not a quiet cringe) from the photographer you will become. How freeing it is to be less precious about what you're making and enjoy the process without that enjoyment being bound to the outcome and the creation of something *great*.

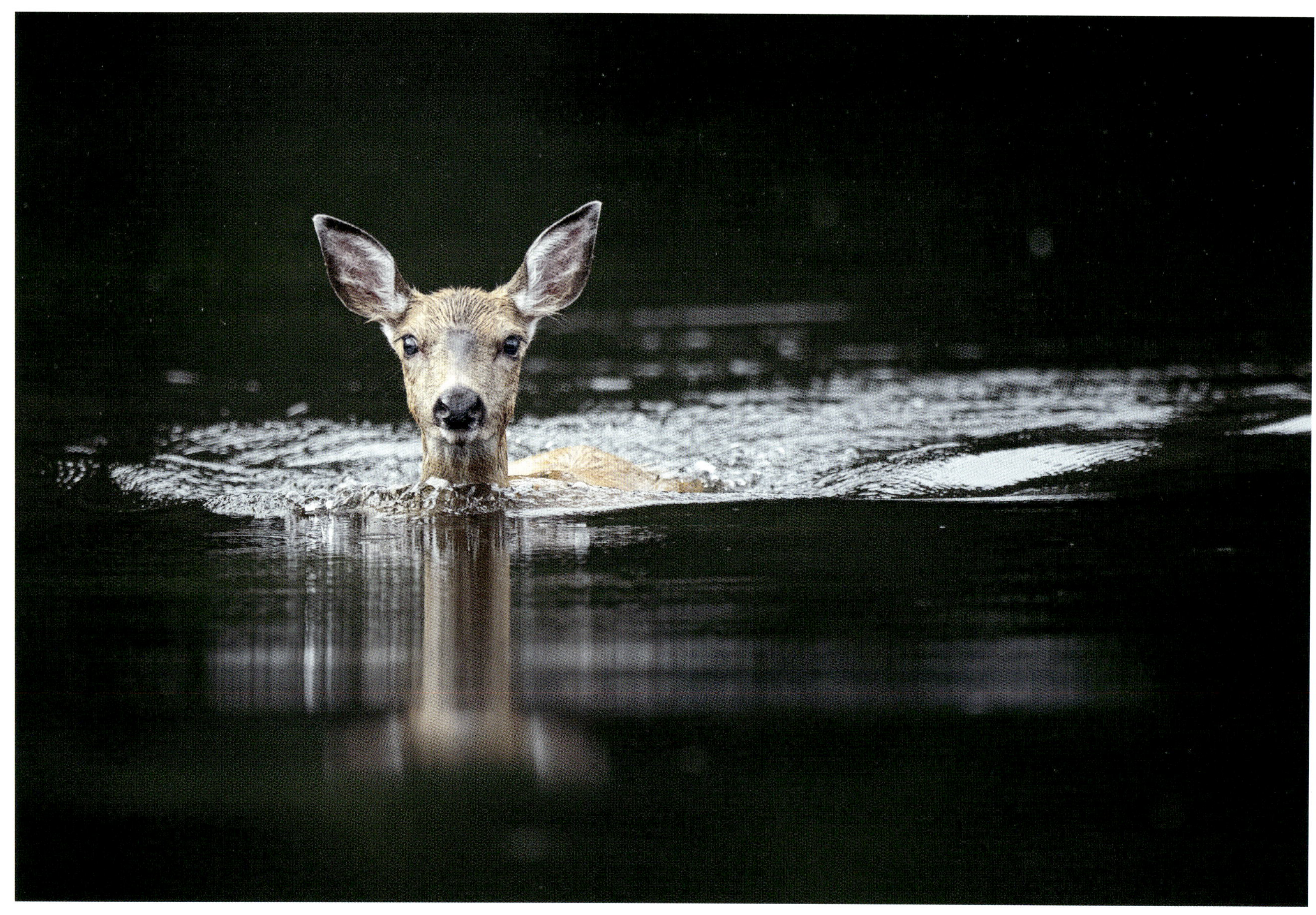

My creative past is littered with detours I do not regret, though I now wish the evidence were not so readily available to others. I had an ill-advised period when I shot everything with a blue-gold polarizing filter, which was truly magical until it wasn't. I spent far too long addicted to the miniaturization effect of my tilt-shift lens. I had months of indiscretions with sepia toning and a long affair with much too much clarity and saturation. And then there are images that elicited brief in-love euphoria for having finally figured out some new technique, the efforts to master it almost inevitably resulting in heavy-handedness. These are milestones, and though yours will look different from mine, they point toward a person willing to try new things and find joy in them before finally learning to embrace a little more subtlety in the approach. They are evidence of risk, and they should be applauded.

Knowing that with my current efforts I am learning and growing and becoming a photographer who will later look back at these same efforts with a raised eyebrow frees me to be less rigid about my work. I can lean into the act of *making* rather than obsessing only about the particular thing being made; I can focus on the process itself and not the product. It is the process that matters, and the lessons you learn in that act of creativity will have greater endurance than most of the final pieces you create.

This isn't easy. We all want to think of ourselves as having more or less arrived, as having reached a point at which our apprenticeship is over. But it's never over, and the freedom in that is a kind of flexibility, a lowering of expectations (though not our standards) about the work we make. We're all so hungry to make a masterpiece when the real effort needs to be directed to *becoming a master*. Whether that photograph you make endures or whether it is a masterpiece, only time will tell. The photographer with a beginner's mind is not so burdened, open as they are to every possibility and free from any sense of what the final photograph *should* look like.

The photographer (or any creative person) must be patient. I've written elsewhere about being patient with the scene and waiting it out, about taking more time and being less hurried. We will one day regret having rushed our way through what little time we had. But we also need to be patient with what we make and with ourselves to find our joy in the making. Being patient with yourself is a way of giving yourself the freedom to learn the lessons you must uncover on the way to making work that, in the end, does endure—the work that is most *you*.

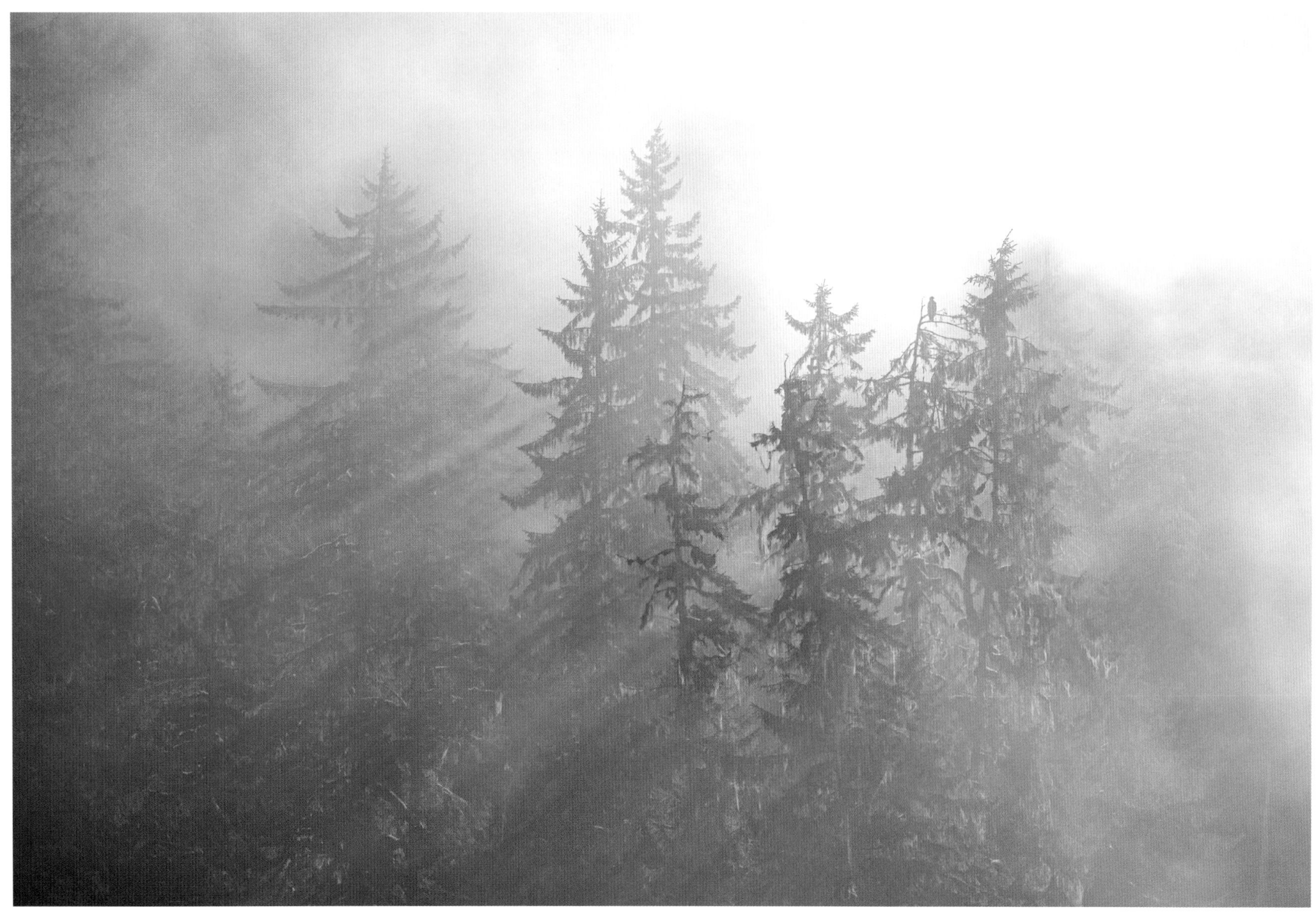

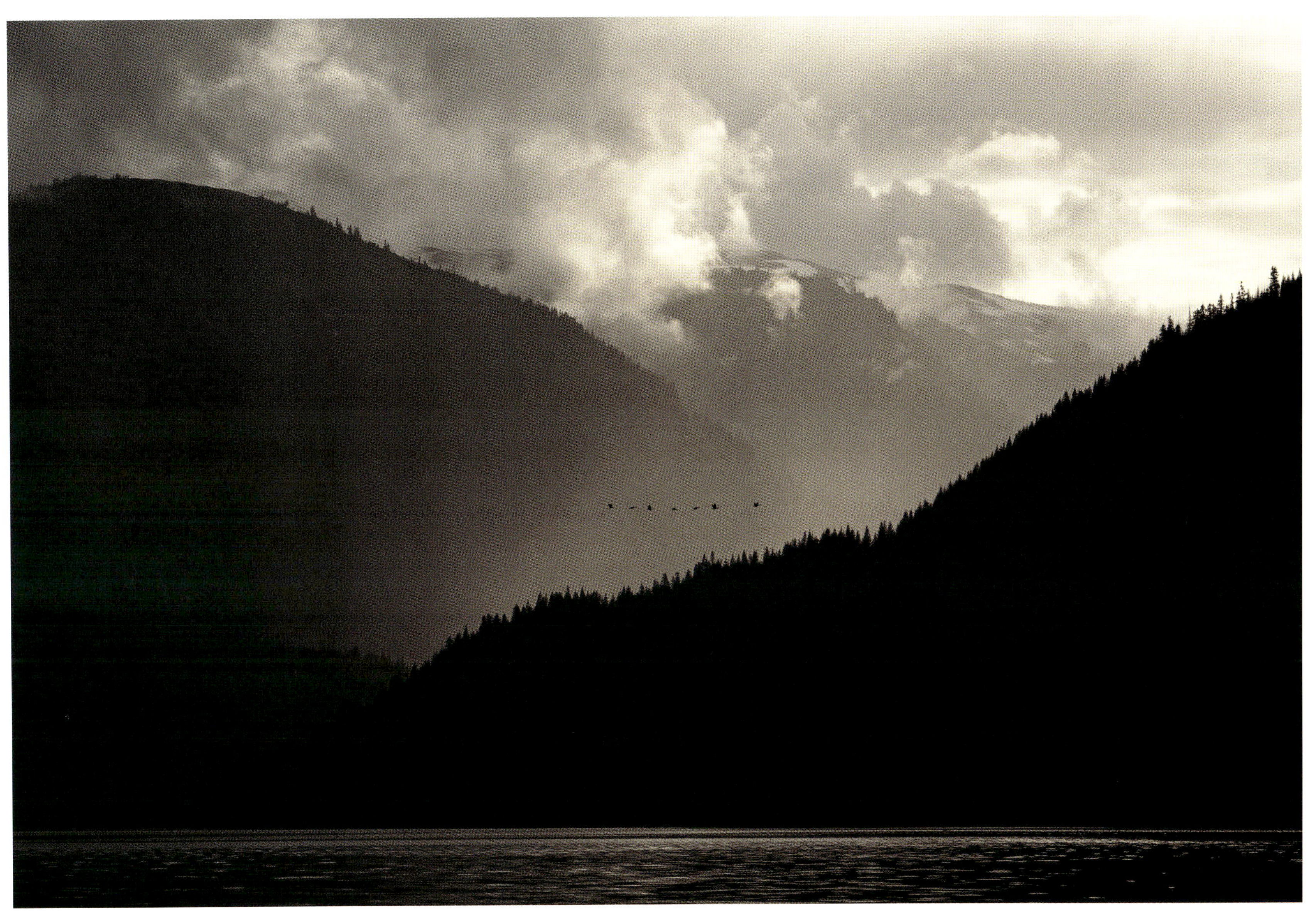

Not everything you make will one day make you cringe or look back and wonder what you were thinking. Some of it will last and resonate with you for much longer. That work is a sign that you're on the right track. Follow that track for long enough and notice what the best of it has in common; you'll begin to see not only your growth but also your voice, as though the shutter were left open long enough to catch all the moments of your evolution and blur them into what is essentially you.

When asked to name her favourite photograph, Imogen Cunningham replied, "The one I'm going to take tomorrow." I suspect she recognized that the photograph she made today would teach her something, open her eyes to new perceptions, and that the one she made tomorrow would be made by a photographer just a little wiser. She also gave a nod to the idea that what she had made was in her past and that her art and art-making were forward-looking.

There is a danger in resting on our so-called laurels. If you look back and don't cringe at some of your work, then what is it that pushes you forward to find both new and interesting perceptions of the world around you and new and challenging ways of using the camera to translate those perceptions into photographs? There is a sacred discontent in making anything; what we create seldom does exactly what we hope, and when it does, that surprise and wonder doesn't often last long. That discontent or dissatisfaction pushes us forward into the challenge of learning what we need to make tomorrow's photograph.

And then, because time marches on, tomorrow's photograph will inevitably become yesterday's photograph. It will initially captivate us, but not for long because tomorrow's photograph is still out there, waiting to be made. It calls us forward, and if you're honest and feel the cringe (or something like it) the way I sometimes do, your older work might also give you a necessary nudge in that direction, moving you ever forward.

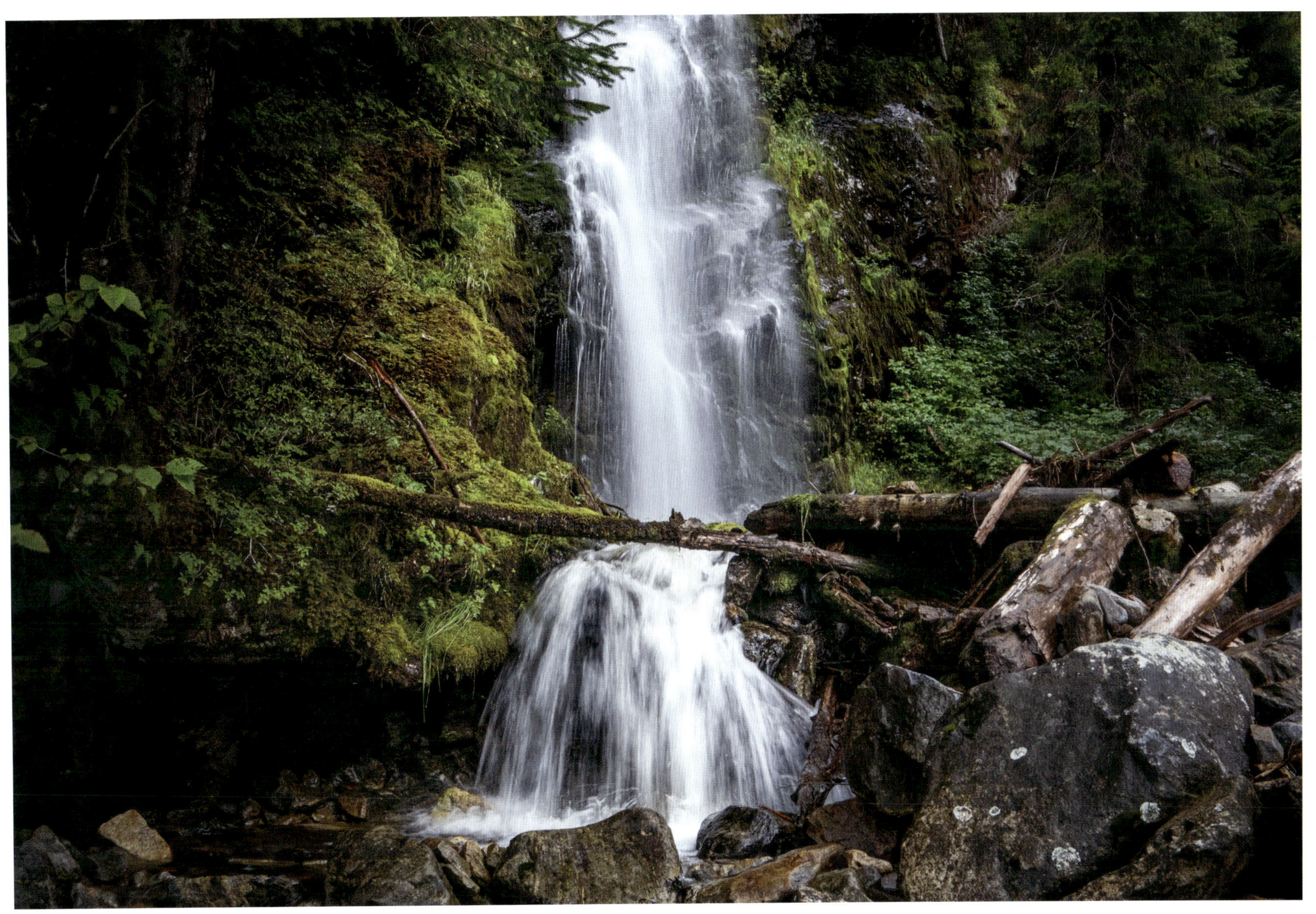

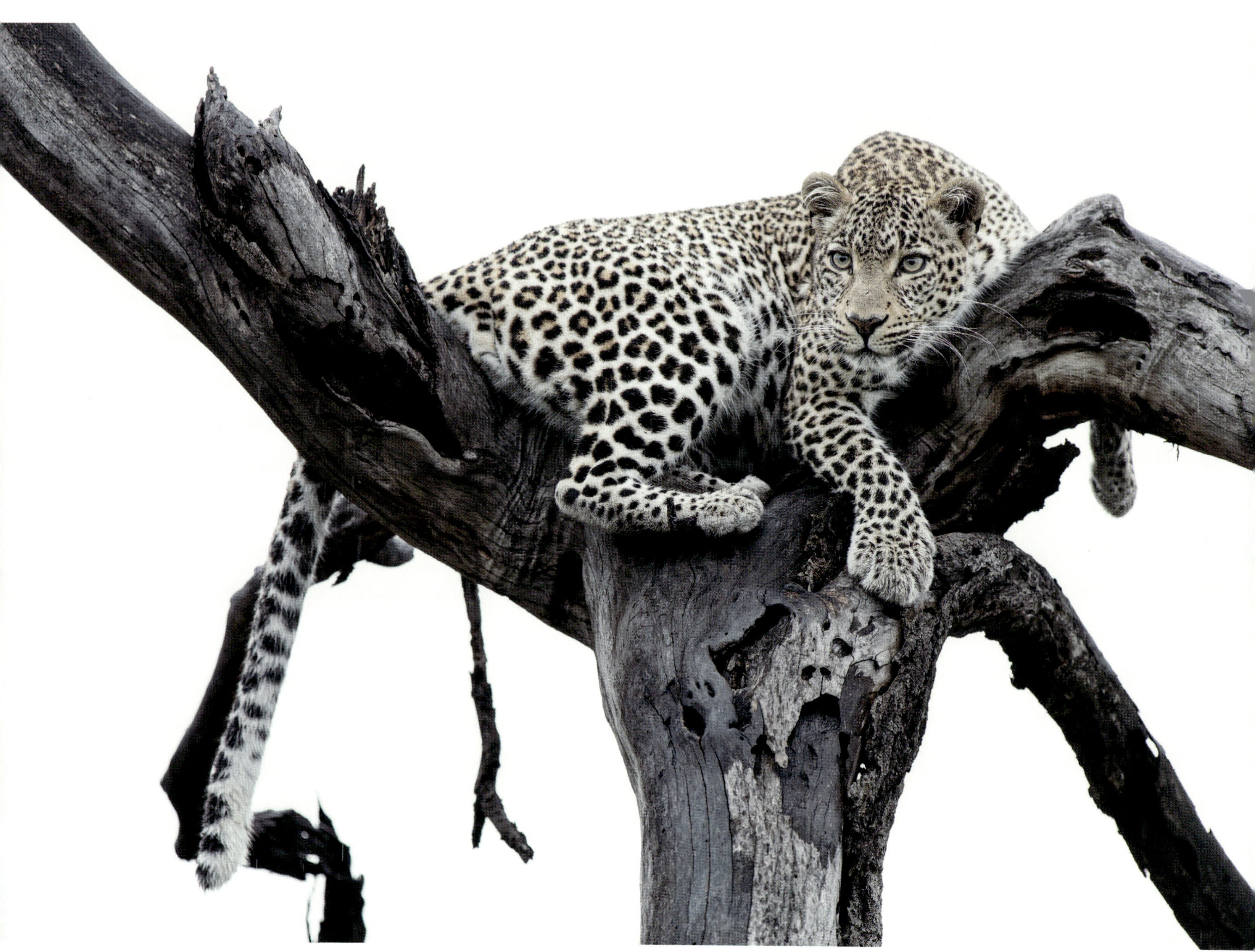

17

Imposters
and Improvisers

At some point, you will feel like an imposter. That might mean you suspect that you aren't what you might consider a *real* photographer. It might mean you feel that you're just faking it. It could also mean that you feel the rest of us know it and think, "You're just making this up as you go along!"

It makes us feel better to think so because we are all just making it up as we go. It's easier when we believe we're not alone—that we're not the only ones groping forward in the darkness without a roadmap. It feels like a dirty little secret we carry, living in fear that we'll be found out: "One day, someone will discover that I have no idea what I'm doing, and they'll revoke my membership card."

The feeling that we're faking it is an honest one because, to a greater or lesser degree, we're all just making it up—and we should be. To live a creative life, whether as a photographer or an artist in another discipline, we must do things that are often new to us. New techniques. New ideas. New visions for our next body of work. If it's new, it's uncertain, and working with uncertainty is where improvisation shines—because if it's old and a sure thing, why would we waste our time on it?

Most of us aren't imposters; we're improvisers, proudly faking it until we make it, if "faking it" means we have no idea how this will work out. It's not that we don't have a foundation of skill or any idea how to use a camera; it's that for *this* moment, for *this* photograph, we don't yet know exactly where it's going or how we're going to get it there. Of course we don't; we've never done it before, and it will take some figuring out. Trial and error. Move the camera. Change the lens. Wait for the light to change. Try again. You know the drill. Uncertainty isn't a sign that you're not the photographer you'd hoped; it's a sign that you've refused to remain the photographer you once were and are moving forward into the unknown to find out what's next.

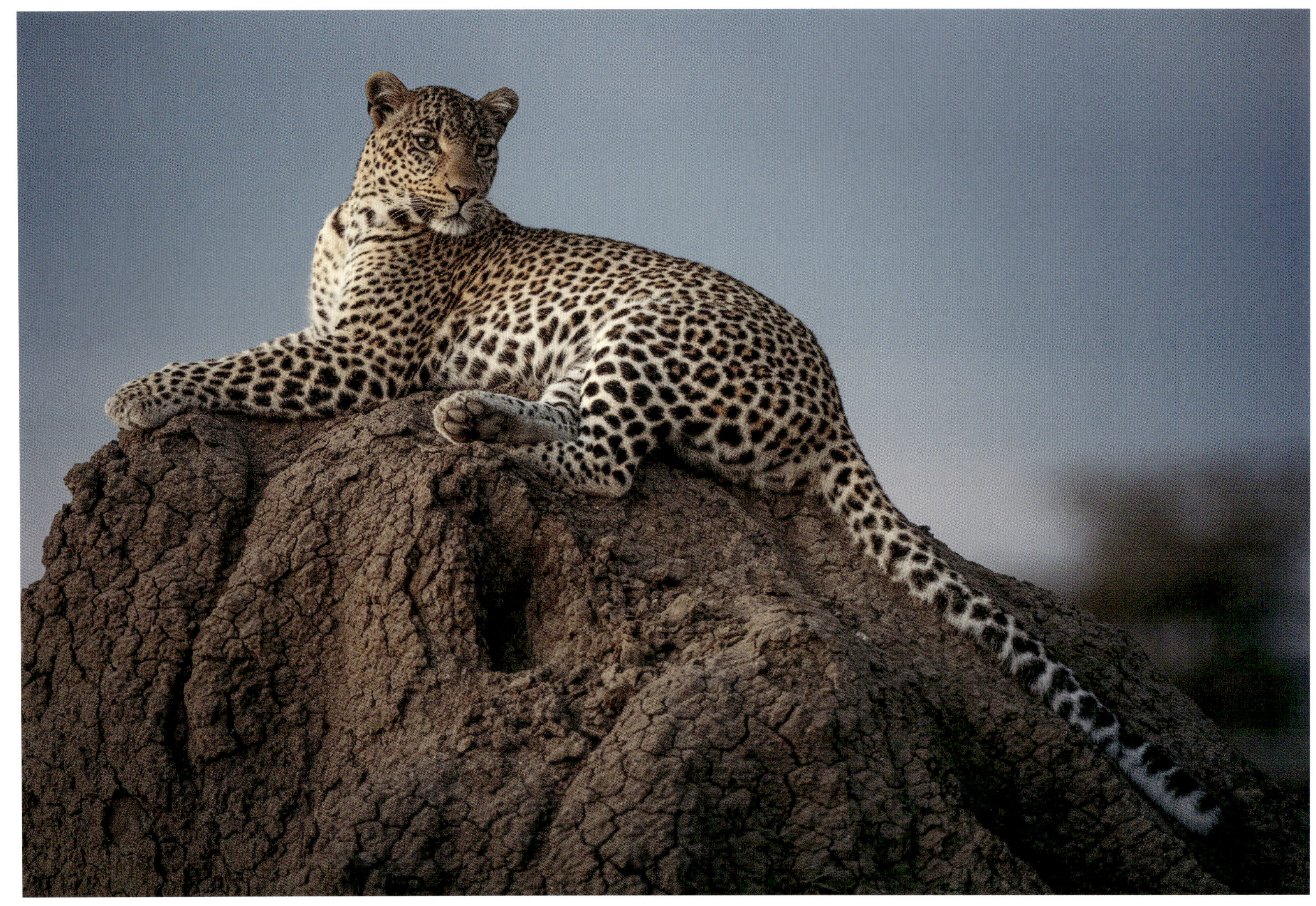

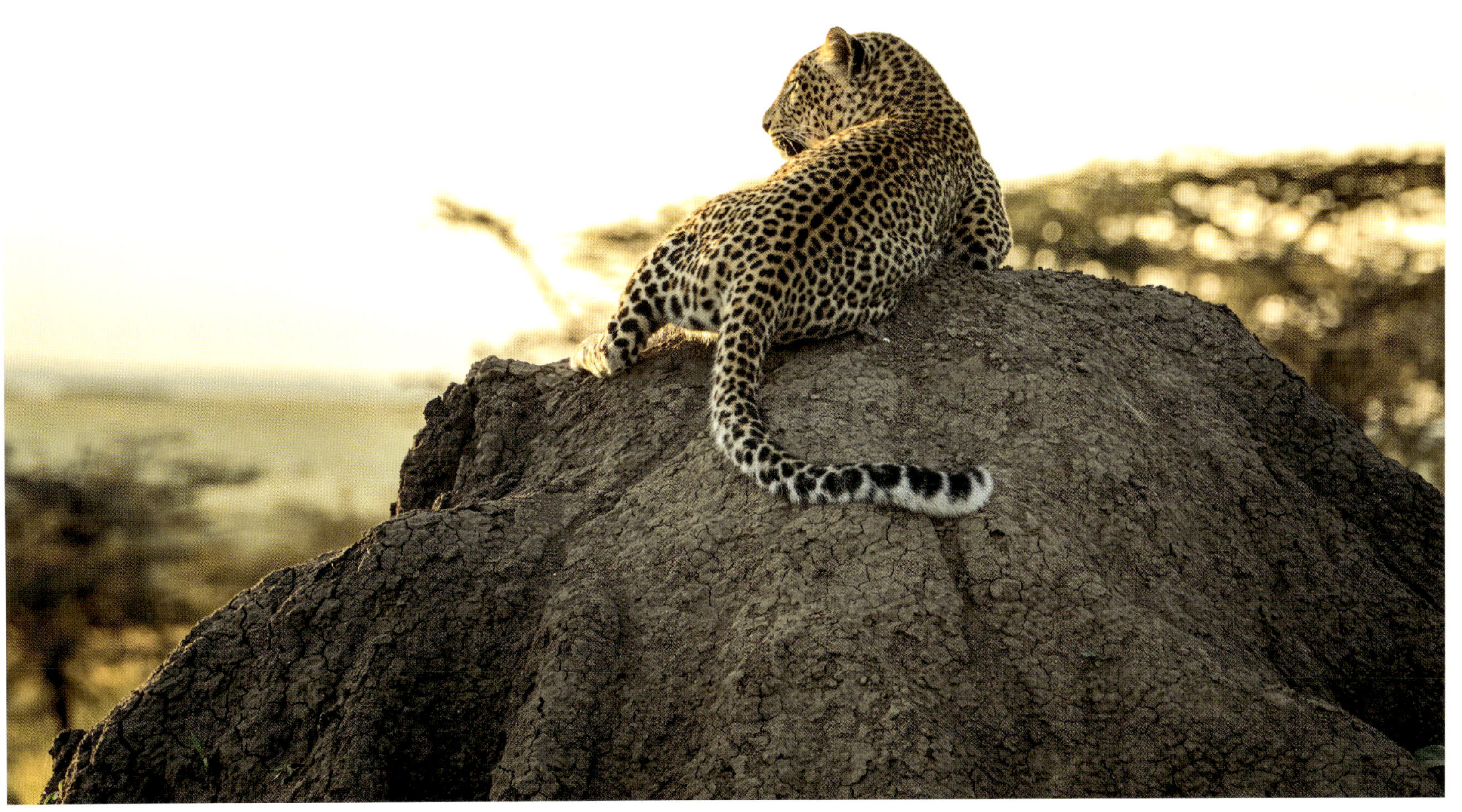

I don't worry about the photographer who fears they're just making it up as they go along; I worry for the one who's so sure they've got it figured out that they never experiment with new ideas or move into unfamiliar territory for fear of looking foolish when they do.

Anyone who has ever stepped foot on an improv stage knows that looking foolish is the cost of doing business to earn the laughs when they do come. It's the knowledge that we're all just trying something new, and it's different every time. Photographers often come to their creativity without the freedom of those lower expectations, though we'd benefit from them. How much freer might we be if we could laugh off the mis-steps and the failed efforts, take a breath—hell, take a bow!—and then try again? How serious we all can be.

Have you ever stood behind your camera and said to yourself, "I thought I had an idea of where this was going, but this just isn't working"? Doesn't everyone? Why are we so surprised, even derailed, by it? For me, after many years, this feeling has faded but never vanished, replaced by a growing confidence that if I've figured it out before, I'll probably figure it out again—or that I'll learn something while trying. It has helped that the time behind the camera, just being there and flexing those improvisational muscles, has become more important to me than the so-called success of my efforts. Sometimes, I make a photograph I love; sometimes, not so much. But if I focus on the process and enjoy it for its own sake, I never put the camera down disappointed. This has allowed me to relax, and though I didn't plan it this way, my work has improved because of it.

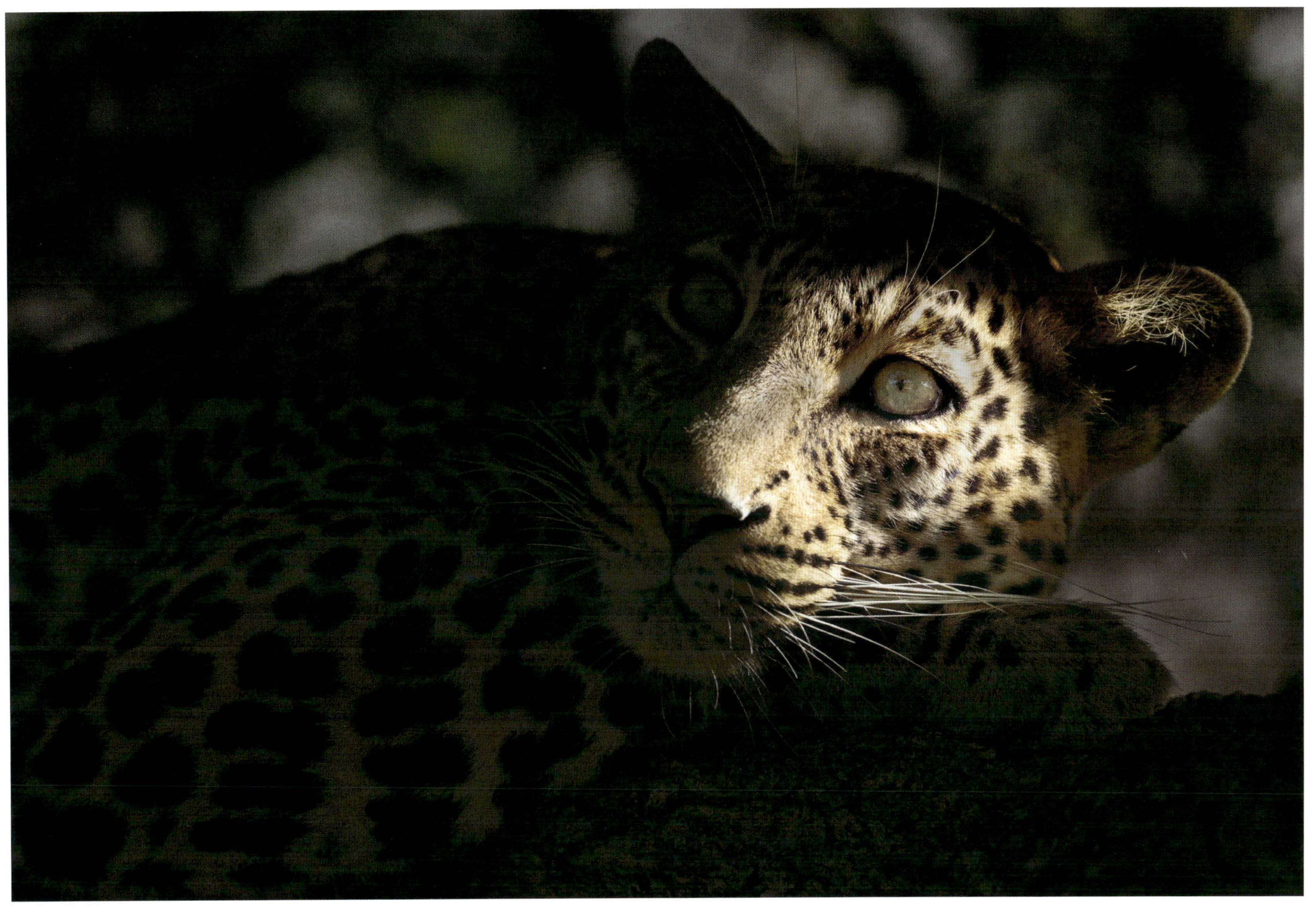

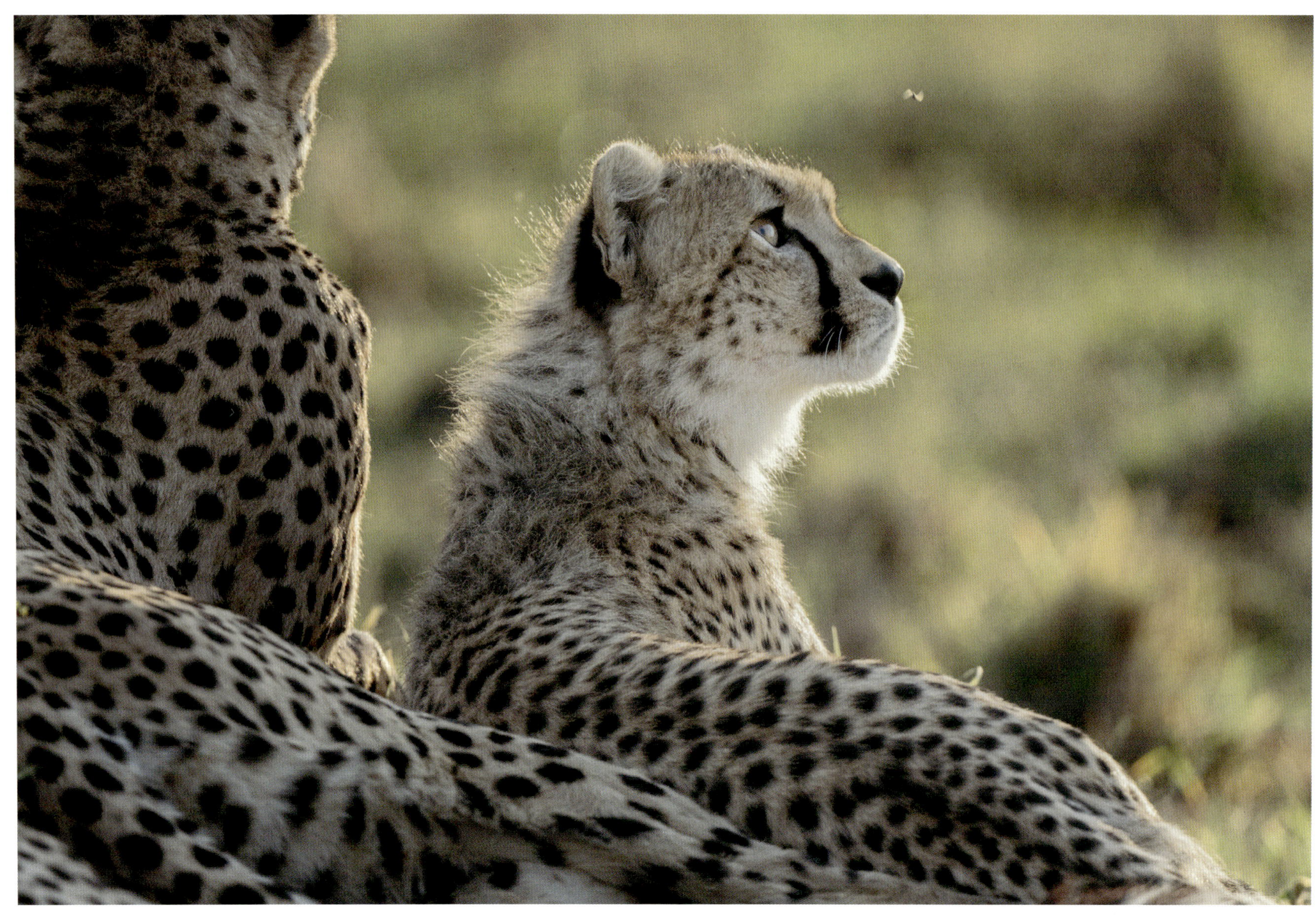

When I look back at my photographs that have endured, the ones I am most proud of, they are preceded mainly by images made while flailing around on the stage of photographic improvisation. What keeps me from feeling like I don't belong is the knowledge that *everyone* on that stage flails around in their own way. Not imposters, but improvisers. My flailing feels somewhat more graceful as the years go by—or perhaps it's just that I've reconciled myself to the happy reality that I'm not on a stage. No one sees my failed efforts. No one sees the disastrous sketch images. The pressure to be the photographer I imagine people think I am (or should be) is made so much lighter by the realization that people aren't thinking about me at all. It's very unlikely that the committee will revoke my membership (or yours) because they, too, are all so busy making it up as they go and hoping no one notices. What freedom!

That freedom allows you to stand behind your camera and, when those voices ask if you have any idea what you're doing, respond with, "I do not. But let's find out."

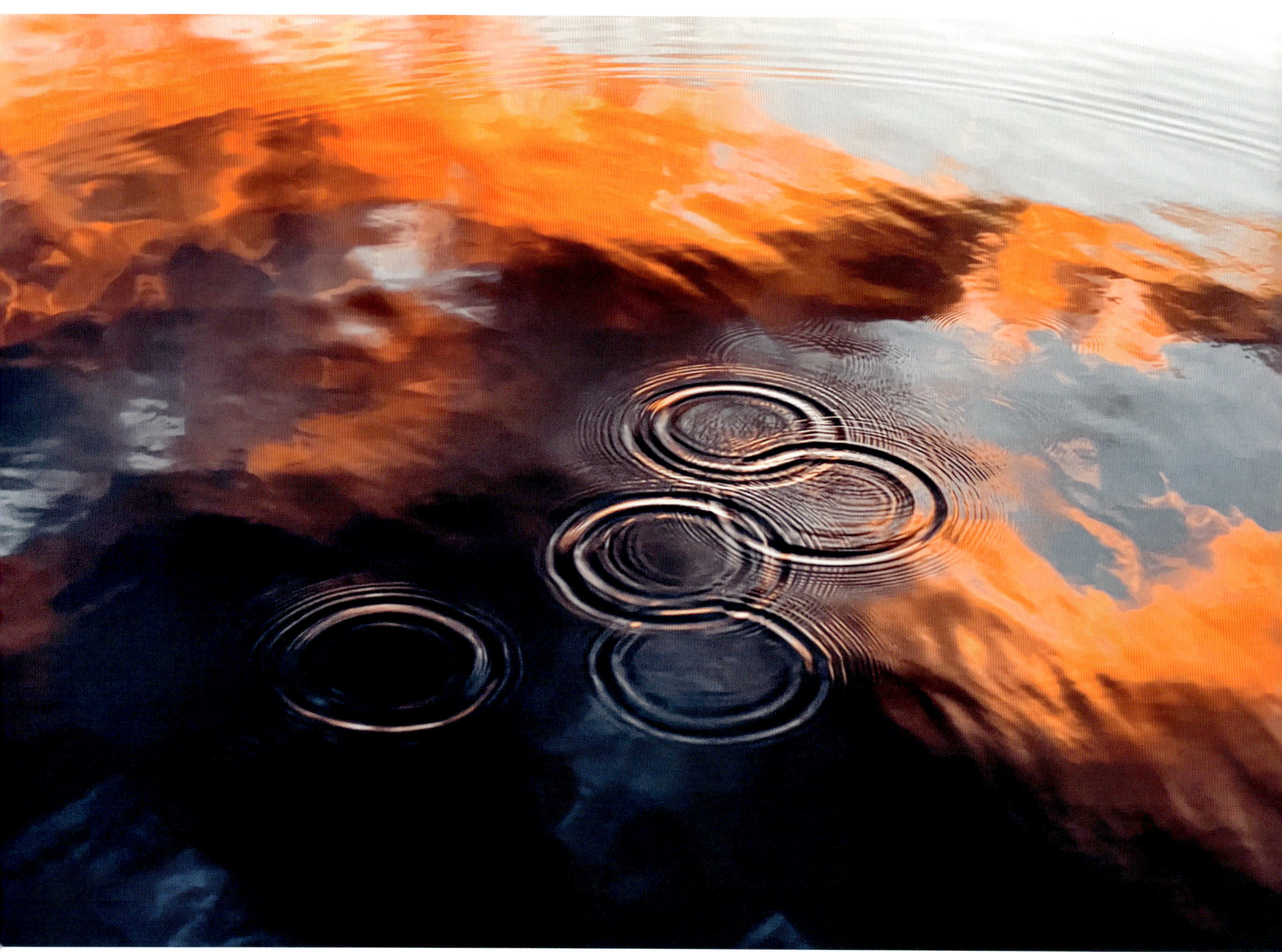

18
Over the Shoulders of Giants

Years ago, I took my battered Land Rover Defender to the Racetrack Playa in Death Valley. I'm sure you've seen photographs of the playa: rocks sitting on parched earth and cracked mud, long trails behind them as if they've moved on their own. This fascinating phenomenon of what are called "sailing stones" is explained by thin sheets of melting ice and powerful winter winds, though that makes it no less mysterious to me. I was there for two nights, taking advantage of that time to feel out the scene, get a sense of the possibilities of the place, and make a photograph or two.

That first evening we were alone, just me and my friend Corwin. Or so we thought. With my tripod set up for an hour or so, I'd found the composition that most intrigued me, and while waiting for twilight, I felt something press against my shoulder. Thinking it was Corwin (and knowing how oblivious I can get to my surroundings when photographing), I turned to say hi. But it wasn't Corwin; it was a random tourist who'd made the long trek out to the playa and, having no better ideas of his own, rested his camera (I'm not making this up) on my shoulder and pressed the shutter.

Click.

The tourist checked the back of his camera and proudly proclaimed, "This might be the best shot I've taken!" Satisfied, he vanished into the dark, and I returned to my work, feeling surreal about the whole thing.

I have admittedly looked over the shoulders of other photographers, though never quite so literally. I have observed them through their social media, online portfolios, and books. I've compared myself and my work to theirs. I've envied their successes, and on my better days, I've celebrated them, learned from them, and become better at what I do because of them.

Others have looked over my shoulder, too, and I feel their breath when I'm shooting. I hear their silent questions when I take a chance with an unconventional choice or creative risk. I wonder if those imaginary people will like what I'm making or understand my choices. Some days, this is all brushed aside so quickly, pushed to the back of my mind as I get into that state of grace when it's all flowing well. On other days, it's harder, and I can't decide which is worse: when the imagined voices chatter loudly or when I can't hear them at all and wonder, "What if no one cares?"

What if no one cares about the work you are making? What if you never find acclaim or leave a legacy? What if no one ever looks over your shoulder or cares enough to chance it?

When I think about those questions long enough, I find myself surprised by the answers that bubble up: what a relief it would be to work in that silent space without the (perceived) chattering expectations of others. What freedom I would find if I could make my many hundreds of sketch images with no one's preferences to consider but my own. Would I find myself holding my breath as often? And how much more joy would I find in the process? How much more present and less rigid would I be in the making of this work? And how much better (or at least how much more truly my own) would the work itself be?

One day, I want my work to have a wider audience. I would like it if others found something meaningful in what I made. And once I'm through the complex process of making something so simple as a photograph, how wonderful it would be if others felt the same wonder I did in the presence of wildness. How many others—the size of that audience—is unimportant. Perhaps it's only you. That would be enough for me. An audience for my *work* would be nice, but not for my *working*.

I can only really pay attention to one thing at a time. I can only have interesting perceptions about one thing at a time, and those are hard enough to come by. I can only make photographs about one thing at a time. I don't have the capacity to simultaneously consider you and what you might think about my work. Hell, I don't even know what *I* think of the work yet. How focused can any of us be when we make work in consideration of others before giving our own thoughts and preferences some serious thought and completing all the experimenting it takes to make a single image or a body of work?

I can't decide which is worse: when the imagined voices chatter loudly or when I can't hear them at all and wonder, "What if no one cares?"

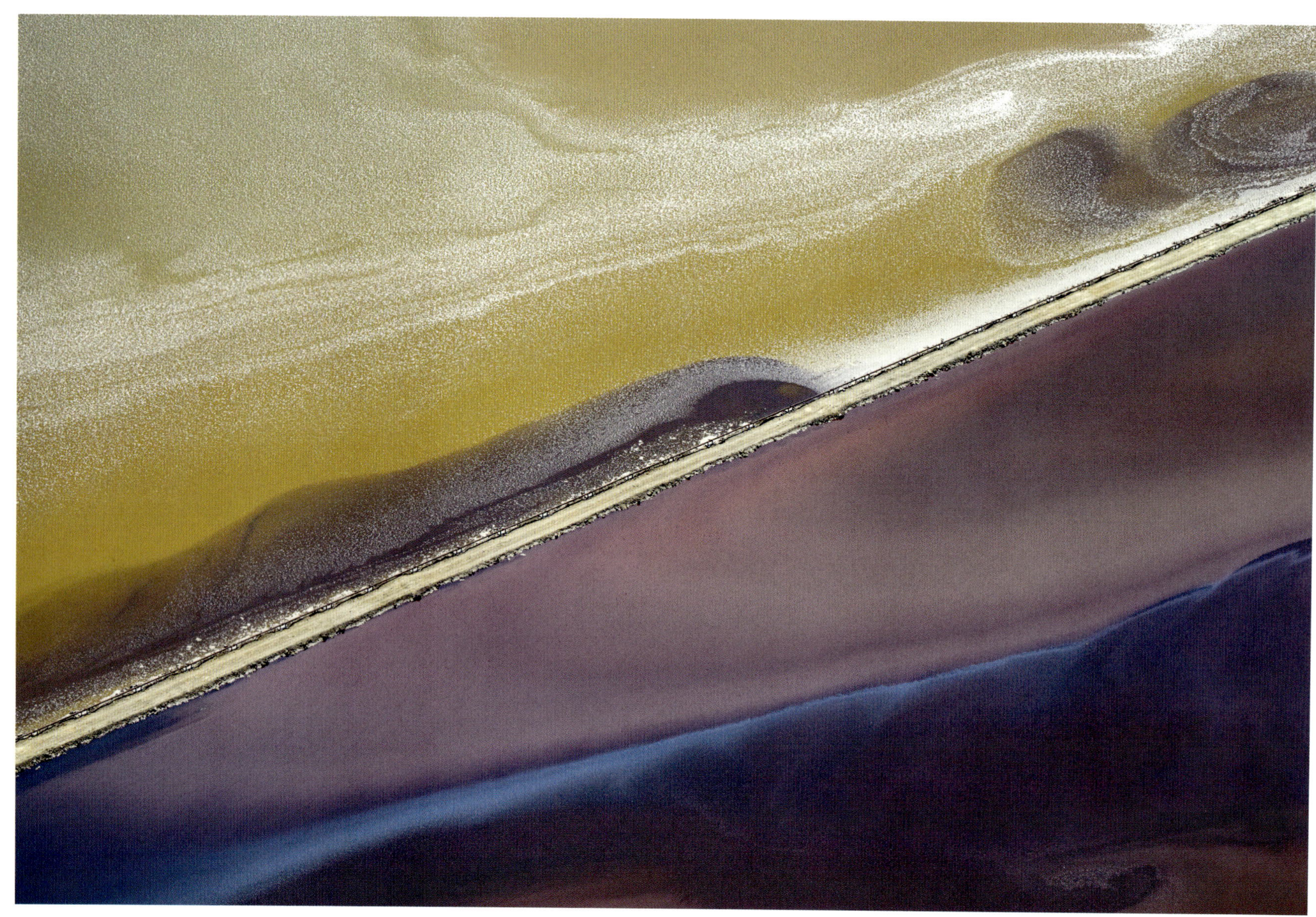

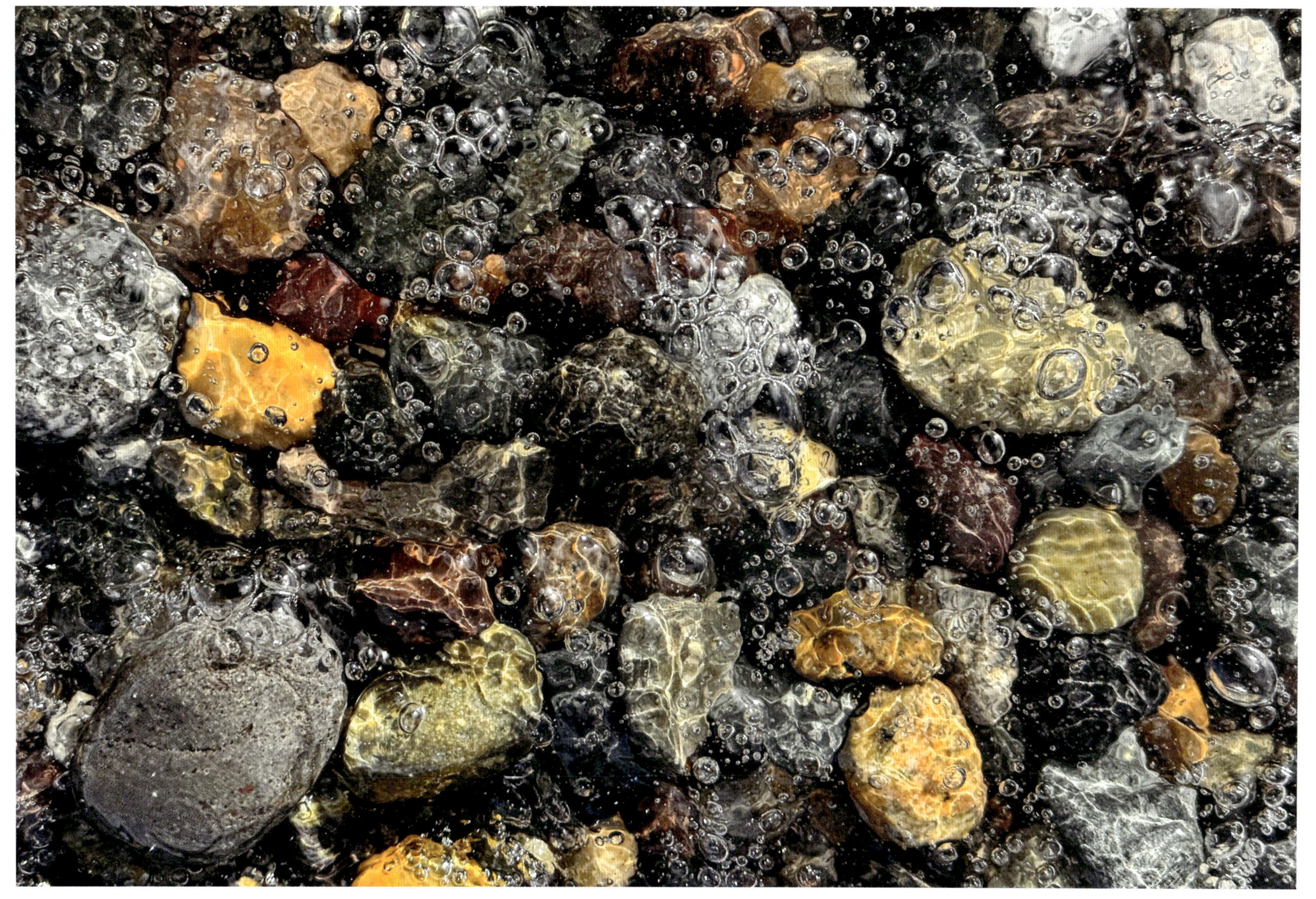

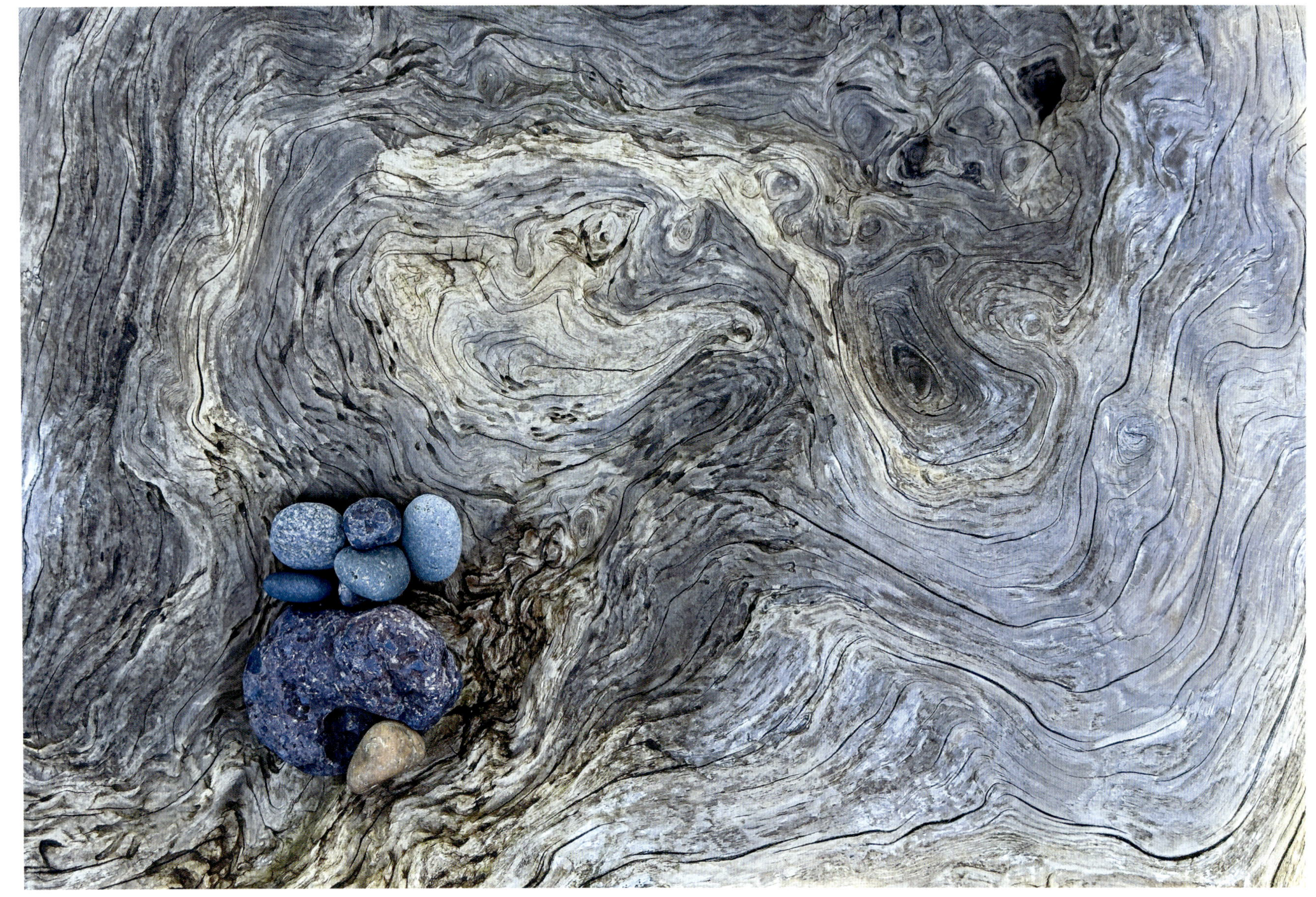

Your audience, however small, will one day thrill to see what you make. But you must not make it *for* them. Not *first* for them. You must make your work for yourself, neither looking over the shoulders of others nor paying attention to those looking over yours. When you work, your focus must be on that work. The thoughts. The what-ifs and the speculations about what all your choices might produce. Those are yours alone. And only once you're unapologetically—and yes, even selfishly—absorbed in those reflections and explorations will you make the work that then deserves its audience.

Audience is a by-product of work that thrills you first, or conjures something from deep within you, or answers to the reasons you picked up the camera in the first place. That's where your gaze needs to be. When the muse arrives, she needs to find you getting your hands dirty, using the camera to make photographs from the interesting perceptions you've had because you've been looking at the object of those perceptions, not the people you believe are waiting for what you create.

As you engage in this process, you do not have the bandwidth for me or anyone else to look over your shoulder. Your process is yours alone, and—forgive the pun—you're not alone if you find photography a more rewarding and productive pursuit when it's solitary, when it's quiet and free of distractions such as other people's opinions.

The creative process, even a single creative thought, is fragile; it needs to be held somewhat gently as it comes into being. It needs to be coaxed out. I've only ever found the best of those thoughts shy in the presence of others; they tend to retreat when conflicting tastes and preferences demand our photographs be one thing or another before we're even sure of what we hope for them.

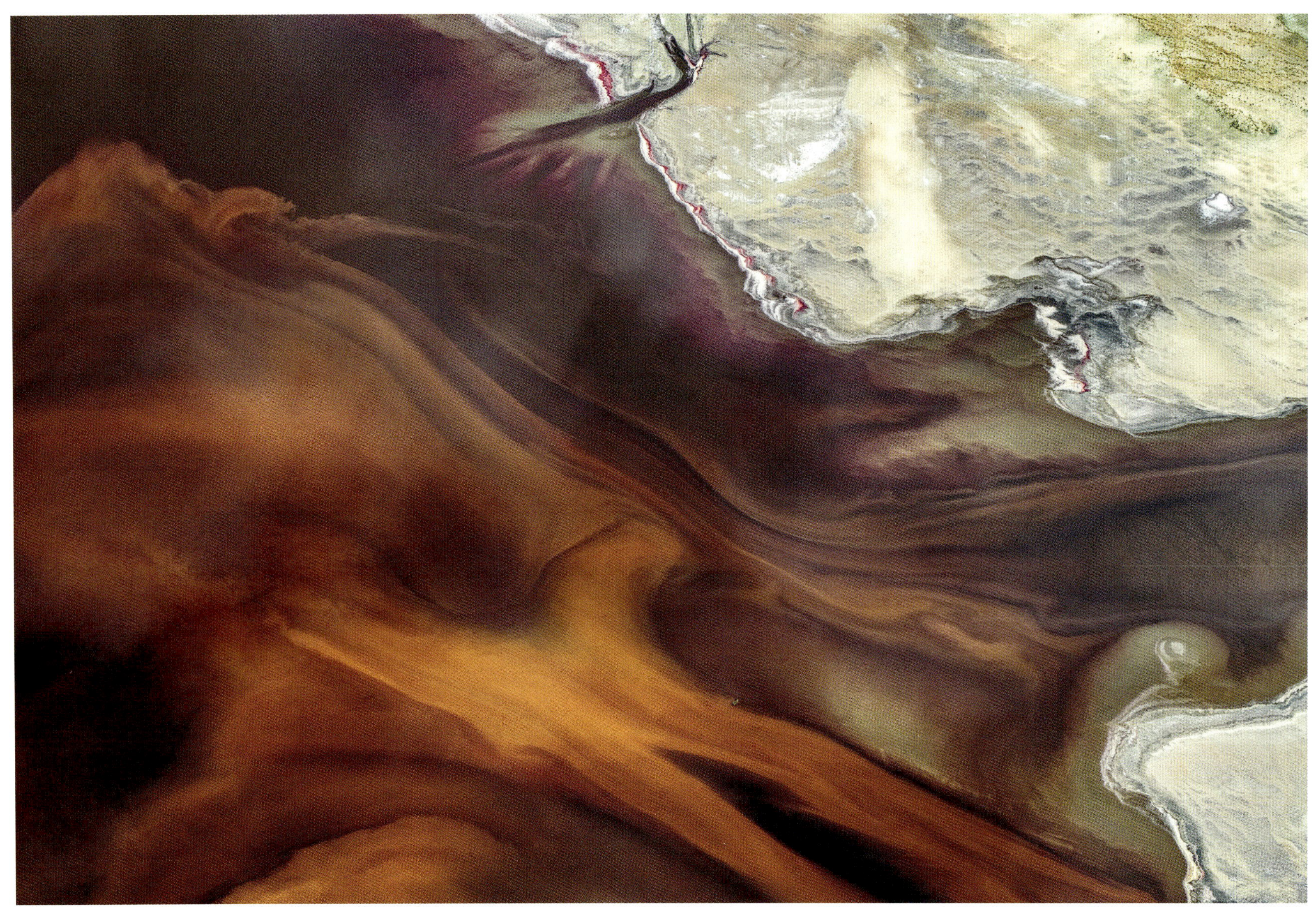

That the guy looking over my shoulder at Death Valley even happened at all amuses me. If that's how he needs to make a photograph, then let him have it. But I wasn't about to ask him his opinion and alter my work because of it, and that's the danger of having an audience of any size, even an audience of one, that is not yourself first. It's hard enough to find your way to your vision or voice without others clamouring for it to be this or that, even when that clamouring is only imagined. Maybe *especially* when those voices are imagined because, unlike Death Valley guy, they rarely give up and take their leave so quickly; they have a persistence that's hard to ignore. But they must be ignored because caring more about the voices of others than about finding and giving expression to *your* voice is moving in the wrong direction, away from what makes you and your work truly your own. It dilutes your personality in the final product and steals the joy of discovering that rare, hidden element in the very best of that work: yourself.

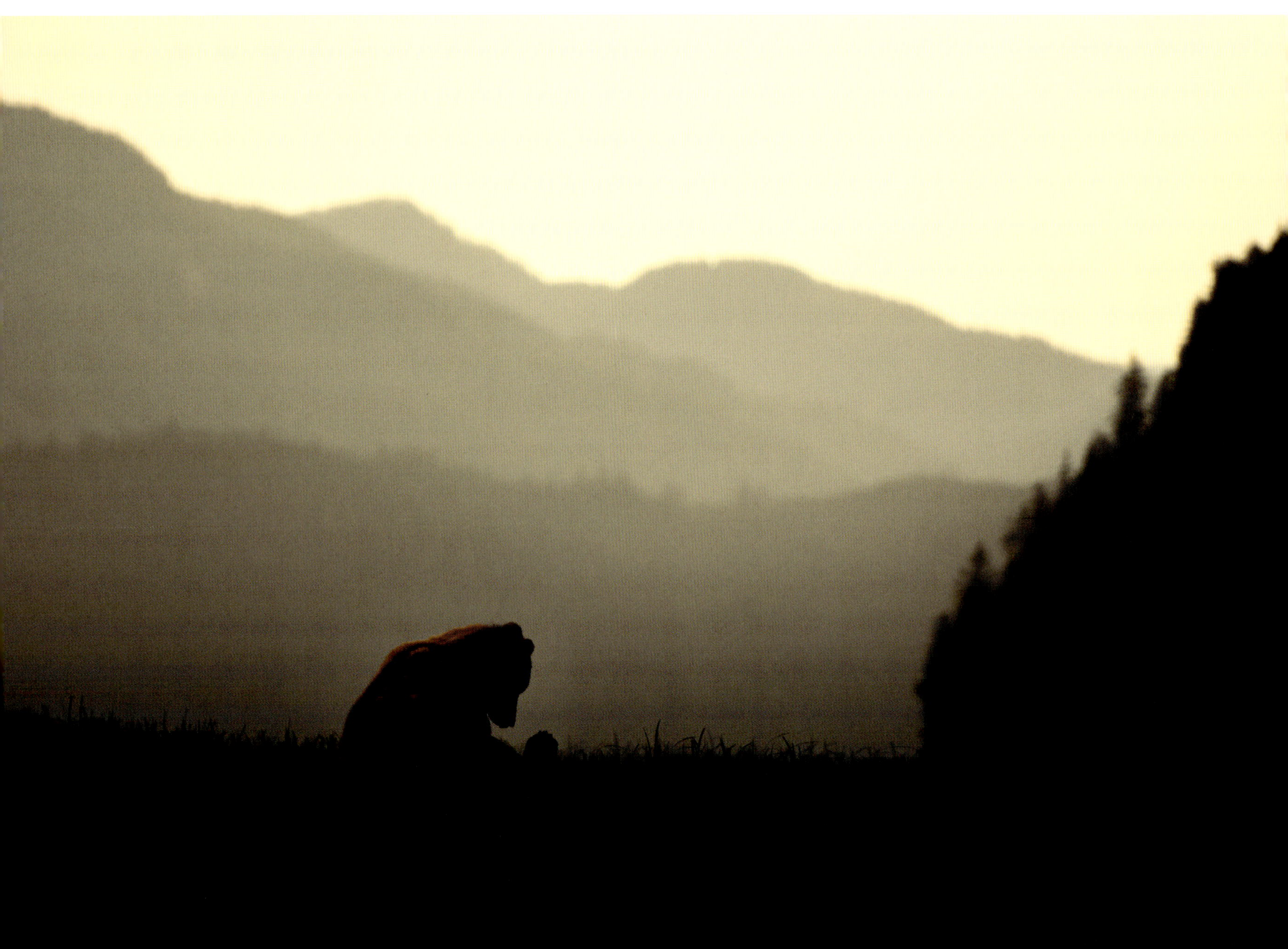

19
Starts
and Stops

The hardest part of any creative endeavour is getting started. Knowing when to finish is hard, too. The messy bit in the middle can also be a challenge. But the most crucial and challenging aspect lies in the start. Picking up the camera and getting to work—even knowing *how* to get to work and which direction to work in—is not only the hard part but also the most important. When you're in the middle of things, even when it's not yet flowing, you have something to react to. If the last choices didn't work, you change your approach. If the last choices felt right, you trust that and follow where they lead. But starting? When there's nothing but possibility and endless what-ifs? That's hard.

Inspiration is the obvious place to find a beginning, but it's rare enough that I'm more interested in asking what we do when that inspiration is lacking. What do you do when your muse is out of sight and you're *not* feeling it? How often have I picked up my camera with nothing more to drive me than a sense that there's beauty afoot and I *should* probably start doing something with it? No bright ideas, no sense of vision, no notion of where to begin, only that I probably *should*.

Even in the most astonishing encounters with people, wildlife, or the land itself, we must begin somewhere. That's usually the choice of one lens, a shutter speed, an aperture, and a place to put the camera. That's not one choice but four, and if you truly care about your work, you've felt the fear whispering, "What if you get it wrong?" which is nonsense because there is no "wrong" from which you can't back out or otherwise change course. Helpfully, changing course from a less-than-perfect first choice is direction. It's momentum. It means you've started and are no longer deliberating; you are working.

The muse—that feeling of inspiration that's so unpredictable we've personified it and treated as its own being external to ourselves for over 2,000 years—appears in our process only when we are working, not before. Ideas arrive in reaction to existing ideas; momentum builds as you make decisions. Right or wrong has nothing to do with it. If you're looking for the spark you feel when, out of the blue, you think, "What if I . . . ?" then it's a sign you need to rub some ideas together, usually the ones that aren't working satisfactorily. The sparks come from the friction between those ideas, often felt as frustration. But when the sparks begin to fly, it's a sign that something's going to change, or rather that we need to change something. A new lens. A slower shutter. A stronger moment.

Beginning is everything: not *where* you begin but *that* you begin. Anywhere. For the love of St. Elliott Erwitt (for whose absence we are so much poorer), do *something*. Begin. We all start ugly. Every chance to make a photograph is a chance to learn how to make this particular photograph in this particular moment—and learning is messy. Always has been. Learning is reacting to failures with the hard-earned insight of what *doesn't* work, of wandering into the unknown and seeing what you find and can experiment with. If you're not learning, there's a chance you're just repeating yourself.

It is far better to make a dozen false starts down poorly chosen roads and let them lead you somewhere—*anywhere!*—than to let paralysis set in. You'll make nothing waiting for inspiration, waiting for the idea to come first. Most photographs are not the result of one single idea that arrives just in time but of many small ideas. Some of them will one day feel intuitive, more like instinct than conscious thought, but even then, you'll have moved on to consciously entertaining new ideas while the basics run in the background. Either way, it's rarely one startling revelation that makes a photograph, but many smaller ideas: a little depth of field, a wider focal length, a move closer to the foreground or slightly to the left. The reaction to those decisions spawns other ideas, and still others as you dial it in. Polarizer on or off? What if you made a double exposure or used a strobe for a pop of light? None of these happen without starting. And how you start—what that first effort looks like—is probably a long way from where you will finish, for which you should be grateful.

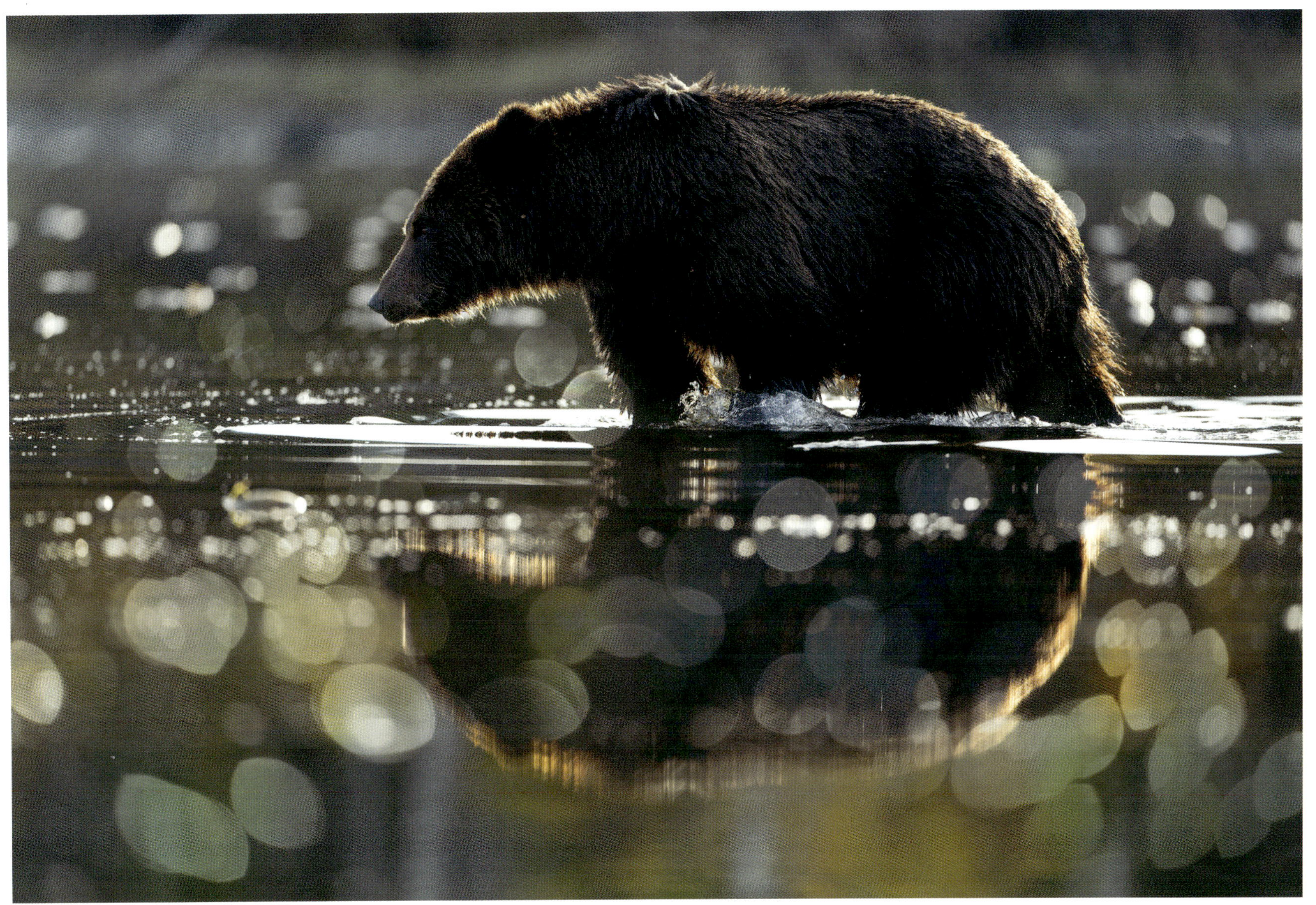

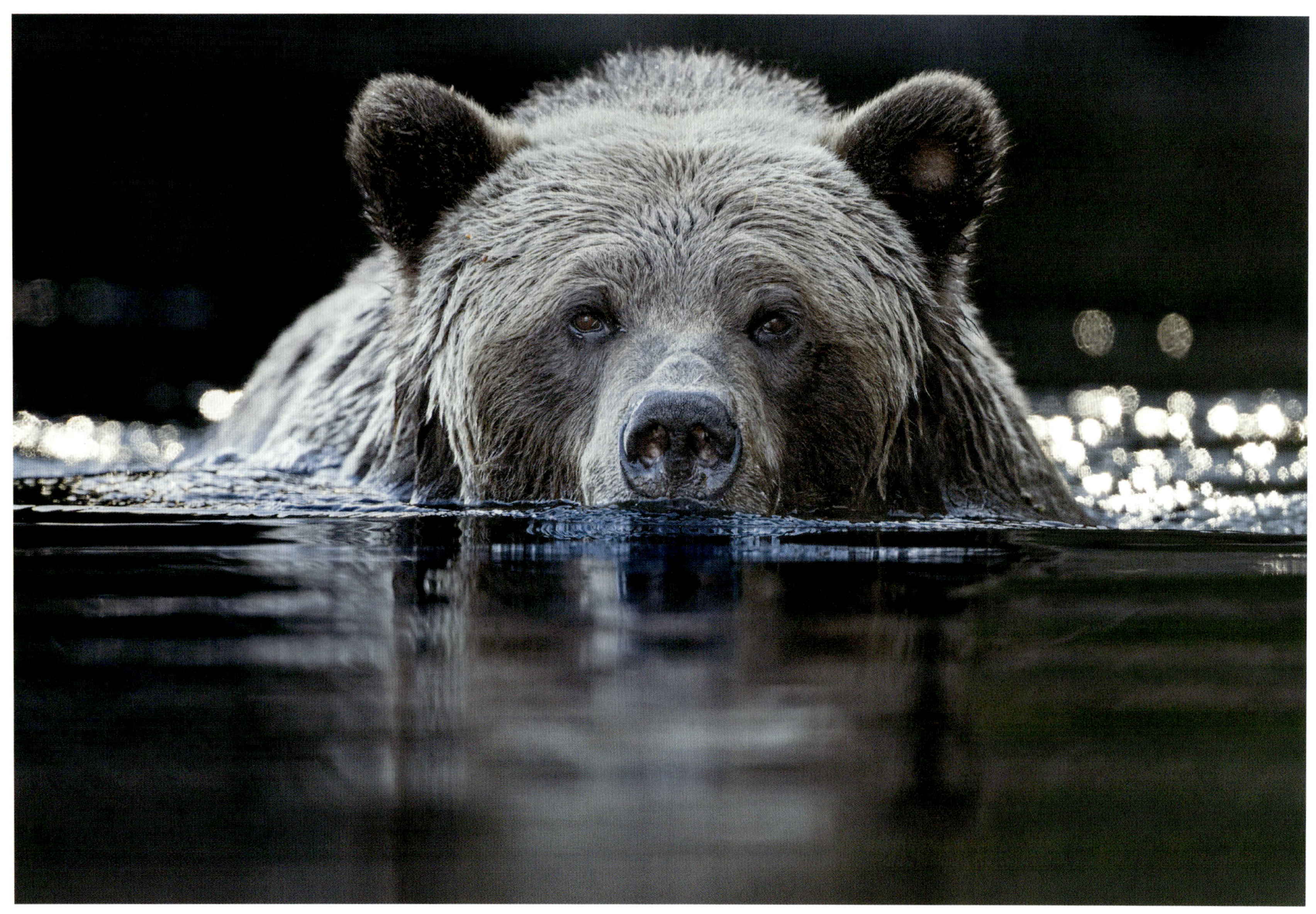

Ideas arrive in reaction
to existing ideas;
momentum builds
as you make decisions.

First steps often falter. I have learned to walk four times in my life, most recently on a prosthetic leg. The first steps, weak and uncertain, looked nothing like my stride now. Those initial movements were small and searching, as if I'd never made them before. I know what walking looks like, and those first steps weren't walking. Not yet. To have judged them as failures would have sabotaged my progress. I needed those first small, ugly steps to be small and ugly to gain skill and confidence. Initial attempts at anything are almost always embarrassingly free from the promise of what they'll one day become. First steps. First efforts at a new language. First moments as a human being. We can argue later about the aesthetics of newborn babies, but I'm grateful most of us get better-looking as we age. New photographs, too. The first frames are often far from the final ones, but they get us there.

Start somewhere. Be uncertain, but start. Pick up the camera and start making choices. Make "bad" choices if you must; they'll get stronger. Move the camera. Wait for stronger moments. Try a different lens. But whatever you do, don't keep pressing the shutter and simply hoping something will change. If you find yourself stuck in a loop of saying, "It's not working," try asking instead, "How can I work it?"

Starting is hard, but the middle isn't necessarily easier; it's where efforts and ideas get refined, where the ugly first steps begin to find their polish. The middle is just as messy and uncertain as the beginning, but it comes with some momentum, and if you've challenged yourself enough and the challenge is equal to your skill, there's a chance it'll come with flow. Flow allows you to be less self-conscious, to lose sense of time, and to recognize that the choices that were once harder to come by feel more graceful. Flow is the sweet spot of creative work, but you can't get there without starting. No one starts in the middle of flow.

And inevitably, you also have to stop at some point; you've got to call it finished and sign your name to it. The struggle in stopping is not in knowing *how* to put the camera down, but *when*. How do you know when you're looking through the viewfinder that you're done? The risk is not in working it for too long but calling it done before it's time. There's no harm done if you overstay the moment, but if you leave before it's really over, you could miss the magic. You can overthink and overwork a project, but I don't think it's possible to overshoot it. Looking back, I'm conscious of the times I left a scene in search of something better, only to find out that the magic happened ten minutes after I left. And I am delighted by memories of wanting to pack it in and move on, but I stayed instead and was rewarded for doing so.

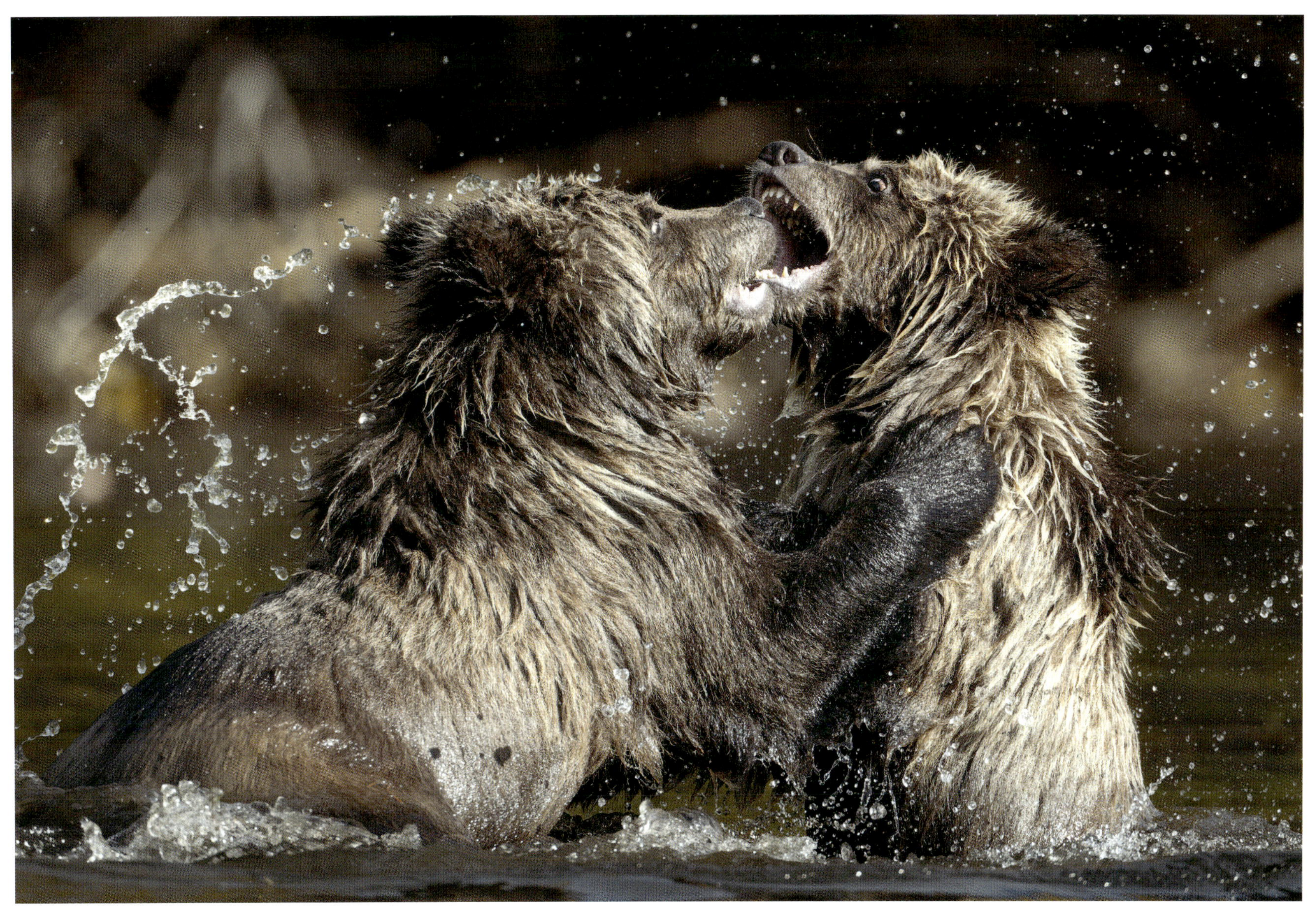

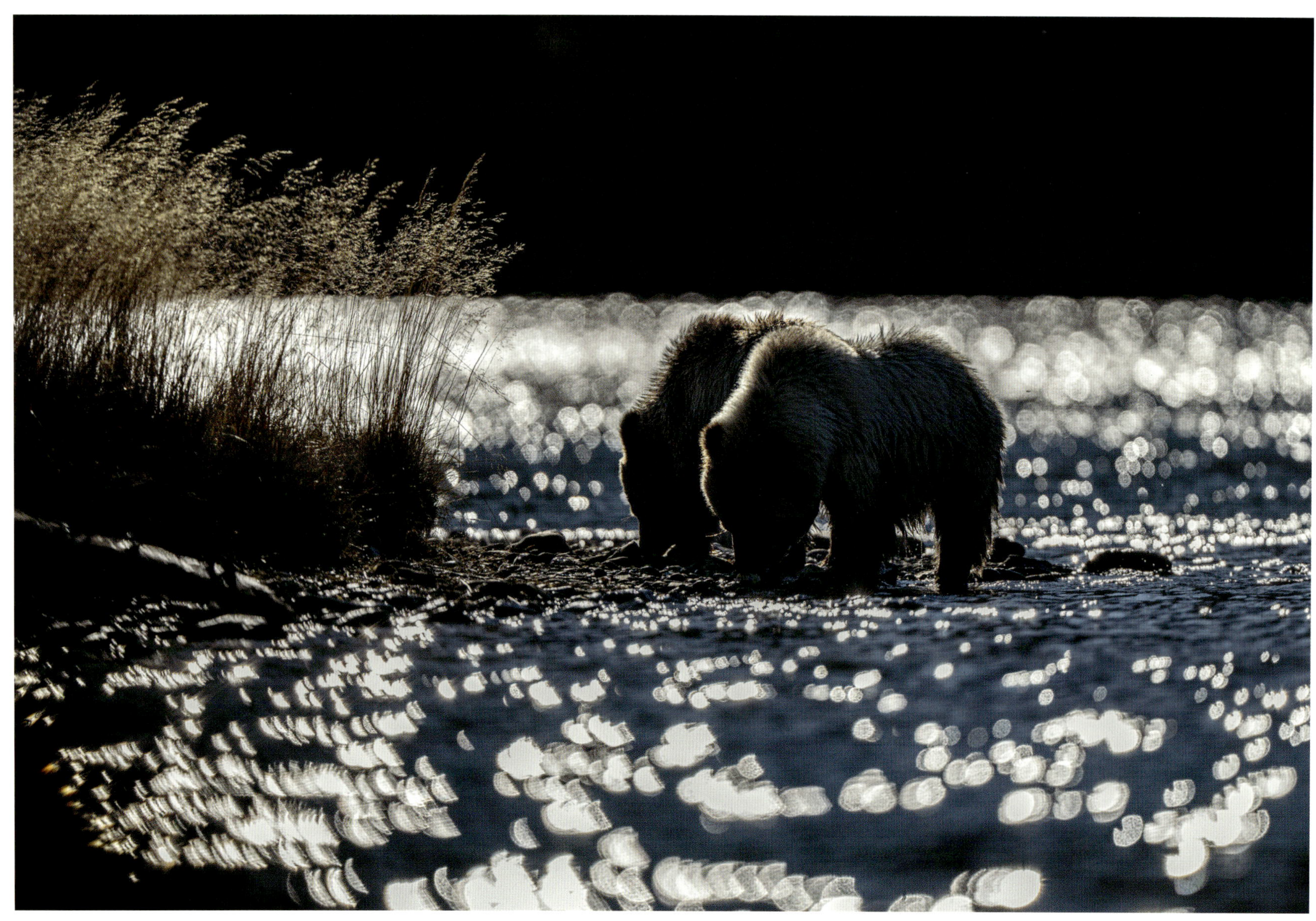

On trips I guide to photograph bears, I'm often asked during long moments of inaction if we should move on. My usual reply is, "You don't leave a bear to go find a bear." It's not always that simple, but I prefer not to leave something I do have in search of something I don't, especially when waiting might bring it to me. I'd rather wait out a great composition that only needs a better moment or light than look for another. Great compositions come less frequently than the light changes. I'd rather stay put.

Sometimes, waiting pays no dividends when you know in your gut that the light is gone, the magic has returned to wherever it is that magic comes from, and the moment has passed. Sometimes, you feel it strongly enough in your bones that the gamble is worth it. But you never *really* know. You can't. Not for sure. If you're looking for guarantees and certainties, photography, with its reliance on real life and its propensity to serendipity and unexpected coincidence, might not be for you. But that's part of the thrill, isn't it? Isn't part of what we do as much about the hunt or the discovery as it is the making of whatever photograph that follows once we find it? Doesn't part of the joy come from starting and not knowing where the effort will lead, which new ideas will come, and which lessons will be learned on the way to the incomparable "I made that" feeling of seeing your finished photograph?

Starting is easier when you're more intentional about your expectations for those beginnings. Expect your first frames to be a path forward rather than the destination itself, and you'll have more patience with yourself and the process. Rather than being surprised by failures, you can anticipate and welcome them like an opportunity rather than treating them like wasted detours. How you think about this part of the process will make it either playful or angst-ridden—the former a chance to take a risk, the latter a chance for self-doubt. I know my first frames are going to be crap, but they're necessary to get the gears moving and help me decide on a direction. It's as essential to know what's *not* working as what is. And that's a start.

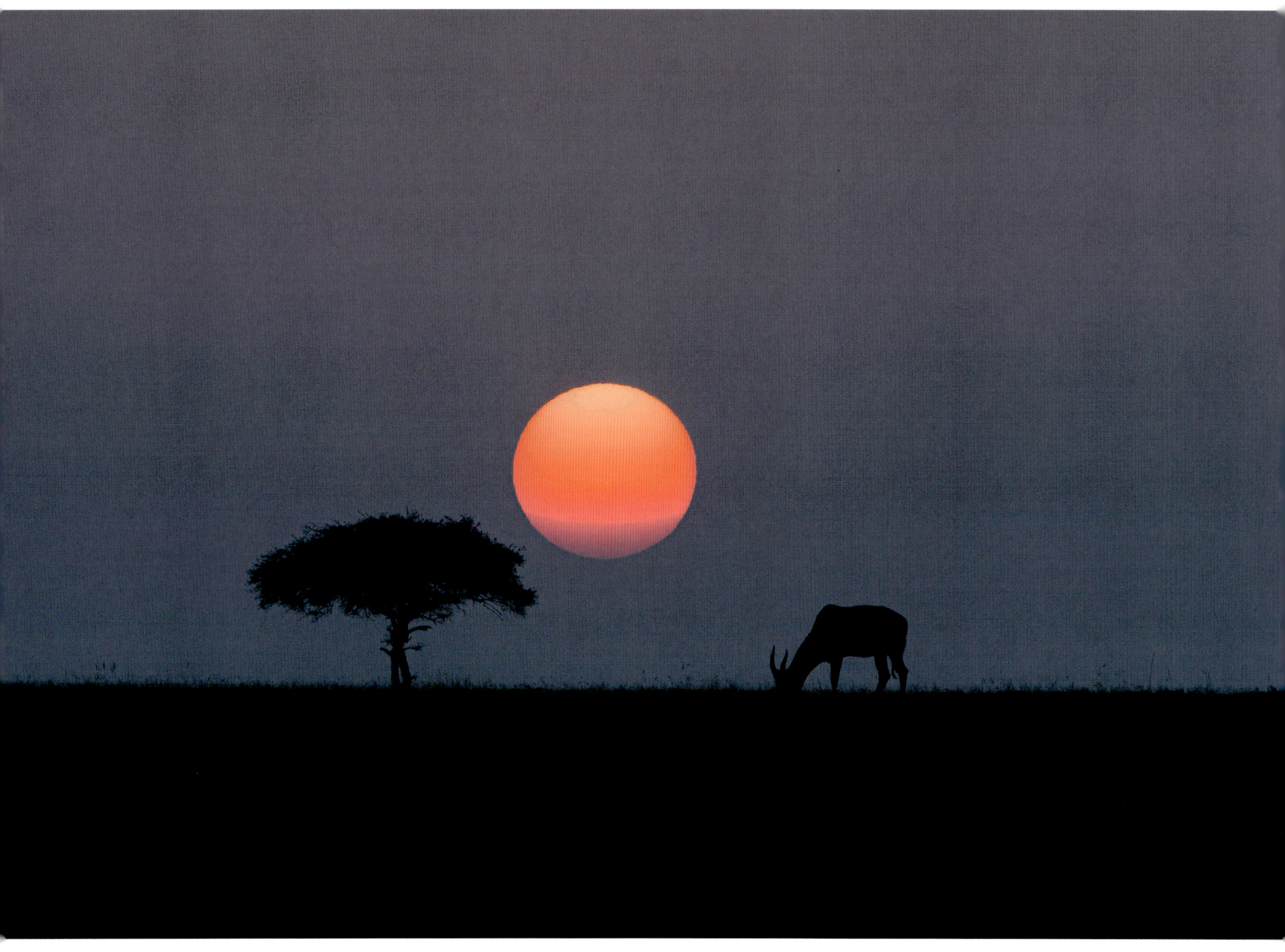

20
Find Your Magic

For the better part of 40 years, photography has been a constant for me, the one thing I never gave up on. Creatively, it will always be my first love, but there is much about photography that I don't love. I can do without most of the culture of competition and the trend toward sameness. The over-the-top geekery confuses me, and while I'm sure there's someone out there who needs to know about "focus breathing," it isn't me. I'm glad those people are out there, though I still end up feeling like a lesser photographer for neither knowing nor caring. I just can't see how knowing those things might change my approach to making photographs.

And the constant posturing about gear? Well, I could do without that as well. If I'm honest, there are times I don't even love *making* photographs. I find it stressful when things aren't flowing, and between the real-world constraints we all wrestle with and my expectations of myself and my work, there are times I'd just rather not get the camera out.

But that reluctance and the pressure I feel probably come from places inside me that are my issues to solve. I've noticed they don't come up so much when they are free from the expectations of others, when my photography is allowed to be more relaxed and more of an optional reaction to what I am experiencing. Maybe I press the button, maybe I don't. As a professional and someone who believes in discipline and the creative value of challenge, I don't always have the luxury of tripping the shutter only when something magical appears in front of me. Sometimes, I need to hunt down the magic, wait for the magic, and even *make* the magic. But those efforts usually come from a work ethic, not from love.

I don't photograph because I love playing with cameras. What I love is being out there with no pressure or agenda, not desperately hunting for something to put in front of my lens. I love the magic of the unexpected that I seem to encounter more when I'm out there with a camera in my hands, like seeing elephants appear out of the fog or turning a corner in some wonderful place and seeing something that wasn't there the day before or something that's been there *every* day but in light I've never seen. I love the coincidence of light, space, and time when it happens and my eyes are open to it. I love the moments afterward, too, when the created picture matches not just what was there in front of me but also the magic of which my imagination caught a glimpse. The feeling. The awe. The wonder. When that happens, I feel more alive and awake to life. Those are the feelings I'm chasing when I photograph.

Too seldom do we experience awe and wonder, but it's the frisson of those emotions and the hope of experiencing them that gets me out of bed before sunrise and into the world with my cameras. I want to feel the magic, to interact with it, and see if I can be a small part of it. I want to look through the lens and not see what a thing looks like, but something more. A galaxy in the backlit bubbles of my dive buddy, or the moment a bear swims through water that looks like colourful and viscous paint, rich with the hues of autumn leaves reflected on the surface.

One of the problems with the culture of popular photography is the underlying assumption that we all photograph for the same reasons—because we don't. Some people do it to play with the gear; there's nothing wrong with that. My work process is better when my gear performs the way it's meant to, and better or different gear means different creative possibilities, so hurray for the gear and thank the gods for those who buy every new camera and fund research and development! But the gear is only how I do my work, not *why*. I photograph to find and feel the magic, to get closer to a life filled with wonder.

I have never felt that magic while labouring to impress others. Quite the opposite, in fact. Under the gaze of others, I've always wilted creatively. I have never felt it while trying to conform to the expectations of others or the belief that to be a "real photographer," I need to own certain things or know specific technical terms. I traveled once with a National Geographic photographer whose photographs I adore, and she freely admitted to not knowing what the Rule of Thirds was. That clearly didn't hold her back; she was too busy looking for and responding to the magic.

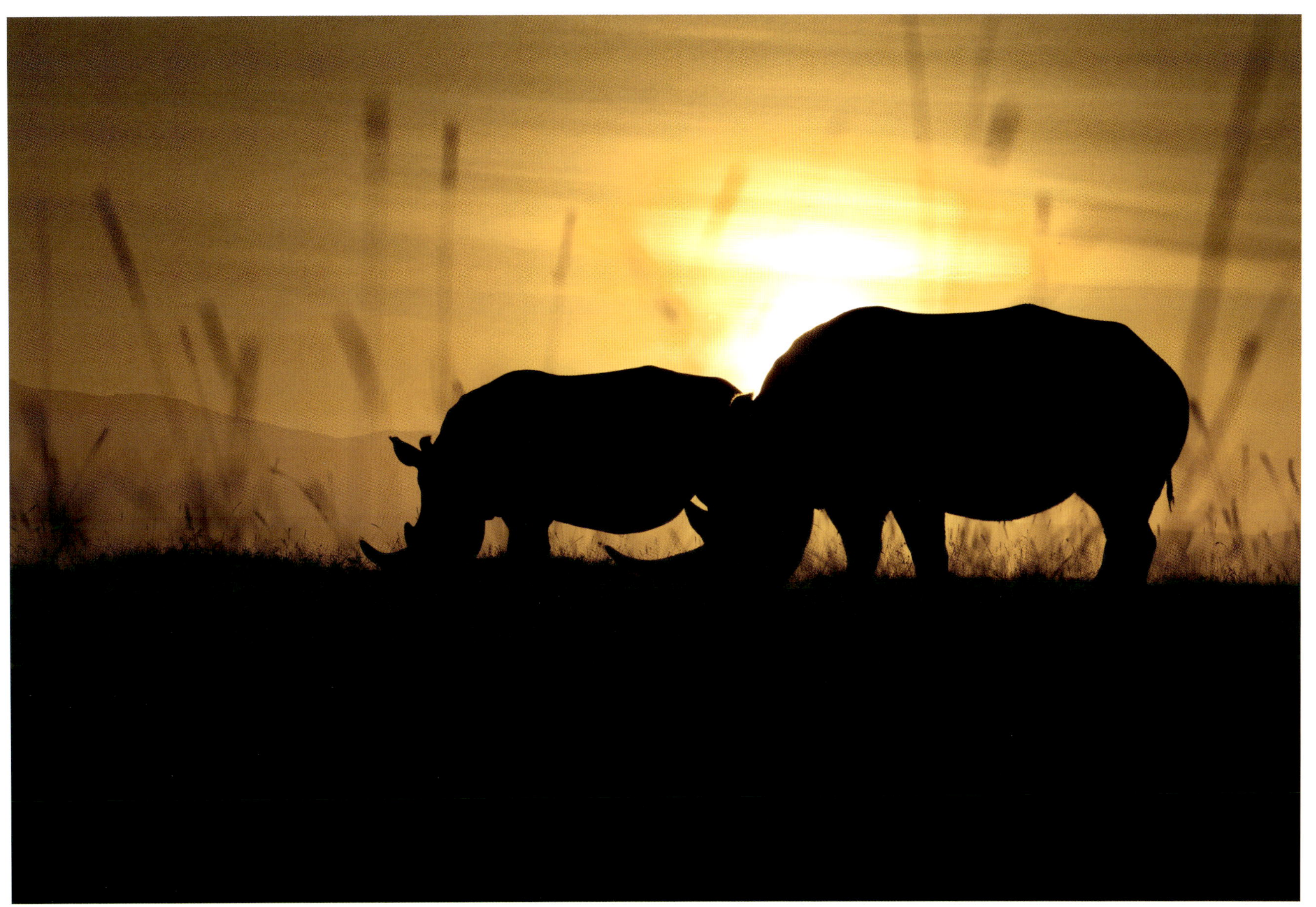

I love the magic of the unexpected that I seem to encounter more when I'm out there with a camera in my hands.

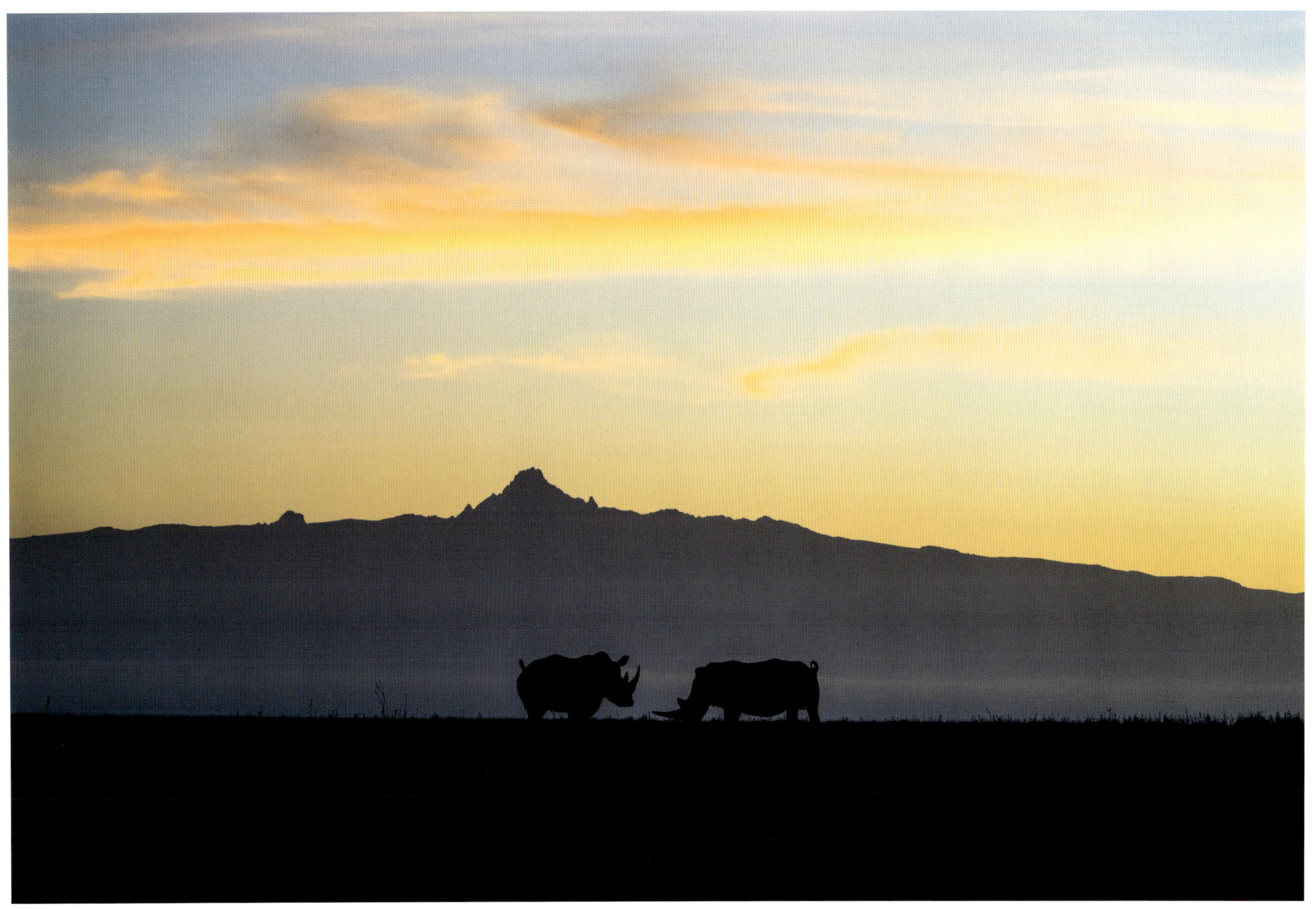

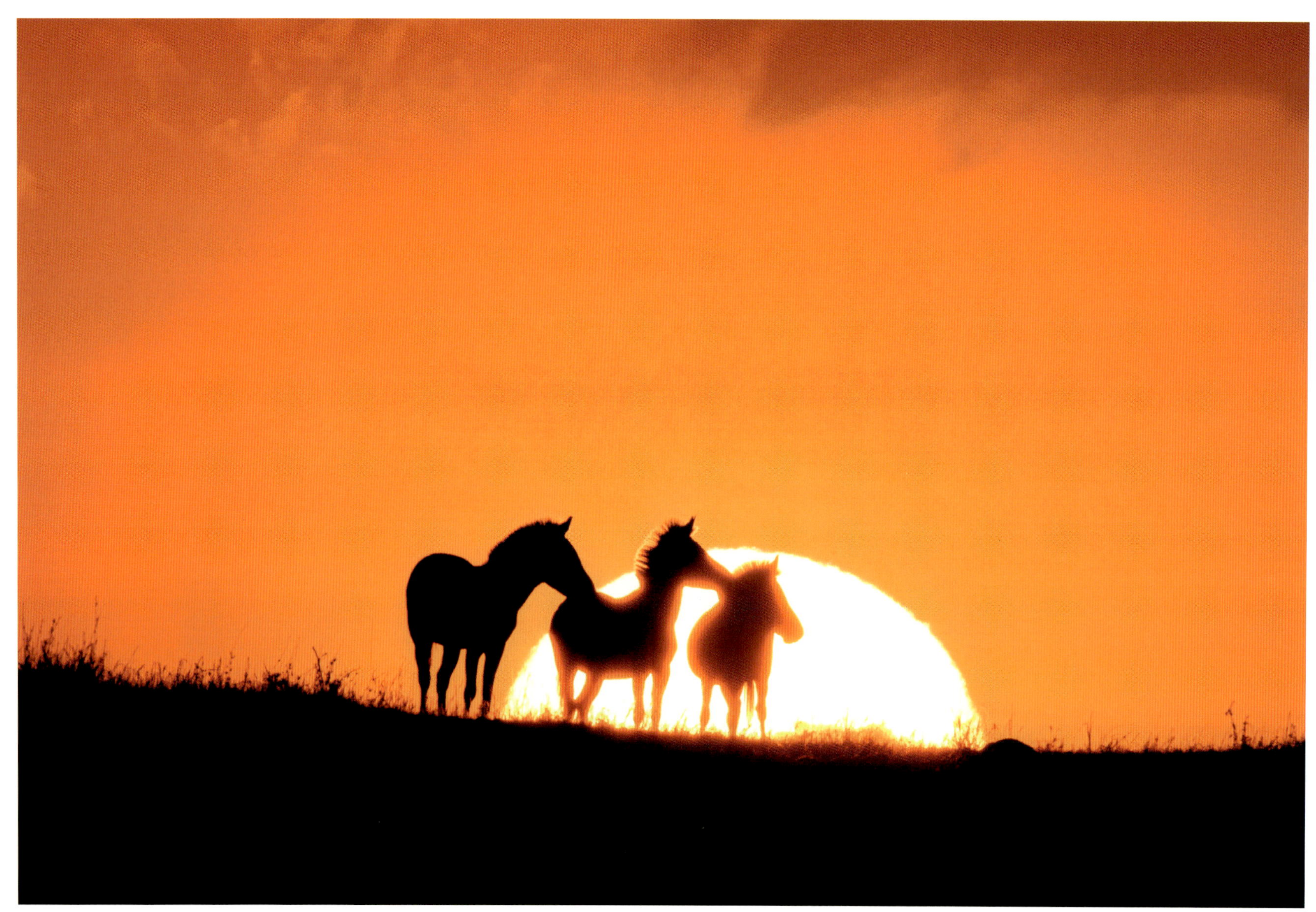

You don't need to know it all. You don't need to own it all. You don't need to win an award, have an exhibit, have the right clients (or *any* clients!), or publish a book. None of these things validate what you do unless, of course, you *want* them to. There is joy in those things if they are where you find your magic. I find mine (and get tremendous joy from) publishing my work in books, but it need not be where you find yours.

As a kid, there were times I couldn't afford film but still went out with my camera, dialing in the settings, playing with compositions, and looking through different lenses to see the world a bit more receptively than without the camera. I also pressed the shutter because, even without film, the magic was still there for me.

You do not need permission to do photography your way. But in case you need a reminder: sometimes your best or most important photograph isn't the one anyone else will praise you for but is instead the one that represents a step forward for you. Maybe that's taking a risk where you have previously played it safe. Maybe you've been learning a new technique and finally figured out how to really make it yours. Those things matter more than how good others believe your work to be, or even how good *you* think it is; the day will come when you look back at that one photograph and, because your craft and vision have surpassed

where you once were, it will no longer resonate the way it once did. The magic is often found while moving forward, and it's good that it sometimes feels slightly out of reach, though I suspect one of the reasons many of us make photographs at all is to look back.

The magic in memories grows as we age, and many of the best photographs of our lives will be those that allow us to relive the magic we might otherwise have forgotten. Objectively speaking, they need not be "good." The composition might be crap, the light nothing special. They might even be out of focus. But the magic persists, lingering in photographs that would be meaningless to anyone but you for reasons all your own. In my darkest times, I return to photographs like those, and will no doubt look back on them in my later years as the most important and enduring pictures of my life. I'd never be able to explain them to you and they wouldn't win any awards, but I bet you also have pictures like that—the ones that are cloaked in magic. Those images may even grow more important with time, but you probably won't remember which camera you used to make them. And knowing what you know these many years later, you might now have chosen different settings or a more sophisticated composition, but it's unlikely those choices would have either amplified the magic or diminished it. Magic is resilient that way.

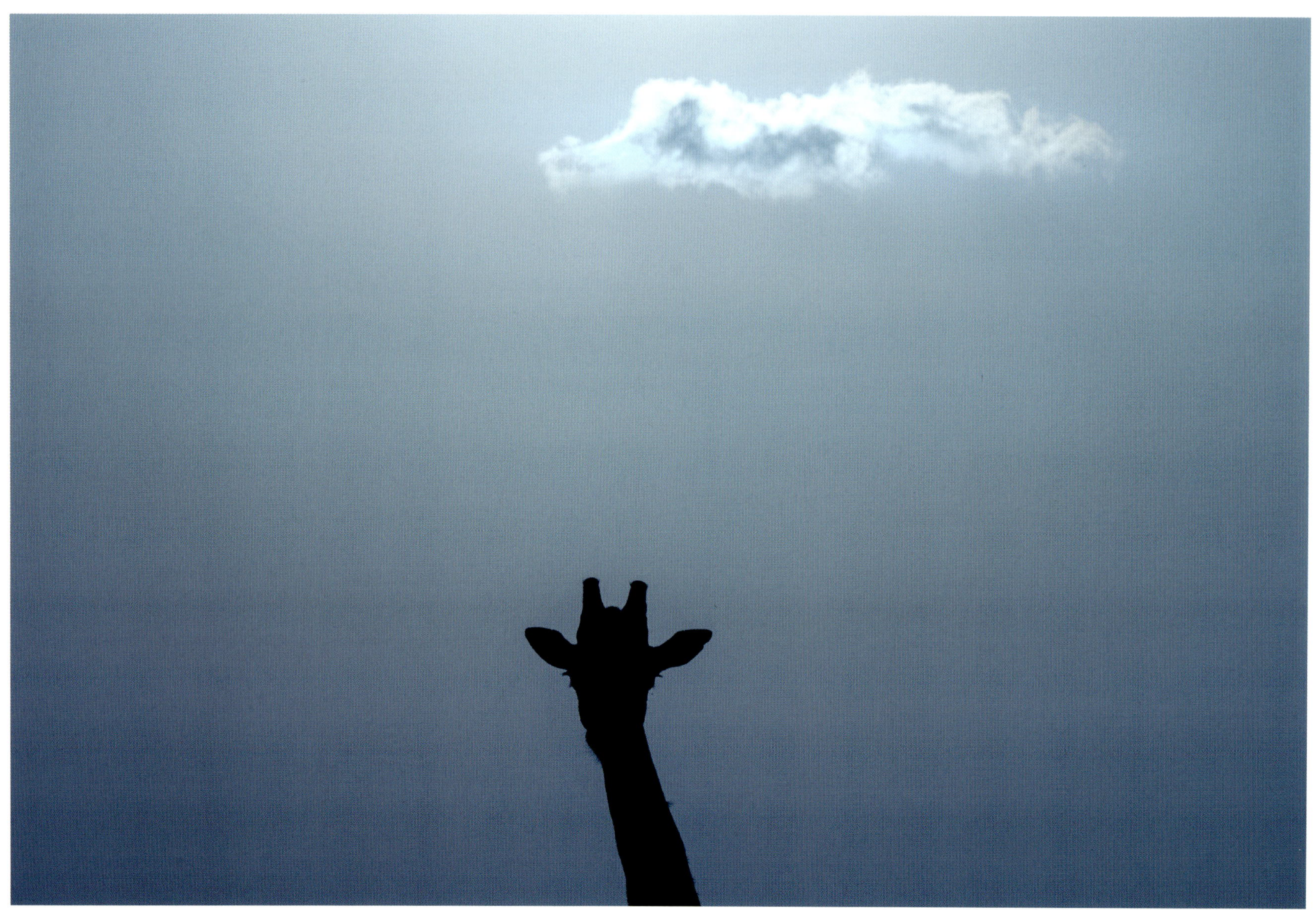

No artist statement could be better than "I made this because I liked it, because it gave me joy or was meaningful."

Find what lights you up inside and do that. Make the photographs that are truly yours, the ones you love for no other reason than that you love them. No artist statement could be better than "I made this because I liked it, because it gave me joy or was meaningful." Don't let the other stuff get in the way. What a loss to be within a truly wonderful moment, one you want to remember and relive, only to miss the photograph because you were fussing or because you left the camera in your pocket because "the light wasn't right" or some other nonsense that won't matter in 20 years when it's the only photograph you have of that friend who is now gone and your memories of the place are beginning to fade.

Some photographs are good; some are magic. Some are both, but I'm finding those rare few come when I chase the one and not the other. Give me a sliver of life that truly lights me on fire, fills me with joy, or makes me feel something deeply over a sharp photograph any day. If I can have both, even better, but what a loss to miss the former in the pursuit of the latter.

Find your magic. Figure out *why* you make photographs. Do more of that. Ignore the rest.

We learn early on to focus our lenses and expose our sensors (or film). What a shame it would be if we never got around to focusing our attention and exposing our souls to those things and experiences that matter most to us—the things that made us more alive while we had the chance, living as we do at this one brief inter-section of light, space, and time.

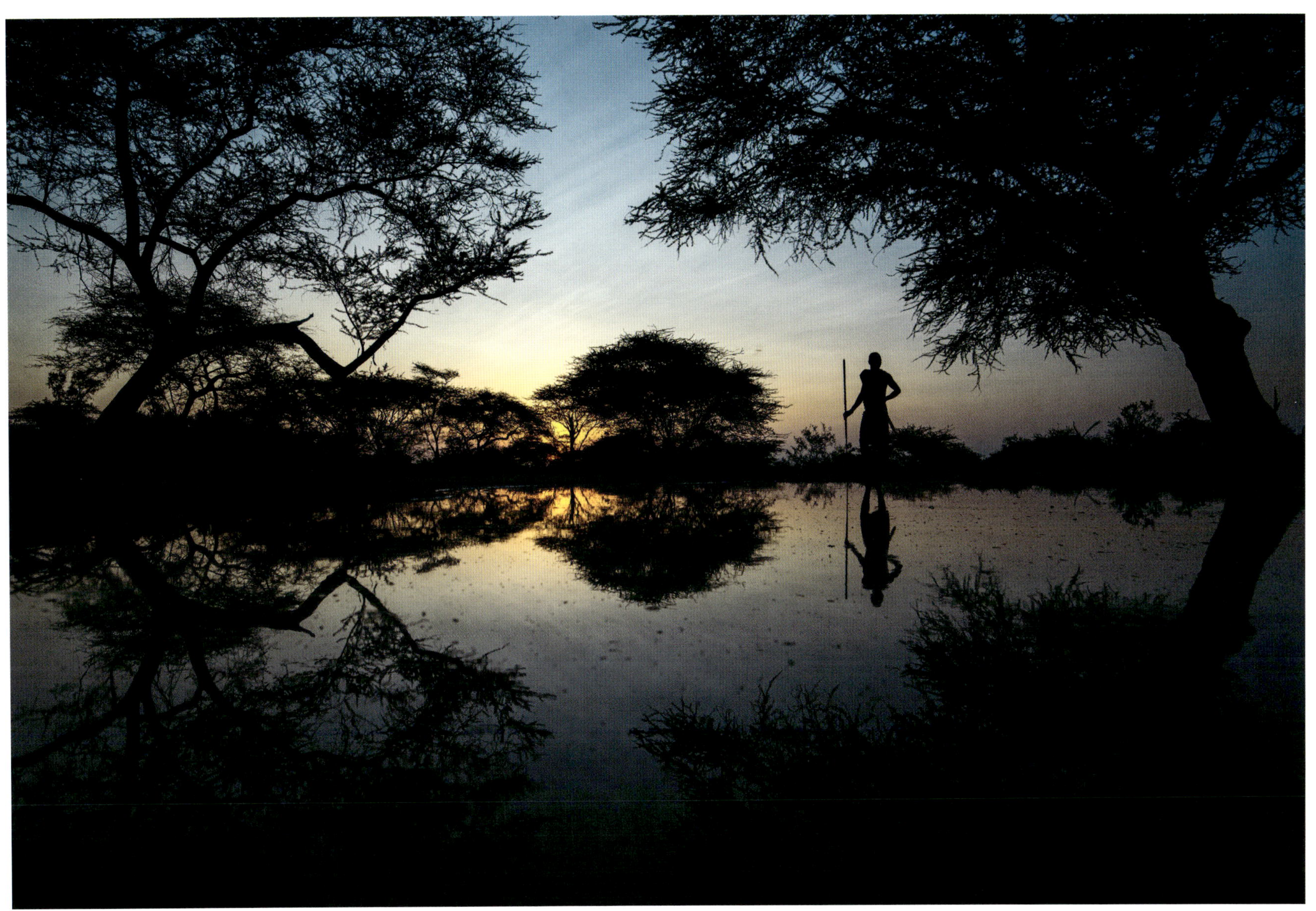

Acknowledgments

What glory is to be had for writing a book goes to the author, but unfairly so. A book like this is a team effort. I am indebted to my team at Rocky Nook, especially to Scott Cowlin and Ted Waitt, the latter of whom has been my editor and valued collaborator since the beginning. Thank you both for believing in me all this time.

To my beloved Cynthia, who polishes my words and saves my readers from the trauma of my many commas—I couldn't do this without you. I love you.

To my friends, most especially Corwin and Jon, thank you for your endless patience as I talk through my ideas, and for saving me from myself over and over again.

And to you, if you're still reading. I write books because I think ideas matter, but without you to read them, I'm not sure I see the point. Thank you for reading my words, and—so many of you—giving me the honour of being part of your creative life.

Mary Oliver, in her brief poem "Instructions for Living a Life," implored us: "Pay attention. Be astonished. Tell about it." Is there any higher wisdom for photographers? I wish you open minds and hearts to see the world, astonishment when you do, and the craft to put that into your photographs in order to spread the wonder.

About the Author

David duChemin is a photographer, writer, and adventurer who makes his home on Vancouver Island, Canada. A former humanitarian photographer, David now turns his lens toward the wilderness. He is the author of best-selling books like *Within the Frame*, *The Soul of the Camera*, and *The Heart of the Photograph*, among others. His work can be found online at DavidduChemin.com.

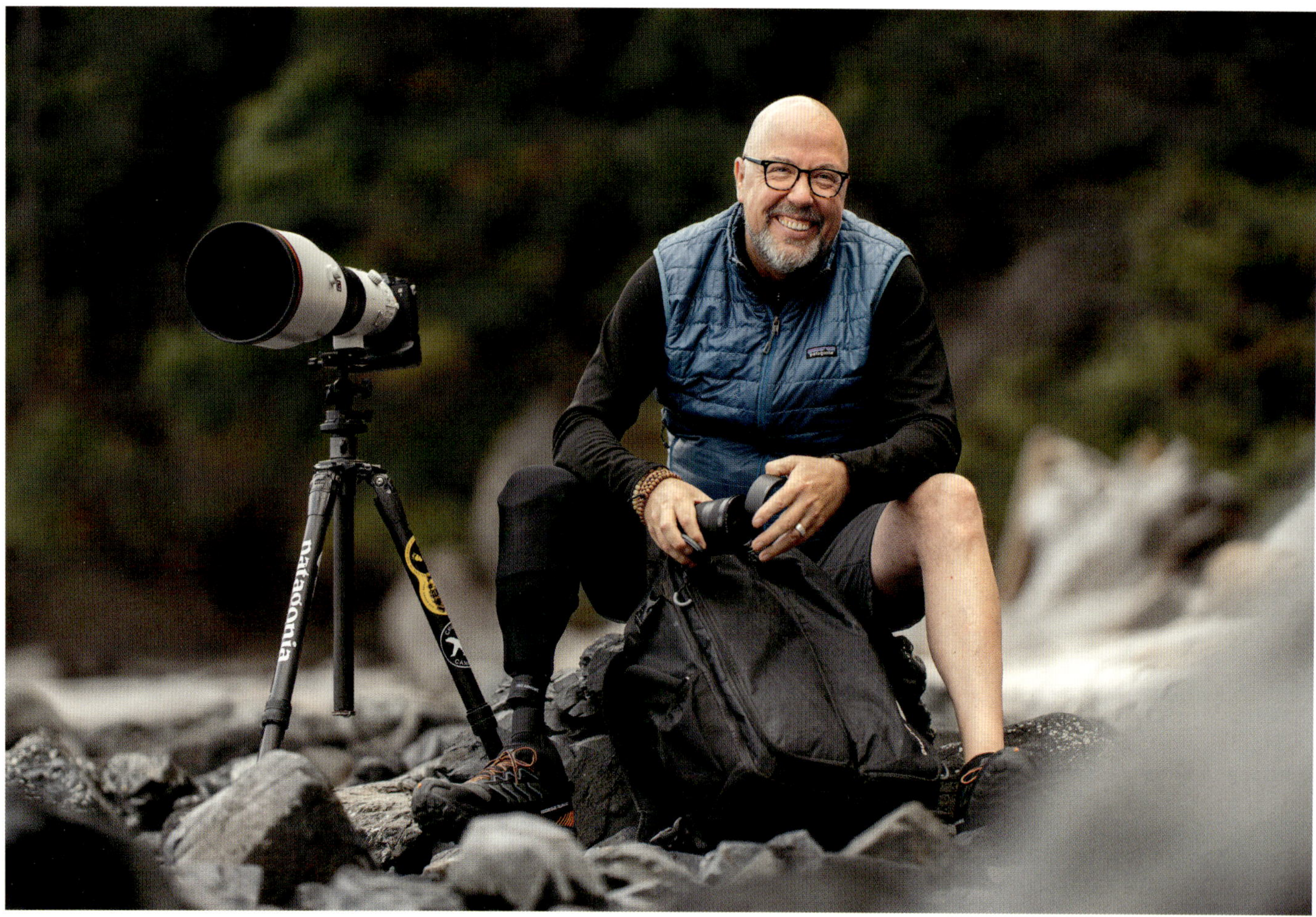

Photo: Peter Holst